COMPANION

WORLD COINS
& CURRENCY

Allen G. Berman

©2006 Krause Publications

Published by

krause publications
An Imprint of F+W Publications

700 East State Street • Iola, WI 54990-0001
715-445-2214 • 888-457-2873

Our toll-free number to place an order or obtain
a free catalog is (800) 258-0929.

Library of Congress Catalog Number: 2006930827
ISBN 13-digit: 978-0-89689-402-0
ISBN 10-digit: 0-89689-402-9

Designed by Kay Sanders
Edited by Dan Brownell

Printed in China

Contents

Dedication

Dedicated to the millions of private collectors, who, over the centuries, have filled our museums and deciphered our history, all for the love of knowledge.

Acknowledgments

Special thanks to Chester L. Krause for generously providing coins and paper money to be photographed, making this full-color book possible.

Abbreviations

AG: About Good
AL: Aluminum
ALB: Aluminum Bronze
AU: About Uncirculated
B: Brass
Bil.: Billon (a copper/silver alloy)
BU: Brilliant Uncirculated
C: Copper
CN: Copper Nickel
CNZ: Nickel Silver (a copper, nickel, zinc alloy)
CU: Crisp Uncirculated
EF: Extra Fine
F: Fine
FR: Fair
G: Good or Gold
l.: Left

mm.: millimeter
MS: Mint State
N: Nickel
ND: Not Dated
Obv.: Obverse (Heads)
PF: Proof
Rev. or Rx: Reverse (Tails)
r.: Right
S: Silver
St.: Steel
Unc.: Uncirculated
VF: Very Fine
VG: Very Good
WM: White Metal (a tin alloy
XF: Extra Fine
Z: Zinc

General Introduction

This book is not intended to be a comprehensive resource about world coins and paper money. In fact, a full library is necessary to answer every question regarding this subject. Rather, it is intended to fill a much needed niche—a very basic introduction, in which a reader can get a quick overview of the hobby and get a general feel for the background, characteristics and values of each of the common categories presented.

Values

Coin and currency prices can be as volatile as the stock market. While some coins and bills remain stable for years, others skyrocket during a period of popularity and then plummet when they fall out of fashion. The listings presented here simply give an idea of the normal retail value at the time of writing. Because the law of supply and demand ultimately rules, the final decision about the value of a coin lies with the buyer and seller.

Dealers are in business to make a living. This means they must pay less than the retail cost listed in this book when they are buying. Depending on the value and demand, a dealer will pay between 10 percent and 90 percent of the retail value of coins or currency listed in this reference.

In this book, the grades chosen to represent average prices are those most likely found in the market or the ones most likely to be sought by the average collector.

Collecting representative samples of world pocket change, past and present, is is an educational and enjoyable hobby. One should be aware, however, that while many higher denomination coins can be collected for investment purposes, most world coins issued to circulate at a value of only a few cents never exceed that in value, even after decades. Many coin dealers have "junk boxes" into which these coins are thrown, and make them available as a service to their customers at 25¢ to one dollar each. Often this does not pay for the time of the counter help to sell them. That is why one should not expect a dealer to pay more than a few cents each for such coins, or often $2 or $3 per pound. Their value is the labor of the dealer. Most of the coins listed at 50¢ to $4 in Unc. and BU fall into the category of poundage when circulated.

Sizes

Not all coins and paper money are shown to scale in this book. Thus, do not rely on the size of the photos for identification, but rather the information stamped or printed on the coins or bills, and the captions and listings accompanying them.

COIN-COLLECTING ONLINE

It is entirely conceivable that in another few years one-third of all numismatic sales will be done over the Internet, yet at the moment, it is a secondary but growing market. Most dealers have constructed Web pages with varying results. Also there are now a couple of services which consolidate a number of dealers' offerings into a series of pages in a common location for ease of searching.

At the moment, both for the dealers and for the collectors in search of dealers, the "net" is still somewhat uncharted territory. So far, it lacks some of the safety mechanisms that exist with periodicals or local shops. There are no customer service awards or standard policies for advertisers, nor are there local Better Business Bureaus to which one can appeal.

This does not mean there are no means by which you can discern legitimate dealers from fly-by-nights. Many of the criteria you would apply to shop, mail order. and show dealers can be applied to net dealers. Many of the more serious dealers on the "Web" will also have active advertising programs in conventional media, permitting you to check with those periodicals. Also the importance of membership in a professional organization still applies. Ask how long the dealer has been in business, not just collecting coins as a hobbyist. Perhaps the most difficult part of selecting dealers on the Web is discerning who is a legitimate, full-time numismatic expert from the skilled home computer buff with the dream of becoming a real coin dealer.

Many auction sites take no responsibility for the transactions which they host, but eBay, for example, does provide one way of screening out some of the worst offenders. Stars are used to indicate the amount of customer feedback the member has. Clicking on the star gives additional information such as whether any customers have left negative comments about their transactions. While even the most honest and knowledgeable dealer may not please everybody, a dealer with more than a few percent of his feedback listed as negative should be regarded with caution. A pair of sunglasses instead of a star indicates a new ID. Some unscrupulous dealers booted off eBay have been known to simply take new identities and start over.

Whatever the medium through which a collector seeks out dealers, a collector who is willing to do some research and ask the right questions is bound to end up with a few dealers in whom he can place confidence and find a certain level of comfort.

The Internet can be used for far more than purchases. E-mail is a wonderfully immediate way to correspond. Basic computer caution should be observed in order to avoid viruses. Never open an unexpected enclosure. Either ask the sender to post an image on a Web site, or verify that it was sent by someone you trust. Simply recognizing the return e-mail address is not enough, as some viruses steal address books.

Ever more powerful search engines are making numismatic research a possibility. Unfortunately, too many collectors are confusing the somewhat random scattering of information on the Internet for a substitute for basic books. It does not even come close. All too often I have heard people say "I tried to look it up on the Internet and couldn't find it." This does not mean that the coin is rare. It more often means that the individual has spent hours using his computer when ten minutes with a *Standard Catalog of World Coins* would have provided a simple answer, and more likely a more accurate one.

The thousands of numismatic Web sites are a great resource. Not only do the nation's most important numismatic organizations all have Web sites, listed in the next section, but a large minority of local coin clubs do as well. Some can even be found through the A.N.A. Web site itself. Discussion groups can also provide for interesting conversations normally only possible at larger coin shows. But remember, protect your security by not revealing an excess of personal information until you know well the trustworthiness of the individual to whom you are about to give your information. Never give out things such as passwords and home addresses. If you are convinced that a firm should be entrusted with your credit card number, send it to them in parts, contained in separate e-mails.

Many of the world's largest mints have sites, including:

United States Mint	www.usmint.gov
Bureau of Engraving and Printing	www.moneyfactory.com
Royal Canadian Mint	www.rcmint.ca
British Royal Mint	www.royalmint.com

If you are doing a search remember, most countries do not have mints at all, but contract their minting to other countries.

CLUBS AND ASSOCIATIONS

As mentioned earlier, coin collecting can be an extremely social hobby, with national, regional, and local clubs. The largest numismatic organization in the world is the American Numismatic Association. It is an institution chartered by Congress to promote numismatic knowledge, and has over the years attracted hundreds of thousands of collectors and dealers. Not only does it provide the arbitration services mentioned above, but holds large conventions twice each year at various locations throughout the country. The summer A.N.A. convention is particularly important being one of the largest coin shows in the world, including not only coin dealers but also representatives of the mints of many foreign countries. Other benefits to A.N.A. membership include a circulating numismatic library, access to its one-week summer seminar in Colorado, and an authentication service. Every member of the A.N.A. also receives a monthly issue of the *Numismatist*, its official journal containing many

popular articles and columns, as well as ads by member dealers. Its
address is:

American Numismatic Association
818 North Cascade Ave.
Colorado Springs, CO 80903
www.money.org.

Another extremely important institution is the American Numismatic
Society, which boasts the most important numismatic library in the
Western Hemisphere. It has played a significant role in the promotion of
original academic numismatic research, and there is little cutting edge
scholarship in which its books or staff are not consulted. It also conducts
a summer seminar for graduate students and scholarships for students
incorporating numismatic research in their theses. Its address is:

American Numismatic Society
96 Fulton Street
New York, NY 10038 in the Financial District
www.numismatics.org.

While a great number of Canadians are active members of the A.N.A.,
there is also an important national level organization founded specifically
for Canadian numismatists. It is:

Canadian Numismatic Association
4936 Younge St., Suite 601
North York, Ontario, Canada M2N 6S3
www.canadian-numismatic.org

A national organization for coin collectors in Mexico is:

Sociedad Numismática de México A.C.
Eugenia 13 - 301
C.P. 03810
México, D.F., Mexico   sonumex@snm.org.mx

Many regional associations exist, and most of them sponsor important
coin shows. One of the largest such organizations is F.U.N. or Florida United
Numismatists, which sponsors a large show of national importance each
January in Orlando. Another large regional organization is the Central
States Numismatic Association which sponsors conventions throughout
the Midwest. The addresses of some e more important regional societies
are:

Florida United Numismatists
POB 951988
Lake Mary, FL 32795

Central States Numismatic Society
POB 841
Logansport, IN 46947

Great Eastern Numismatic Association
1805 Weatherstone Drive
Paoli, PA 19301

New England Numismatic Association
POB 586
Needham, MA 02192

Pacific Northwest Numismatic Association
P.O. Box 4718
Federal Way, WA 98063-4718

Many state level organizations exist that are too numerous to list here.

There is also a good chance that a coin club meets regularly in your town or county. There are hundreds of such organizations throughout the U.S. and Canada, and most meet in an informal manner. Many such organizations are members of the A.N.A., so contacting the A.N.A. may be a way of getting in touch with one. Also ask at a local library or coin shop.

HANDLING AND TREATMENT OF COINS

How a collector treats his coins can greatly affect how well they hold their value. Metal is more reactive and softer than most people think.

The human body contains many corrosive chemicals. In some cases, simply touching a coin can contribute to its deterioration. This is especially true of coins exhibiting mint luster or iridescent toning. Touching a bright copper surface with a sweaty thumb can easily result in the appearance of a dark thumbprint several weeks or months later.

All this being said, it is easy to understand why the first lesson of coin collecting is to **never touch a coin on its surface**. If one needs to pick up a coin with bare skin, touch only its edge. In the case of proof coins, even greater precaution must be taken. The highly reflective surfaces are so sensitive that one should avoid even breathing directly on a coin. This will create small black dots that coin collectors call "carbon spots." Also, do not leave coins exposed to dust, sunlight, or changes in temperature.

To Clean or Not to Clean Coins?

Many new collectors ask the question "How do I remove the toning?" While it can be done, it is not recommended. While there are rare exceptions when it is beneficial, it should generally be stated that one should **never clean a coin**. It is highly likely that more harm than good will result. Toning is actually part of the coin. It is molecularly bonded to the metal, and the only way to remove the toning is to remove part of the coin. This is the way in which most coin dips work, by means of a mild acid. Physical cleaning is even worse, as microscopic striations almost inevitably are scraped into the coin's surface even using materials as mild as a tissue!

Coin Storage

Coins can be stored in many ways. One of the most convenient is in two-inch square plastic "flips." These are transparent holders with two pockets, one to contain the coin, one to contain a cardboard ticket on which information can be recorded. It folds over on itself into a size two inches by two inches. Originally, they were made only of a PVC formula plastic. This material was particularly flexible and easy to work with, but eventually it would break down, depositing a green slime on the coins it contained.

Today both the PVC formula and a new, more inert Mylar formula are available. The Mylar type is prone to cracking, but so far has not been found to damage coins. The PVC type is still popular because it is more flexible, but it is now usually used only by dealers and auction houses for temporary storage. Collectors usually repackage coins purchased in such holders before placing the coins into long-term storage.

Another common coin holder is the "two-by-two." This is a pair of cardboard squares with an adhering film of relatively inert plastic on one side. The coin is sandwiched between the two layers of plastic, and the two halves are stapled together. While this does not permit the coin to be removed and touched as easily as storage in flips, it does permit the coin to be viewed on both sides without opening the holder.

It is important to be very careful when removing coins from these holders so the coin is not accidentally scratched on the exposed ends of the staples that poke out when the holder is pulled apart. These careless staple scratches have ruined tens of thousands of good coins.

Both flips and two-by-twos fit nicely into specially made boxes. They also fit into plastic pages designed to hold 20 of either holder. The pages are transparent and will fit into most loose-leaf binders. It is important to remember not to place coins loose in the pages, as they are often of PVC plastic. Moreover, the thumb-cuts made to help remove the coins are large enough for some coins to fall through.

Many specialized coin folders and albums are designed not only to store and exhibit a collection, but to guide collectors. Each coin in the series is individually labeled, making the holder very convenient. It is widely believed that one of the main reasons coin collecting was able to catch on with the American middle class in the 1930s is the invention of the "penny board," a one-sheet predecessor of these modern coin folders and albums.

Old folders and albums are made by different processes than present ones. Older ones contained substances in the cardboard that tone the coins, although actual corrosion is rare. Today, most manufacturers omit these materials from their albums.

The toning also occurs with the long-term use of the orange-brown two-inch coin envelopes, although it is less of a problem with those of other colors. The toning in this case is caused by sulfur in the paper.

It is best to store a coin collection in a cool, dry environment. Of course, not everyone lives in such a climate. One common answer to this is to store a packet of silica gel in the same container as the coin collection. The gel is a desiccant and will absorb the moisture from the air. It can sometimes be obtained at photo shops, if not as easily through your local coin dealer.

SECURITY

For anyone who collects something of value, security is a major issue. Realize that no house is theft proof and take reasonable precautions. Make sure all doors are locked and that access cannot be gained through open windows. Many collectors choose to install alarm systems. If this is what you choose, do not neglect to place a sticker to that effect in the window. Most alarm companies provide them automatically. If your collection warrants it, you may wish to consider a home safe of suitable size.

Perhaps more important than locks and alarms is being discrete. Do not tell everyone you meet that you are a coin collector. Even if your collection is relatively inexpensive, some potential thieves may presume that all coin collections are valuable, and if they hear of your collection third hand, they may not realize they have stolen a $100 collection instead of a $10,000 one until it is gone.

The most intelligent choice is to keep all your more valuable coins in a safe deposit box in a bank. If your bank is conveniently located to your home or work, you are sacrificing only a little convenience in exchange for peace of mind. When choosing a safe deposit box, it is important to consider the environment. It is better to have a box on an inside wall of the vault rather than along the outside wall of the building. This will reduce the exposure to temperature fluctuations. Also do not forget to place a small packet of silica gel in each box. You may find it more convenient to have multiple boxes of moderate size rather than one large box if your collection is particularly heavy.

Last, if you are buying coins through the mail, do not give out your home address. Use a post office box. Not only does this provide you with a security barrier, it also provides a safe place for your coins to sit if they arrive while you are away.

DETECTING COUNTERFEITS

Counterfeiting is on the rise, although most counterfeits have both their origin and circulation overseas. Detailed discussion will be made throughout this edition of a great many of these new and sometimes dangerous counterfeits. Here are the basics.

There are three kinds of counterfeits the collector should be aware of. Some are more dangerous than others. The oldest type of counterfeit is often called a forgery. It is a false coin or piece of paper money made with the intent of passing it in circulation. It is usually of adequate quality not to be obvious at a casual inspection, but is often imperfect. As a counterfeiter successful at making such a product can at most hope to gain face value of the item he is replicating, he is limited as to the expense he is willing to lay out and still make a satisfactory profit for his risk.

One corollary of this type of counterfeit is imitations and evasions. These are made to circulate but are often not faithful to the original because they are made for use in communities which for various reasons have come to *expect* that some of their coinage will be counterfeit. Imitations vary only due to style, evasions deliberately modify some aspect of the inscription or design to provide a meager legal defense against a charge of counterfeiting. All of these may fool a collector at first glance but they are usually imperfect enough to not pass close scrutiny. Many of them are historically significant and are frequently collected along with or instead of the original series. As such they are called "contemporary counterfeits" because they were struck contemporary to those coins with which they were intended to circulate.

A far greater danger to the collector is the true numismatic counterfeit. These are counterfeits of higher quality created with great care to fool numismatic experts. Many counterfeits are made by casting, even though the original coin may have been made by striking. Look for seams along the edge. They may not be centered and obvious but can be hidden to one side or the other. Also examine the surface under magnification for a multitude of faint pimples or unnatural porosity. The precise shapes of letters are also something often neglected by counterfeiters. On modern coins an inaccurate weight, or incorrect alloy (revealed by specific gravity testing) can be a giveaway. Ancient and medieval coins can vary much more in weight. Be aware that a great many counterfeiters have sought to hide their imperfections by heavy cleaning. The idea is that a collector examining a very rare coin will attribute the problems to abuse, rather than forgery.

The last type of counterfeit is of virtually no threat to collectors, but pity the poor tourist! These are counterfeits made as souvenirs. This is not to say they are never created to pass off as authentic coins, but that the forger is presuming either total credulity on the part of the buyer, or an unwillingness to give a critical inspection. Even the color of the metal is often incorrect. Tens of thousands of these, replicating ancients, have been sold at archaeological sites in Turkey and the Middle East. Other similar counterfeits are found in Italy replicating 19th century silver dollar sized coins. Often these types of replicas (the more accurate name) are sold clearly marked as such in museum shops, or through legitimate vendors. Often they are even marked COPY to prevent confusion with the real thing. Since the passage of the Hobby Protection Act, replicas made in the United States have been required to display this word.

CONDITION AND GRADING

The value of a coin is in part determined by its "grade," or how well preserved it is. The most basic part of grading is determining how much a coin is worn. Numismatists have agreed on a series of terms to describe the amount of wear. Unlike United States and Canadian coins, there are few grading guides for world coins. Below are some general standards that should prove useful for most coins.

In grading world coins, there are two main factors to consider: 1) loss of design details, such as hair, feathers, designs on coats of arms, or beads on the arches of a crown, and 2) how well the coin was struck. Just because the die had certain details does not mean that they were properly impressed into the coin. Knowing the type of coin will help determine how well it was struck. The age or rarity of a coin should not be a consideration in grading.

Some coins will not wear equally on both sides. To accurately describe such a coin, most numismatists will indicate the grade of each side, separated by a slash. VF/F means the coin has a Very Fine obverse and a Fine reverse. In terms of value, however, many "split grade" coins trade nearer to the value of the lower graded side.

Uncirculated (Unc.) or ***Mint State (MS)*** coins are those with no wear at all, as though they had just come from the mint. Even a magnifying glass should reveal no evidence of wear.

Before their release from the mint, coins hit each other while stored in bags, leaving minute scuffs. These scuffs are called "bag marks." Bag marks can be described on a scale from MS-70, meaning a perfect coin, fully struck and free from bag marks, to MS-60, meaning a coin very much scuffed, often having nicks and discoloration.

The numerical grading system was designed for U.S. coins, but many world coin collectors use it as well. More common among world collectors, however, is simply describing the coin. An almost perfect Uncirculated coin is described as "gem," one nicer than average is called "choice," and one with heavy bag marks is called "baggy."

Brilliant Uncirculated (BU) means a mint-state coin that still has its original bright mint luster.

About Uncirculated (AU) describes coins with such slight signs of wear that some people may in fact need a mild magnifying glass to see them. A trace of luster should be visible. One should be careful not to take an attractive AU coin for Uncirculated.

Extremely Fine (EF, XF) is the highest grade coin that exhibits wear heavy enough to be seen easily by the unaided eye. It is a coin on which 90 percent to 95 percent of the minute details will still be extremely sharp and clear. Many will exhibit luster but it is not required.

Very Fine (VF) coins will show obvious signs of wear. Nevertheless, most detail in the design will still be clear. It is an overall pleasant coin.

Fine (F) is the lowest grade most people would consider collectible. About half the design details will show for most types. All lettering should be legible, but may be somewhat weak.

Very Good (VG) coins exhibit heavy wear. All design outlines are clear, as is generally the rim. Perhaps a quarter of the internal detail will also show, but most will be worn off.

Good (G) coins are generally considered uncollectible except for novelty purposes. There will be little or no internal detail to the design at all. Some of the rim may also be worn out.

About Good (aG) and Fair (Fr) are grades in which only truly scarce coins are collected. Many collectors would rather do without a coin than to add it to their collections. The rim will be worn down and some outline to the design may be gone.

Sometimes treated as a grade, but technically not one at all is **Proof (PF)**. Proof quality is a special way of making coins for presentation. A proof coin is usually double struck with highly polished dies on polished blanks, usually yielding a mirror-like finish. These days, proof coins are mass marketed by mints to collectors. Cameo proof is a particular kind of proof that has been struck with dies polished only in the fields, but with the details such as the portrait deliberately given a dull finish. For some coins, these cameo proofs have a premium value above regular proofs. Proofs often grade MS-65 or higher.

Other miscellaneous factors can affect the quality of a coin, and should always be described. The presence of all or part of the original luster usually increases a coin's value. Be careful, however, not to be fooled by a coin that has been cleaned or dipped in a brightener in order to simulate this luster artificially. Toning can be either good or bad. If the toning a coin has acquired is dull, irregular or splotchy, it is likely to be considered unpleasant, and many collectors may choose to avoid it even if it is a high-grade coin. On the other hand, if it is mild or displays a "halo effect" around the edge of the coin, or is composed of pleasant iridescent shades, many collectors and dealers would consider paying a premium to obtain it based on its "eye appeal."

Even on circulated coins, few collectors wish to have coins with corrosion, scratches, or edge nicks. These will occur even more frequently on larger coins or on coins with reeded edges. Depending on extent, such coins may be discounted by a little or a lot.

Of course, coins with damage are worth far less than coins without. Many coins have been mounted for use in jewelry, and even when the loop or bezel has been removed, they still may show slight signs of this unfortunate experience. While discounted heavily, a few collectors consider these opportunities to acquire coins with high-grade detail for a fraction of the cost. It should be remembered that the same heavy discount will apply when that collector goes to sell his coins.

CANADIAN COINS

EVOLUTION OF CANADIAN COINAGE

Like the situation south of the border in the United States and formerly in the thirteen colonies, Canadian coinage before the 1870s was a hodgepodge of various coins and tokens struck by a number of authorities, firms, countries, and individuals. Throughout the 1700s and early 1800s, the British policies of mercantilism prevented the royal government from shipping reasonable quantities of sterling to British North America. By the time the idea was seriously considered, there was already chaos.

When official coinage was finally struck by the various pre-Confederation colonial provinces, they had already recognized slightly different standards, sometimes as much as 20 percent different from each other in value. The first coins to be struck in the name of "Canada" were not struck by the Canadian Confederation, but rather by the Province of Canada. This was the collective name for Upper Canada (Ontario) and Lower Canada (Quebec). Bronze cents and silver five, ten, and twenty cents were struck in 1858-59. In the intervening years before these two provinces combined with New Brunswick and Nova Scotia to form the independent Canadian Confederation in 1867, all of them had already struck their own unique coins. Despite all this complexity of coinage, there still persisted a shortage of small change in circulation. Neither bank tokens nor poorly made "blacksmith" counterfeits could be suppressed.

During the American Civil War, when U.S. silver coins were being discounted in terms of gold, some firms bought them up in quantity and imported them. Unfortunately it soon became the tool of scams, whereby they were paid out at par, but only taken for deposit at a discount. Finally in 1869-70, a three-step program was used to cure this dilemma.

The United States silver was bought up and four million dollars worth re-exported south. An order was placed with the Royal Mint for an issue of millions of new sterling silver Canadian 5¢, 10¢, 25¢, and 50¢ pieces. Lastly a temporary issue of fractional paper money redeemable in gold was released immediately to make due until the new coins arrived. (This small paper money proved so popular that it continued to be issued until the 1930s.)

The new Canadian silver coins, nominally valued at one United States dollar worth of gold per Canada dollar, were struck in quantity, except for the depression of the late 1870s, supplemented by a large initial issue of cents in 1876. These were slightly heavier than the Province's old cents, and continued from 1881 onward. The standards for cents and silver remained unchanged until World War I.

During the 1800s, Canadian coins were struck at the Royal Mint in London, and sometimes by contract at the Heaton Mint, Birmingham, England. In 1908, after years of agitation, a branch of the Royal mint was opened in Ottawa. With it came the ability to mint the gold then being mined in Canada into internationally recognized British design sovereigns, and soon after that a domestic gold coinage was initiated.

While the basic designs for most Canadian coins remained fairly stable from the beginning until 1937, many smaller changes occurred as needed. Of course with the passing of each monarch, a new royal portrait was designed, one for Edward VII in 1902, another for George V in 1911. The gold sovereigns only, instead of using the crowned busts, used bareheaded ones to match British gold sovereigns. There was a bit of a ruckus in 1911 when the new obverse of George V was found to be lacking the Latin *Dei Gratia* for "by the grace of God." The mint responded to the public outcry and beginning 1912 these titles were added. World War I and its aftermath resulted in more modifications.

The large cent was replaced in 1920 by a small cent, and in 1922 , the 5¢ silver was replaced by one of pure nickel, both similar in size to their American counterparts. Also, as a result of a wartime increase in the price of silver, the alloy of coins in that metal was reduced from 92.5 percent pure (sterling) to 80 percent beginning with 1920.

The entire visual style of Canadian coins began to change in 1935, when a new, artistic commemorative silver dollar for the jubilee of George V was released. It depicted the now famous design of a fur trapper and an Indian paddling a canoe. When the obverses were changed to portray the new King George VI in 1937, the opportunity was taken to revise all the reverses of the smaller denominations with creative and distinctly Canadian designs. The cent was given a more naturalistic sprig of maple leaves, the five cents a beaver on its dam, a schooner graced the ten-cent pieces and the bust of a caribou the 25 cent. The 50-cent coins displayed a more conservative coat of arms. Because of the time taken to design the new coinage, some 1936 dated coins were struck in 1937 bearing a minute dot to distinguish them. These are quite rare. The reverses introduced in 1937 have, with some alteration, continued in use today.

Like World War I, the Second World War had its effects on the coinage. Shortages of nickel caused the five-cent piece to be struck in a brass alloy called tombac, and later in chromium-plated steel. It was finally restored to its old nickel composition in 1955. A special reverse design was used to boost wartime morale, that of a torch superimposed on a V for victory. Because of the time taken to modify the royal titles to reflect the independence of India, some 1947 coins were struck in 1948 with a tiny maple leaf after the date. While not at all rare, these are quite popular.

No monarch has had as many different portraits on Canadian coins as Elizabeth II. The first portrait, designed by Mary Gillick, had some minor difficulties in striking, and as a result, was subtly modified after being placed in production. In 1965 a new bust wearing a tiara was introduced, years before Britain itself began using it. When a mature head of the Queen was desired, the Canadian choice for the first time differed from that of Britain. A design with an open crown, by Canadian artist Dora de Pédery-Hunt was used beginning 1990. It was replaced in mid-2003 by a bareheaded, grandmotherly portrait designed by Susanna Blunt.

The centennial of Canadian independence was cause for issue of some of Canada's most beautiful and dignified wildlife coins. Animals emblematic of Canada shown against stark open backgrounds were portrayed on the reverses of the 1967 issues, along with a $20 gold piece with the national arms. Unfortunately, the rising price of silver forced these animal coins out of circulation. In mid-year, the 10¢ and 25¢ pieces were reduced to 50 percent pure, and beginning in 1968, pure nickel replaced all circulating silver.

Throughout the 1970s to the 1990s, various modifications were made to reduce the expense of producing coins, which no longer had any tie to their intrinsic value. The cent went through several modifications in weight and shape before it was switched to copper-plated zinc in 1997, later supplemented by issues in copper plated steel. In 1982, the five-cent piece was changed from nickel to cupro-nickel, then to nickel-plated steel in 2000, along with the 10¢, 25¢, and 50¢ pieces. Radical new dollar and two dollar coins were introduced to save the expense of producing perishable paper money. A small golden-bronze-plated nickel dollar was introduced in 1987 depicting a swimming loon. In 1996 a two dollar coin depicting a polar bear and composed of a nickel ring surrounding an aluminum bronze center followed. Today these two coins are popularly known as the "loonie" and "twonie" respectively.

Since the 1970s Canada has had an aggressive collector coin program, with several different designs in various precious metals being offered in quality strikings each year. Some of these are quite scarce and are made in limited quantities, while others, particularly those of the 1970s are so common as to be frequently melted for scrap. Some of the more unusual pieces are the silver Canadian Aviation series, which actually boasts a small portrait inlay of gold. This decade also saw the old cellophane packaged proof-like sets supplemented with the more market-oriented cased proof sets.

Circulating commemoratives were struck for the 125th anniversary of the Canadian Confederation in 1992. While most coins just bore the 1867-1992 legend, an extremely popular series of 25¢ coins bore reverses emblematic of each province and territory. A dollar depicting children before parliament was issued as well.

As one of the world's richest nations in terms of precious metals, it is not surprising to note that Canada has for years produced some of the world's most popular bullion coins. Silver one ounce, gold 1/20 to one ounce, and platinum 1/20 to one ounce pieces are struck bearing an intricate and difficult to counterfeit maple leaf reverse.

CANADIAN MINT MARKS

C	Ottawa, Ontario
H	Heaton, Birmingham, England
none (1858-1907)	Royal Mint, London
none (1908-	Ottawa, Ontario
none (1968)	Philadelphia, USA
none (1973-)	Hull, Quebec
none (1975-)	Winnipeg, Manitoba
P (1999-)	Plated on steel blank
W (1998-)	Winnipeg, Manitoba

GRADING CANADIAN COINS

Certain convenient key reference points greatly facilitate the grading of Canadian coins. On Queen Victoria's portraits, it is the hair over or braid below the ear. In the case of both Edward VII and George V, it is the band of the crown.

Two special bits of wisdom should be imparted to those who would grade Canadian coins. First, even though the reverse of a pre-1937 Canadian coin is usually in better grade than the obverse, the value of a coin in the marketplace is primarily determined by the grade of its obverse. Second, pure nickel George V five-cent pieces are very difficult to grade. Because of nickel's hardness, the dies did not always leave a sharp impression. Thus, the understanding of the texture and surface of the metal is always useful in grading this series.

Uncirculated coins with particularly unpleasant bag marks, color, or toning may trade at a heavy discount.

MS-65 or Gem—This is the highest grade one is likely to encounter. It has utterly no wear. It has no significant bag marks, particularly in open areas such as the field or cheek. Copper must have luster.

MS-63 or Choice Uncirculated—This is a pleasant coin with absolutely no wear, but enough bag marks to be noticed. Still, there are few enough bag marks not to be considered marred, particularly few in open areas such as the field or cheek.

MS-60 or Uncirculated—While there is technically no wear at all on an MS-60 coin, it is not necessarily attractive. It will bear scuffs and bagmarks acquired from handling at the mint before release. Copper will usually be toned and some coins of either metal may be discolored.

AU or Almost Uncirculated—This describes a coin with such slight signs of wear that some people may in fact need a mild magnifying glass to see them. One should be careful not to confuse an attractive AU coin for uncirculated. Look for the texture of the metal.

XF or Extremely Fine—This is the highest grade of coin that exhibits wear significant enough to be seen easily by the unaided eye. It still exhibits extremely clear minute detail. In the case of Victorian coins, the hair over ear and jewels of diadem, or segments of braid, are sharp. In the case of Edward VII and George V, the jewels in the band of the crown are sharp. George VI coins will have only the slightest wear in the hair over the ear.

VF or Very Fine—These coins show obvious signs of wear. Nevertheless, most of the detail of the design is still clear. In the case of Victorian coins, the hair over ear, or segments of braid, are visible but not sharp. The same is true of the jewels in the diadem. In the case of Edward VII and George V, the jewels in the band of the crown are visible but not sharp. George VI coins will have about 80 percent of hair detail visible.

F or Fine—This is the lowest grade most people would consider collectible. About half the design detail will show for most types. In the case of Victorian coins, the strands of the hair over ear or segments of braid begin to run into each other. Some of the details in the diadem will be obscured. In the case of Edward VII and George V, the jewels in the band of the crown will be unclear, but the band will be distinct from the head. George VI coins will have only about half the hair detail visible.

VG or Very Good—These coins exhibit heavy wear. All outlines are clear, as is generally the rim. Some internal detail will also show, but most will be worn off. On Victorian coins, the details in the strands of the hair over ear or segments of braid will be obscured. Most details in the diadem will be obscured. In the case of Edward VII and George V, the band of the crown will be worn through at its center. George VI coins will have only about one third of the hair detail visible.

G or Good—These coins are generally considered uncollectible except for novelty purposes. There will usually be little or no internal detail to the design. Some of the rim may also be barely visible on silver. With Victorian coins, the hair over ear or the braid will be very much obscured, as will the majority of the diadem. On Edward VII and George V, the band of the crown will be worn through along most of its width. George VI coins will have no hair detail at all.

BOOKS ON CANADIAN COINS

Charlton, J.E., *Canadian, Colonial Tokens*.
Cross, W.K., *Charlton, Standard Catalogue: Canadian Coins*.
Harper, David C., ed., *North American Coins & Prices*.
Haxby, James, *The Royal Canadian Mint and Canadian Coinage: Striking Impressions*.
Haxby, James, and Willey, R.C., *Coins of Canada*.

PERIODICAL

Canadian Coin News.

CENTS

One-inch-wide large cents were among the first coins to be struck by the Province of Canada in 1858-59 before the formation of the Confederation. These coins with a young head of Queen Victoria were struck in such quantities that they were still in bank coffers until 1875. The following year, another large order for cents was placed, this time with a heavier weight and a mature head of the queen. This order lasted for five years. Since 1881, Canadian cents have been struck almost continuously.

With the passing of Queen Victoria a new portrait was designed for Edward VII in 1902, and another for George V in 1911. There was a bit of a ruckus in 1911 when the new obverse of George V was found to be lacking the Latin *Dei Gratia* for "by the grace of God." The mint responded to the public outcry, and beginning in 1912 these titles were added. More public complaint was heard about the traditional size of the cent. The large cent was replaced in 1920 by a small cent much like America's.

When the obverse was changed to portray the new King George VI in 1937, the opportunity was taken to revise the reverse of the cent. It was given a more naturalistic sprig of maple leaves, designed by G.E. Kruger-Gray. Because of the time taken to design the new cents, some 1936 dated coins were struck in 1937 bearing a minute dot to distinguish them. These are quite rare. The reverse introduced in 1937 has, with some alteration, continued in use today.

Because of the time taken to modify the royal titles to reflect the independence of India, some 1947 cents were struck in 1948 with a tiny maple leaf after the date. While not at all rare, these are quite popular.

No monarch has had as many different portraits on Canadian coins as Elizabeth II. The first portrait, designed by Mary Gillick, had some minor difficulties in striking, and as a result, was subtly modified after being placed in production. In 1965 a new bust wearing a tiara was introduced, years before Britain itself began using it. When a mature head of the Queen was desired, the Canadian choice differed from that of Britain. A design with an open crown, by Canadian artist Dora de Pédery-Hunt was used beginning 1990. It was replaced in mid-2003 by a bareheaded, grandmotherly portrait designed by Susanna Blunt.

As part of a set of wildlife coins struck for the centennial of Canadian independence, the 1967 cent depicted a rock dove. For its 125th anniversary, the double date 1867-1992 was displayed.

In an economy measure, the weight of the cent was reduced in 1979, 1980, and 1982. Its copper alloy was switched to copper-plated zinc in 1997. Most years since 1999, these cents were supplemented by some struck on copper-plated steel. The latter are marked with a P on the obverse. From 1982 to 1996, Canadian cents were twelve-sided.

Known Counterfeits: The 1936 dot variety is a prime target.

Victoria 1859 1 Cent

George V Large 1911 1 Cent

Edward VII 1905 1 Cent

George V Small 1920 1 Cent

VICTORIA

	VG	VF
1858	35.00	65.00
1859, 9 over 8	22.00	45.00
1859, Narrow 9	1.75	4.50
1859, Double punched 9 (2 vars.).	32.00	65.00
1876H	1.50	4.00
1881H	2.50	5.00
1882H	1.50	3.50
1884	2.00	4.00
1886	3.25	7.50
1887	2.50	5.00
1888	1.50	3.50
1890H	4.00	12.00
1891 Large date	4.50	11.00
1891 Small date, large leaves	40.00	85.00
1891 Small date, small leaves	30.00	60.00
1892	3.00	6.00
1893	2.00	4.00
1894	5.50	13.00
1895	3.00	7.00
1896	1.75	3.75
1897	2.00	5.00
1898H	4.00	8.00

	VG	VF
1899	1.50	3.50
1900	5.00	12.00
1900H	1.50	3.75
1901	1.50	3.50

EDWARD VII

	VG	VF
1902	1.25	3.00
1903	1.25	2.50
1904	1.50	3.25
1905	2.50	5.00
1906	1.25	2.50
1907	1.50	3.00
1907H	6.00	16.00
1908	2.25	4.00
1909	1.25	2.00
1910	1.25	2.00

GEORGE V—LARGE

	F	XF
1911	1.25	3.50
1912	1.00	2.50
1913	1.00	2.50
1914	1.40	3.50
1915	1.10	2.75

	F	XF
1916	.65	2.00
1917	.50	1.50
1918	.50	1.50
1919	.50	1.50
1920	.75	2.00

GEORGE V—SMALL

	F	XF
1920	.50	2.00
1921	.75	4.00
1922	10.00	22.00
1923	16.25	34.00
1924	4.00	10.50
1925	17.00	28.00
1926	3.00	8.75
1927	1.25	4.00
1928	.25	1.50
1929	.25	1.50
1930	1.80	5.00
1931	1.00	3.50
1932	.25	1.50
1933	.25	1.50
1934	.30	1.50
1935	.30	1.50
1936	.25	1.50
1936 Dot below date		rare

GEORGE VI

	XF	MS-63
1937	1.50	6.00
1938	.85	6.50
1939	.85	5.00
1940	.65	6.00
1941	.85	40.00
1942	.70	30.00
1943	.70	15.00
1944	.85	45.00
1945	.50	5.00
1946	.55	5.00
1947	.50	6.00
1947 Maple leaf	.50	5.00
1948	.80	12.00
1949	.45	4.00
1950	.35	4.00
1951	.35	4.00
1952	.35	4.00

Elizabeth II 1994 1 Cent

ELIZABETH II

	MS-63
1953 without fold	2.00
1953 with fold	35.00
1954 without fold...*Prooflike only*	250.00
1954 with fold	4.00
1955 without fold	950.00
1955 with fold	1.50
1956	.90
1957	.70
1958	.70
1959	.50
1960	.50
1961	.25
1962	.20
1963	.20
1964	.20
1965	.40
1966	.20
1967 *Centennial*	.20
1968	.20
1969	.20
1970	.20
1971	.20
1972	.20
1973	.20
1974	.20
1975	.20
1976	.20
1977	.20
1978	.20
1979	.20
1980	.15
1981	.15
1982	.15
1983	.15
1984	.15
1985	.15
1986	.15
1987	.15

	MS-63
1988	.15
1989	.15
1990	.15
1991	.15
1992 "1867-1992"	.15
1993	.15
1994	.15
1995	.15
1996	.15
Copper-plated Zinc &	
Copper-plated Steel	
1997	.15
1998	.15
1998 Bronze in sets only	.75
1998W	1.75
1998 Large Cent as 1908	16.50
1999	.15

	MS-63
1999P	8.00
2000	.15
2000W	*PL* 1.75
2001	.15
2001 Bronze	*proof only* 2.75
2001P Steel	*PL* 1.75
2002 "1952-2002"	.15
2002P "1952-2002"	.15
2003 Crowned bust	.15
2003P Crowned bust	.15
2003 Bare head	.15
2003P Bare head	.25
2003WP Bare head	1.50
2004	.15
2004P	.15

THREE CENTS

This most unusual denomination for the Canadian series commemorates the 150th anniversary of the first Canadian postage stamp. It is a collector issue struck in gold plated silver. Depicted is a beaver from that stamp.

	PF
2001	30.00

FIVE CENTS

Tiny sterling silver five-cent pieces were among the first coins to be struck by the Province of Canada in 1858 before the formation of the Confederation. These coins bore a young head of Queen Victoria. Twelve years later the new Confederation started issuing five-cent silver coins, making no significant changes from the earlier provincial piece.

With the passing of Queen Victoria, a new portrait was designed for Edward VII in 1902, followed the next year by a change of the reverse crown from St. Edward's to the Imperial crown. There was a bit of a ruckus in 1911 when the new obverse with George V's portrait was found to be lacking the Latin *Dei Gratia* for "by the grace of God." The mint responded to the public outcry, and beginning in 1912 these titles were added.

As a result of a World War I increase in the price of silver, the alloy was reduced from 92.5 percent pure (sterling) to 80 percent beginning with 1920. Public complaint persisted about the small size of this coin. Not only were they prone to loss and fumbling, their thinness resulted in the dents, edge dings, and bends, which collectors object to today. It was replaced in 1922 by a larger coin much like America's but of pure nickel.

When the obverse was changed to portray the new King George VI in 1937, the opportunity was taken to revise the reverse of the five-cent piece. A naturalistic beaver on its dam was portrayed, designed by G.E. Kruger-Gray. This new reverse, with some alteration, is still used today.

Like World War I, the Second World War had its effects on the coinage. Shortages of nickel caused the five cent piece to be struck in a brass alloy called tombac in 1942-44, and in chromium-plated steel in 1944-45 and 1951-54. A special reverse design, that of a torch superimposed on a V for victory, was used to boost wartime morale.

Because of the time taken to modify the royal titles to reflect the independence of India, some 1947 coins were struck in 1948 with a tiny dot or maple leaf after the date. The dot is scarce, the leaf common, but both are quite popular.

No monarch has had as many different portraits on Canadian coins as Elizabeth II. The first portrait, designed by Mary Gillick, had some minor difficulties in striking and as a result, was subtly modified after being placed in production. In 1965, a new bust wearing a tiara was introduced, years before Britain itself began using it. When a mature head of the Queen was desired, the Canadian choice differed from that of Britain. A design with an open crown, by Canadian artist Dora de Pédery-Hunt was used beginning 1990. It was replaced in mid-2003 by a bareheaded, grandmotherly portrait designed by Susanna Blunt.

As part of a set of wildlife coins struck for the centennial of Canadian independence, the 1967 five-cent piece depicted a rabbit running. For its 125th anniversary, the double date 1867-1992 was displayed. Recently, a series of commemorative reverse five-cent pieces has been struck in silver.

In an economy measure, the alloy of the five-cent coin was changed to 75 percent copper, 25 percent nickel in 1982. It was switched to nickel-plated steel gradually from 1999 to 2001, with proofs being struck in sterling.

Modern counting machines occasionally leave an X-shaped scratch on these coins, and such damaged coins are virtually worthless unless they are scarcer dates.

Known Counterfeits: For the small-size pieces, only the 1921, most of which were remelted. For the large-size, crude, contemporary counterfeits are occasionally encountered.

Victoria 1900	Edward VII 1910	George V Silver 1911
5 Cents	5 Cents	5 Cents

VICTORIA

	VG	VF
1858	10.00	35.00
1858 Large date over small date	100.00	250.00
1870 Flat rim	8.00	35.00
1870 Wire rim	8.00	35.00
1871	9.00	35.00
1872H	6.00	35.00
1874H Plain 4	12.50	55.00
1874H Crosslet 4	10.00	40.00
1875H Large date	125.00	325.00
1875H Small date	80.00	250.00
1880H	4.00	20.00
1881H	4.00	25.00
1882H	5.00	30.00
1883H	11.50	80.00
1884	75.00	275.00
1885	7.50	40.00
1886	4.50	25.00
1887	12.50	50.00
1888	3.50	17.00
1889	13.50	70.00
1890H	4.50	22.00
1891	3.00	16.00
1892	4.50	20.00
1893	3.00	12.00
1894	9.50	50.00
1896	3.50	15.00
1897	3.50	10.00
1898	8.00	37.00
1899	2.50	10.00
1900 Oval 0s	2.50	10.00
1900 Round 0s	13.00	50.00
1901	2.50	10.00

EDWARD VII

	VG	VF
1902	1.50	3.25
1902H Broad H	2.00	4.00

	VG	VF
1902H Narrow H	5.50	20.00
1903	4.00	14.00
1903H	1.75	7.00
1904	1.75	7.00
1905	1.75	6.00
1906	1.50	4.00
1907	1.50	4.00
1908	4.00	18.00
1909	2.00	7.00
1910	1.50	3.25

GEORGE V—SILVER

	VG	XF
1911	1.75	10.00
1912	1.50	6.00
1913	1.25	5.00
1914	1.50	7.00
1915	6.50	45.00
1916	2.75	15.00
1917	1.25	4.00
1918	1.25	4.00
1919	1.25	4.00
1920	1.25	4.00
1921	1,600.00	4,000.00

GEORGE V—NICKEL

	VG	XF
1922	.25	7.00
1923	.40	12.00
1924	.30	7.00
1925	35.00	155.00
1926 Near 6	3.00	45.00
1926 Far 6	65.00	325.00
1927	.25	6.50
1928	.25	6.50
1929	.25	6.50
1930	.25	6.50

George V Nickel 1927 5 Cents

George VI 1947 5 Cents

	VG	XF
1931	.25	10.25
1932	.25	10.50
1933	.40	12.50
1934	.25	10.75
1935	.25	6.50
1936	.25	6.50

GEORGE VI

	XF	Unc.
1937	2.50	9.00
1938	7.00	60.00
1939	4.50	35.00
1940	2.25	14.00
1941	2.25	17.00
1942 Nickel	1.75	14.00
1942 Brass	1.75	3.00
1943 Brass	.85	2.00
1944 Brass		*rare*
1944 Steel	1.00	2.00
1945 Steel	1.00	2.00
1946	2.00	10.00
1947	1.25	8.00
1947 Dot	50.00	180.00
1947 Maple leaf	1.25	7.50
1948	2.00	13.00
1949	.75	4.00
1950	.75	4.00
1951 Steel	.85	2.50
1951 Nickel	.50	1.75
1952 Steel	.85	3.00

ELIZABETH II

	BU
1953 Steel, without strap	3.00
1953 Steel, with strap	3.50
1954 Steel	4.00
1955	2.50

	BU
1956	1.50
1957	1.25
1958	1.25
1959	.55
1960	.35
1961	.20
1962	.20
1963	.20
1964	.20
1965	.20
1966	.20
1967 Centennial	.20
1968	.20
1969	.20
1970	.35
1971	.20
1972	.20
1973	.20
1974	.20
1975	.20
1976	.20
1977	.20
1978	.20
1979	.20
1980	.20
1981	.20

Cupro-Nickel

	BU
1982	.20
1983	.20
1984	.20
1985	.20
1986	.20
1987	.10
1988	.10
1989	.10
1990	.10

	XF	Unc.
1991		.20
1992 "1867-1992"		.10

Elizabeth II 1994 5 Cents

	XF	Unc.
1993		.10
1994		.10
1995		.10
1996		.20
1996 Silver	proof only	5.50
1997		.10
1997 Silver	proof only	5.50
1998		.10
1998 Silver	proof only	4.00
1998W		2.75
1998 "1908-1998" Silver		2.75
1999		.10

	XF	Unc.
1999 Silver	proof only	4.00
1999P		8.00
2000		.10
2000 Silver	proof only	4.00
2000P		1.50
2000W	PL	2.75
2000 Voltigeurs, Silver	proof only	12.00
2001		.20
2001 Silver	proof only	4.00
2001 Military Colleges, Silver	proof only	12.00
2001P		.20
2002P "1952-2002"		.20
2002 "1952-2002" Silver	proof only	2.50
2002 Vimy Ridge, Silver	proof only	13.50
2003P crowned portrait		.20
2003 crowned portrait, Silver		3.00
2003P bare portrait		.20
2003 bare portrait, Silver		3.00
2003WP bare portrait		1.50
2004P		.20
2004 D-Day, Silver		40.00

TEN CENTS

Sterling silver ten-cent pieces were among the first coins to be struck by the Province of Canada in 1858 before the formation of the Confederation. These coins bore a young head of Queen Victoria. Twelve years later the new Confederation started issuing ten-cent silver coins, making no significant changes from the earlier provincial piece.

With the passing of Queen Victoria, a new portrait was designed for Edward VII in 1902. There was a bit of a ruckus in 1911 when the new obverse with George V's portrait was found to be lacking the Latin *Dei Gratia* for "by the grace of God." The mint responded to the public outcry and beginning in 1912 these titles were added.

As a result of a World War I increase in the price of silver, the alloy was reduced from 92.5 percent pure (sterling) to 80 percent beginning with 1920.

When the obverse was changed to portray the new King George VI in 1937, the opportunity was taken to revise the reverse of the ten-cent piece. A fishing schooner under sail is depicted, designed by Emmanuel Hahn. Because of the time taken to design the new reverse, some 1936 dated coins were struck in 1937 bearing a minute dot to distinguish them. These are quite rare. This new reverse is, with some alteration, still in use today.

Because of the time taken to modify the royal titles on the dies to reflect the independence of India, some 1947 coins were struck in 1948 with a maple leaf after the date. These are common, but are quite popular.

No monarch has had as many different portraits on Canadian coins as Elizabeth II. The first portrait, designed by Mary Gillick, had some minor difficulties in striking and as a result was subtly modified after being placed in production. In 1965 a new bust wearing a tiara was introduced, years before Britain itself began using it. When a mature head of the Queen was desired, the Canadian choice differed from that of Britain. A design with an open crown, by Canadian artist Dora de Pédery-Hunt was used beginning 1990. It was replaced in mid-2003 by a bareheaded, grandmotherly portrait designed by Susanna Blunt.

As part of a set of wildlife coins struck for the centennial of Canadian independence, the 1967 ten-cent piece depicted a mackerel. Unfortunately, the rising price of silver forced the centennial coins out of circulation. In mid-year the ten-cent piece was reduced to 50 percent pure, and beginning in 1968 to pure nickel. It was switched to nickel-plated steel in 2001, with proofs being struck in sterling.

For the Confederation's 125th anniversary, the double date 1867-1992 was displayed on the regular type. The 1997 issue, commemorating the voyages of John Cabot, begins a series of commemorative ten-cent pieces.

Modern counting machines occasionally leave a circular scratch on these coins, and such damaged coins are virtually worthless unless they are scarcer dates.

Known Counterfeits: The 1936 dot should be examined by an expert. 1930 circulation counterfeits are known.

Victoria 1874H 10 Cents

George V 1936 10 Cents

VICTORIA

	VG	VF
1858, 8 over 5	425.00	975.00
1858	16.50	55.00
1870 Narrow 0	12.00	55.00
1870 Wide 0	17.00	90.00
1871	15.00	90.00
1871H	18.00	95.00
1872H	70.00	225.00
1874H	8.00	40.00
1875H	175.00	675.00
1880H	6.00	50.00
1881H	8.00	50.00
1882H	8.00	60.00
1883H	25.00	175.00
1884	140.00	625.00
1885	22.00	200.00
1886 Small 6	12.00	90.00
1886 Large 6	15.00	100.00
1887	23.00	175.00
1888	6.00	40.00
1889	400.00	1,500.00
1890H	11.50	75.00
1891, 21 leaves	12.00	75.00
1891, 22 leaves	12.00	75.00
1892/1	115.00	400.00
1892	9.50	37.50
1893 Flat top 3	14.00	120.00
1893 Round 3	425.00	1,800.00
1894	13.00	90.00
1896	6.00	45.00
1898	6.00	45.00
1899 Small 9s	6.00	32.00
1899 Large 9s	10.00	55.00
1900	6.00	30.00
1901	6.00	30.00

EDWARD VII

	VG	VF
1902	4.50	25.00

	VG	VF
1902H	2.75	12.50
1903	9.00	60.00
1903H	4.00	25.00
1904	6.50	30.00
1905	6.00	40.00
1906	3.75	22.00
1907	3.50	18.50
1908	7.00	37.00
1909 Victorian leaves	3.50	28.00
1909 Broad leaves	5.50	35.00
1910	2.75	12.50

GEORGE V

	VG	XF
1911	4.00	40.00
1912	1.75	22.00
1913 Large leaves	75.00	650.00
1913 Small leaves	1.50	17.50
1914	1.50	18.50
1915	4.00	80.00
1916	1.25	11.00
1917	1.25	8.75
1918	1.25	8.75
1919	1.25	8.75
1920	1.25	9.00
1921	1.25	12.50
1928	1.00	10.00
1929	1.00	9.50
1930	1.25	14.00
1931	1.25	10.00
1932	1.50	20.00
1933	2.00	25.00
1934	3.00	50.00
1935	3.50	50.00
1936	.75	8.00
1936 Dot		*four known*

GEORGE VI

	XF	Unc.
1937	3.75	10.00

Elizabeth II 1968 10 Cents

	XF	Unc.
1938	6.50	40.00
1939	6.00	35.00
1940	3.00	13.00
1941	6.00	35.00
1942	4.00	25.00
1943	4.00	11.00
1944	4.50	18.00
1945	4.00	11.00
1946	4.50	20.00
1947	6.00	27.00
1947 Maple leaf	3.00	9.50
1948	14.00	37.00
1949	2.00	7.00
1950	1.50	6.00
1951	1.50	4.50
1952	1.50	4.00

ELIZABETH II

	XF	BU
1953 without straps	1.25	2.50
1953 with fold	1.25	3.00
1954	2.25	6.00
1955	.75	2.50
1956	.75	2.50
1956 Dot below date	5.00	10.00
1957	—	1.25
1958	—	1.25
1959	—	1.25
1960	—	.75
1961	—	.75
1962	—	.75
1963	—	.75
1964	—	.75
1965	—	.65
1966	—	.65
1967 Centennial	—	.65
1968	—	.50

Nickel

	XF	BU
1968	—	.25

	XF	BU
1969	—	.25
1970	—	.65
1971	—	.25
1972	—	.25
1973	—	.25
1974	—	.25
1975	—	.25
1976	—	.25
1977	—	.25
1978	—	.25
1979	—	.25
1980	—	.25
1981	—	.25
1982	—	.25
1983	—	.25
1984	—	.25
1985	—	.25
1986	—	.25
1987	—	.25
1988	—	.25
1989	—	.25
1990	—	.25
1991	—	.25
1992 "1867-1992"	—	.25
1993	—	.25
1994	—	.25
1995	—	.25
1996	—	.25
1996 Silver	*proof only*	5.50
1997	—	.25
1997 Silver	*proof only*	5.50
1997 John Cabot, Silver	*proof only*	16.50
1998	—	.25
1998 Silver	*proof only*	4.00
1998O Silver	*proof only*	4.00
1998W	—	.25
1998 "1908-1998" Silver	—	5.50
1999	—	.35
1999 Silver	*proof only*	4.00
1999P	—	10.00
2000	—	.35
2000 Silver	*proof only*	4.00
2000P		*14 known*
2000W		*PL* 1.75
2000 Credit Unions, Silver	*proof only*	11.00
2001 Silver	*proof only*	4.00
2001P	—	.35

	XF	BU
2001 Volunteer,		
Silver . . . . *proof only*	. . .	**11.00**
2001P Volunteer. . . . . —	. . . . . .	**.50**
2002P "1952-2002" . . . . —	. . . . . .	**.35**
2002 "1952-2002"		
Silver . . . . *proof only*	. . . .	**4.00**
2003P Crowned portrait . . . —	. . . . . .	**.35**

	XF	BU
2003 Crowned portrait,		
Silver . . . . *proof only*	. . . .	**4.00**
2003P Barehead. . . . . —	. . . . . .	**.35**
2003 Barehead,		
Silver . . . . *proof only*	. . . .	**4.00**
2004P . . . . —	. . . . . .	**.35**
2004 Silver . . . . *proof only*	. . . .	**4.00**

TWENTY CENTS

Sterling silver twenty-cent pieces were the largest of the first coins to be struck by the Province of Canada in 1858 before the formation of the Confederation. These coins bore a young head of Queen Victoria. During the American Civil War, when U.S. silver coins were being discounted in terms of gold, some firms bought them up in quantity and imported them into Canada. With so many United States quarters circulating at the same time, it became easy to confuse the twenty-cent piece with them. Because of this it, was decided to withdraw the denomination in 1870.

It has since become one of the most desirable and saleable Canadian coins.

Known Counterfeits: Few.

	VG	VF
1858	**45.00**	. . . **100.00**

TWENTY-FIVE CENTS

Sterling silver twenty-five cent pieces were first struck in 1870 after the decision to abandon the old twenty-cent denomination. The new coin was more in harmony with the flood of United States quarters that had been imported into Canada during the American Civil War. These coins bore an older head of Queen Victoria. They saw hard service, not being actively replaced by the government as they wore out, hence they are more difficult to find than one would expect in middle to upper grades.

With the passing of Queen Victoria, a new portrait was designed for Edward VII in 1902. There was a bit of a ruckus in 1911 when the new obverse with George V's portrait was found to be lacking the Latin *Dei Gratia* for "by the grace of God." The mint responded to the public outcry and beginning in 1912 these titles were added.

Because of a World War I increase in silver prices, the alloy was reduced from 92.5 percent pure (sterling) to 80 percent beginning with 1920.

When the obverse was changed to portray the new King George VI in 1937, the opportunity was taken to revise the reverse of the twenty-five cent piece. A caribou's bust is depicted, designed by Emanuel Hahn. Because of the time taken to design the new reverse, some 1936 dated coins were struck in 1937 bearing a minute dot to distinguish them. These are quite rare. This reverse is, with some alteration, still in use today.

Because of the time taken to modify the royal titles on the dies to reflect the independence of India, some 1947 coins were struck in 1948 with a tiny dot or maple leaf after the date. The dot is scarce, the leaf is not, but both are quite popular.

No monarch has had as many different portraits on Canadian coins as Elizabeth II. The first portrait, designed by Mary Gillick, had some minor difficulties in striking, and as a result, was subtly modified after being placed in production. In 1965 a new bust wearing a tiara was introduced, years before Britain itself began using it. When a mature head of the Queen was desired, the Canadian choice differed from that of Britain. A design with an open crown, by Canadian artist Dora de Pédery-Hunt was used beginning in 1990. It was replaced in mid-2003 by a bareheaded, grandmotherly portrait designed by Susanna Blunt.

As part of a set of wildlife coins struck for the centennial of Canadian independence, the 1967 twenty-five cent piece depicted a bobcat. Unfortunately, the rising price of silver forced the centenial coins out of circulation. In mid-year this coin was reduced to 50 percent pure, and beginning in 1968 to pure nickel. It was switched to nickel-plated steel in 2000, with proofs being struck in sterling.

A special reverse was used in 1973 to commemorate the centenary of the Royal Canadian Mounted Police. A whole set of circulating commemorative twenty-five cent pieces was struck for the 125th anniversary of the Canadian Confederation in 1992. While one of the coins simply bore a "1867-1992" legend, a dozen others of the extremely popular series bore reverses emblematic of each province and territory. A series of monthly "Millennium" 25¢ pieces was initiated in 1999 and 2000, with the approach of the new millennium, and were struck in the old nickel composition.

Most common 1912-1968 pieces in Very Good or lower are worth only their scrap value. Modern counting machines occasionally leave a circular scratch on these coins, and such damaged coins are virtually worthless unless they are scarcer dates.

Known Counterfeits: The 1936 dot should be examined by an expert.

Victoria 1872H 25 Cents   George V 1911 25 Cents

Edward VII 1902 25 Cents

EDWARD VII

	VG	VF
1902	7.00	40.00
1902H	5.00	32.00
1903	8.00	50.00
1904	13.00	120.00
1905	7.00	95.00
1906 Small crown	3,000.00	6,000.00
1906 Large crown	6.00	38.00
1907	4.00	38.00
1908	7.00	65.00
1909	5.00	40.00
1910	3.50	26.00

GEORGE V

	F	XF
1911	14.00	70.00
1912	3.50	40.00
1913	3.50	40.00
1914	4.00	50.00
1915	33.00	330.00
1916	4.25	30.00
1917	3.00	20.00
1918	3.00	20.00
1919	3.00	20.00
1920	4.00	22.00
1921	16.00	185.00
1927	38.00	185.00
1928	4.00	28.00
1929	2.75	28.00
1930	3.50	35.00
1931	3.50	40.00
1932	5.00	40.00
1933	5.00	50.00
1934	6.00	55.00
1935	5.00	42.00
1936	3.50	18.00
1936 Dot	60.00	275.00

VICTORIA

	VG	VF
1870	19.00	75.00
1871	19.00	95.00
1871H	25.00	135.00
1872H	9.00	45.00
1874H	9.00	45.00
1875H	250.00	1,250.00
1880H Narrow 0	40.00	250.00
1880H Wide 0	125.00	475.00
1880H Wide over narrow 0	95.00	375.00
1881H	25.00	95.00
1882H	25.00	110.00
1883H	17.00	75.00
1885	95.00	400.00
1886, 6 over 3	25.00	125.00
1886	19.00	95.00
1887	95.00	450.00
1888	20.00	75.00
1889	125.00	500.00
1890H	25.00	125.00
1891	85.00	350.00
1892	15.00	75.00
1893	95.00	395.00
1894	25.00	110.00
1899	9.00	40.00
1900	7.00	35.00
1901	7.00	38.00

GEORGE VI

	XF	Unc.
1937	4.00	10.00
1938	6.50	45.00
1939	5.50	40.00
1940	3.50	10.00
1941	3.50	12.00
1942	3.50	13.00
1943	3.00	14.00
1944	4.00	17.00
1945	3.00	10.00
1946	5.00	35.00
1947	7.00	36.00
1947 Dot after date	110.00	200.00
1947 Maple leaf	4.00	12.00
1948	5.00	40.00
1949	2.00	7.00
1950	2.00	6.50
1951	2.00	5.00
1952	2.00	5.00

ELIZABETH II

	XF	BU
1953 Without strap	1.75	4.00
1953 With strap	2.00	6.00
1954	4.00	15.00
1955	—	3.50
1956	—	3.00
1957	—	2.00
1958	—	2.00
1959	—	1.75
1960	—	1.50
1961	—	1.50
1962	—	1.50
1963	—	1.50
1964	—	1.50
1965	—	1.50
1966	—	1.50
1967 Centennial	—	1.50
1968	—	1.25
Nickel		
1968	—	.50
1969	—	.50
1970	—	1.25
1971	—	.50
1972	—	.50
1973 R.C.M.P.	—	.50
1974	—	.50

	XF	BU
1975	—	.50
1976	—	.50
1977	—	.50
1978	—	.50
1979	—	.50
1980	—	.50
1981	—	.50
1982	—	.50
1983	—	.75
1984	—	.50
1985	—	.50
1986	—	.50
1987	—	.65
1988	—	.65
1989	—	.50
1990	—	.60
1991	—	8.00
1992 "1867-1992"	—	12.50
1992 Alberta	—	.50
1992 Alberta Silver Proof	—	7.50
1992 British Columbia	—	.50
1992 Br. Columbia Silver Proof	—	7.50
1992 Manitoba	—	.50
1992 Manitoba Silver Proof	—	7.50
1992 New Brunswick	—	.50
1992 New Brunswick Silver Proof	—	7.50
1992 Newfoundland	—	.50
1992 Newfoundland Silver Proof	—	7.50
1992 North West Terr.	—	.50
1992 North West Terr. Silver Proof	—	7.50
1992 Nova Scotia	—	.50
1992 Nova Scotia Silver Proof	—	7.50
1992 Ontario	—	.50
1992 Ontario Silver Proof	—	7.50
1992 Prince Edward Island	—	.50
1992 Prince Edward Island Silver Proof	—	7.50
1992 Quebec	—	.50
1992 Quebec Silver Proof	—	7.50

Elizabeth II 1994 25 Cents

	XF	BU
1992 Saskatchewan	—	.50
1992 Saskatchewan Silver Proof	—	7.50
1992 Yukon	—	.50
1992 Yukon Silver Proof	—	7.50
1993	—	.65
1994	—	.65
1995	—	.65
1996	—	.65
1996 Silver	proof only	6.50
1997	in sets only	4.00
1997 Silver	proof only	5.00
1998	in sets only	6.00
1998 Silver	proof only	5.50
1998O Silver	proof only	5.50
1998W	—	5.00
1998 "1908-1998" Silver	—	15.00
1999	in sets only	3.50
1999 Silver	proof only	6.00
1999P	—	16.00
1999 January	—	.50
1999 January Silver	proof only	8.50
1999 February	—	.50
1999 February Silver	proof only	8.50
1999 March	—	.50
1999 March Silver	proof only	8.50
1999 April	—	.50
1999 April Silver	proof only	8.50
1999 May	—	.50
1999 May Silver	proof only	8.50
1999 June	—	.50
1999 June Silver	proof only	8.50
1999 July	—	.50
1999 July, Silver	proof only	8.50
1999 August	—	.50
1999 August, Silver	proof only	8.50
1999 September	—	.50

	XF	BU
1999 September, Silver	proof only	8.50
1999 October	—	.50
1999 October, Silver	proof only	8.50
1999 November	—	.50
1999 November, Silver	proof only	8.50
1999 December	—	.50
1999 December, Silver	proof only	8.50
2000	—	4.00
2000P	two known	
2000 Silver	proof only	8.00
2000W	PL Only	5.00
2000 Health	—	.50
2000 Health, Silver	proof only	8.50
2000 Freedom	—	.50
2000 Freedom, Silver	proof only	8.50
2000 Family	—	.50
2000 Family, Silver	proof only	8.50
2000 Community	—	.50
2000 Community, Silver	proof only	8.50
2000 Harmony	—	.50
2000 Harmony, Silver	proof only	8.50
2000 Wisdom	—	.50
2000 Wisdom, Silver	proof only	8.50
2000 Creativity	—	.50
2000 Creativity, Silver	proof only	8.50
2000 Ingenuity	—	.50
2000 Ingenuity, Silver	proof only	8.50
2000 Achievement	—	.50
2000 Achievement, Silver	proof only	8.50
2000 Natural Legacy	—	.50
2000 Natural Legacy, Silver	proof only	8.50
2000 Celebration	—	.50
2000 Celebration, Colorized	—	50.00
2000 Celebration, Silver	proof only	8.50
2000 Pride	—	.50
2000 Pride, Colorized	—	15.00

	XF	BU		XF	BU
2000 Pride, Silver.. *proof only*	....	**8.50**	2003 Crowned portrait,		
2001	—	.65	Silver .... *proof only*	....	**4.00**
2001 Silver .... *proof only*		**6.50**	2003P Crowned portrait ...	—	.65
2001P	—	.50	2003P Canada Day		
2001P Canada Day			reverse, Colorized	—	.8.00
Reverse, Colorized	—	**12.00**	2003 Bare portrait,		
2002 "1952-2002"			Silver .... *proof only*	....	**4.00**
Silver .... *proof only*		**6.50**	2003P Bare portrait........	—	.65
2002P "1952-2002"	—	.65	2003WP	—	**2.75**
2002P Canada Day			2004	—	**2.75**
reverse	—	.65	2004 Silver .... *proof only*	....	**4.00**
2002P Canada Day			2004P	—	.65
reverse, Colorized	—	.8.00	2004P Canada Day reverse,		
			Colorized	—	.8.00

FIFTY CENTS

    Sterling silver fifty-cent pieces were the largest coin struck for domestic circulation from the beginning of Confederation coinage in 1870 until 1912. These coins bore a portrait of an older Queen Victoria. Initial mintages were moderate, and for some time it was not the government's policy to replace worn out coins, so these coins saw hard service. They are more difficult to find than one would expect in middle to upper grades.

    With the passing of Queen Victoria a new portrait was designed for Edward VII in 1902. The very first coin struck at the new Canadian mint in 1908 was one of these pieces. There was a bit of a ruckus in 1911 when the new obverse with George V's portrait was found to be lacking the Latin *Dei Gratia* for "by the grace of God." The mint responded to the public outcry, and beginning in 1912 these titles were added.

    As a result of a World War I increase in the price of silver, the alloy was reduced from 92.5 percent pure (sterling) to 80 percent beginning with 1920. Most 1921 pieces were melted before they could be released, and no more fifty-cent pieces were struck until 1929. The 1921 fifty-cent pieces are today one of the greatest of Canadian rarities.

    When the obverse was changed to portray the new King George VI in 1937, the opportunity was taken to revise the reverse of the fifty-cent piece. The crowned coat of arms of Canada was selected, as designed by George Kruger-Gray. This new reverse motif has, with significant alterations, continued in use today.

Because of the time taken to modify the royal titles on the dies to reflect the independence of India, some 1947 coins were struck in 1948 with a tiny maple leaf after the date. This is not common and quite popular.

No monarch has had as many different portraits on Canadian coins as Elizabeth II. The first portrait, designed by Mary Gillick, had some minor difficulties in striking and as a result was subtly modified after being placed in production. In 1965 a new bust wearing a tiara was introduced, years before Britain itself began using it. When a mature head of the Queen was desired, the Canadian choice differed from that of Britain. A design with an open crown, by Canadian artist Dora de Pédery-Hunt was used beginning 1990. It was replaced in mid-2003 by a bareheaded, grandmotherly portrait designed by Susanna Blunt.

During this reign, the coat of arms on the reverse went through its own evolution. A version with a motto and more elaborate crest was introduced in 1959, only to be modified the next year. The 1959 version was heraldically inaccurate, using the symbol for blue instead of white in the lowest section. In 1997, an additional collar was added around the shield.

As part of a set of wildlife coins struck for the centennial of Canadian independence, the 1967 fifty-cent piece depicted a howling wolf. Unfortunately, the rising price of silver forced the centennial coins out of circulation. Production of the silver fifty-cent piece was suspended, and beginning in 1968 it was reduced in size and produced in pure nickel. It was switched to nickel plated steel in 2000, with proofs being struck in sterling.

For the Confederation's 125th anniversary, the double date "1867-1992" was displayed on the regular type. Since then, commemoratives have become more common, with most placed on sale at a premium.

Most common 1937-1968 pieces in Fine or lower condition are worth only their scrap value.

Known Counterfeits: Any 1921 should be examined by an expert.

George V 1917 50 Cents

George VI 1952 50 Cents

VICTORIA

	VG	VF
1870	550.00	1,800.00
1870 LCW	40.00	180.00
1871	65.00	275.00
1871H	90.00	400.00
1872H	40.00	175.00
1872H Inverted A over V	150.00	700.00
1881H	45.00	200.00
1888	150.00	500.00
1890H	700.00	2,000.00
1892	50.00	250.00
1894	250.00	990.00
1898	65.00	300.00
1899	95.00	500.00
1900	38.00	175.00
1901	42.00	185.00

EDWARD VII

	VG	VF
1902	11.00	85.00
1903H	18.00	110.00
1904	85.00	300.00
1905	100.00	435.00
1906	10.00	70.00
1907	10.00	70.00
1908	15.00	125.00
1909	13.00	150.00
1910 Victorian leaves	9.00	80.00
1910 Edwardian leaves	8.00	65.00

GEORGE V

	F	XF
1911	55.00	455.00
1912	16.00	200.00
1913	16.00	210.00

	F	XF
1914	45.00	400.00
1916	12.00	115.00
1917	9.00	90.00
1918	8.00	70.00
1919	8.00	70.00
1920	8.50	90.00
1921	17,000.00	23,000.00
1929	8.00	80.00
1931	22.00	190.00
1932	130.00	625.00
1934	25.00	200.00
1936	22.00	150.00

GEORGE VI

	XF	Unc.
1937	8.00	22.00
1938	22.00	95.00
1939	13.50	60.00
1940	4.00	20.00
1941	4.00	20.00
1942	4.00	20.00
1943	4.00	20.00
1944	4.00	20.00
1945	4.00	20.00
1946	7.50	45.00
1946 Hoof in 6	100.00	900.00
1947 Straight 7	10.00	58.00
1947 Curved 7	10.00	58.00
1947 Straight 7, maple leaf	55.00	140.00
1947 Curved 7, maple leaf	1,900.00	3,000.00
1948	80.00	125.00
1949	7.00	30.00
1949 Hoof over 9	50.00	275.00
1950	16.00	130.00

	XF	Unc.
1950 Lines in 0	4.00	9.00
1951	3.50	7.50
1952	3.50	7.50

ELIZABETH II

	XF	MS-60
1953 Small date, without strap	2.50	5.00
1953 Large date, without strap	9.50	60.00
1953 Large date, with fold	4.00	10.00
1954	7.00	20.00
1955	4.00	10.00
1956	3.00	4.50
1957	—	3.50
1958	—	3.00
1959	—	3.00
1960		3.00
1961		3.00
1962		3.00
1963		3.00
1964		3.00
1965		3.00
1966		3.00
1967 Centennial		3.00

Nickel

1968	.75
1969	.75
1970	.75
1971	.75
1972	.75
1973	.75
1974	.75
1975	.75
1976	.75
1977	1.35
1978	.75
1979	.75
1980	.75
1981	.75
1982	.75
1983	.75
1984	.75
1985	.75
1986	1.00
1987	1.00
1988	1.00
1989	1.00
1990	1.00
1991	.85
1992 "1867-1992"	1.00

Elizabeth II 1994 50 Cents

	XF	MS-60
1993		.85
1994		.75
1995		.75
1995 Puffin, Silver	proof only	15.00
1995 Whooping crane, Silver	proof only	15.00
1995 Gray jays, Silver	proof only	20.00
1995 Ptarmigans, Silver	proof only	20.00
1996		.75
1996 Silver	proof only	7.50
1996 Moose calf, Silver	proof only	14.00
1996 Wood ducklings, Silver	proof only	14.00
1996 Cougar kittens, Silver	proof only	14.00
1996 Black bear cubs, Silver	proof only	14.00
1997		.75
1997 Silver	proof only	7.00
1997 Duck tolling Retriever, Silver	proof only	10.00
1997 Labrador retriever, Silver	proof only	10.00
1997 Newfoundland, Silver	proof only	10.00
1997 Eskimo dog, Silver	proof only	10.00
1998		.75
1998 Silver	proof only	6.00
1998W	in sets only	3.00
1998 "1908-1998" Silver		15.00
1998 Skaters, Silver	proof only	12.50
1998 Ski jumper, Silver	proof only	12.50
1998 Soccer players, Silver	proof only	12.50
1998 Race car, Silver	proof only	12.50
1998 Killer whales, Silver	proof only	10.00
1998 Humpback whale, Silver	proof only	10.00

Elizabeth II 2000 50 Cents

Elizabeth II 2000 50 Cents

	XF	MS-60

1998 Beluga whales,
   Silver . . . . *proof only* **10.00**
1998 Blue whale, Silver . . *proof only* **10.00**
1999 . . . . **.75**
1999 Silver . . . . *proof only* **4.00**
1999P **8.00**
1999 Golfers, Silver . . . . . *proof only* **13.50**
1999 Yacht race, Silver . . *proof only* **12.00**
1999 Football, Silver . . . . *proof only* **12.00**
1999 Basketbal, Silver . . . *proof only* **12.00**
1999 Cymric cat, Silver . . *proof only* **15.00**
1999 Tonkinese cat, Silver *proof only* **13.50**
1999 Cougar, Silver . . . . . *proof only* **13.50**
1999 Lynx, Silver . . . . *proof only* **13.50**
2000 . . . . **.75**
2000 Silver . . . . *proof only* **6.00**
2000P . . . . *approximately 200 struck*
2000W . . . . *in sets only* **2.00**
2000 Hockey, Silver . . . . . *proof only* **12.00**
2000 Curling, Silver . . . . . *proof only* **12.00**
2000 Steeplechase, Silver *proof only* **12.00**
2000 Bowling, Silver . . . . *proof only* **12.00**
2000 Great horned owl,
   Silver . . . . *proof only* **13.50**
2000 Red-tailed hawk,
   Silver . . . . *proof only* **13.50**
2000 Osprey, Silver . . . . . *proof only* **13.50**
2000 Bald eagle, Silver . . *proof only* **13.50**
2001 Silver . . . . *proof only* **7.50**
2001P **1.00**
2001 Quebec Winter Carnival,
   Silver . . . . *proof only* **15.00**
2001 Nunavut Toonik Tyme,
   Silver . . . . *proof only* **15.00**
2001 Newfoundland Folk Festival,
   Silver . . . . *proof only* **15.00**
2001 P.E.I. Festival, Silver *proof only* **15.00**
2001 The Sled, Silver . . . . *proof only* **17.00**
2001 The Maiden's Cave,
   Silver . . . . *proof only* **17.00**
2001 Les Petits Sauteux,
   Silver . . . . *proof only* **17.00**

	XF	MS-60

2002 Silver . . . . *proof only* **8.00**
2002P "1952-2002" **1.75**
2002 "1952-2002," Silver **17.50**
2002 Nova Scotia Festival,
   Silver . . . . *proof only* **16.00**
2002 Ontario Stratford
   Festival, Silver . . . . *proof only* **16.00**
2002 Manitoba Folklorama,
   Silver . . . . *proof only* **16.00**
2002 Alberta Calgary
   Stampede, Silver . . . . *proof only* **16.00**
2002 British Columbia
   Squamish Days, Silver *proof only* **16.00**
2002 The Pig... over the
   Stile, Silver . . . . *proof only* **18.00**
2002 Shoemaker in Heaven,
   Silver . . . . *proof only* **18.00**
2002 Le Vaisseau Fantome,
   Silver . . . . *proof only* **18.00**
2002 Tulip Festival, Gilt
   Silver . . . . *proof only* **50.00**
2003 Crowned portrait. **1.00**
2003 Crowned portrait,
   Silver . . . . *proof only* **5.00**
2003 Bare portrait, Silver . *proof only* **5.00**
2003W Bare portrait **1.00**
2003WP Bare portrait **2.00**
2003 Yukon Festival,
   Silver . . . . *proof only* **16.00**
2003 Manitoba Back to
   Batoche, Silver . . . . . . *proof only* **16.00**
2003 Saskatchewan Arts
   Festival, Silver . . . . *proof only* **16.00**
2003 New Brunswick Festival,
   Silver . . . . *proof only* **16.00**
2003 N.W.Terr. Festival,
   Silver . . . . *proof only* **16.00**
2003 Daffodil, Gilt Silver *proof only* **25.00**
2004 . . . . **2.00**
2004, Silver **5.00**
2004 Easter Lily, Gilt
   Silver . . . . *proof only* **25.00**

DOLLARS

Despite patterns having been produced as early as 1911, Canada did not issue a silver dollar until 1935. The entire visual style of Canadian coins began to change then, when a new artistic, commemorative dollar for the jubilee of George V was released. It depicted the now famous Voyageur design of a fur company agent and an Indian paddling a canoe past an islet. This design was retained when the reverses of all the other denominations were modernized with appearance of the new George VI portrait in 1937.

Because of the time taken to modify the royal titles to reflect the independence of India, some 1947 dollars were struck in 1948 with a tiny maple leaf after the date. This variety is both scarce and popular. The 1950-52 Arnprior varieties have only 1½ water lines to the right of the canoe, due to over-polishing of the die.

No monarch has had as many different portraits on Canadian coins as Elizabeth II. The first portrait, designed by Mary Gillick, had some minor difficulties in striking and as a result was subtly modified after being placed in production. In 1965 a new bust wearing a tiara was introduced, years before Britain itself began using it. When a mature head of the Queen was desired, the Canadian choice differed from that of Britain. A design with an open crown, by Canadian artist Dora de Pédery-Hunt was used beginning 1990. It was replaced in mid-2003 by a bareheaded, grandmotherly portrait designed by Susanna Blunt.

The 1967 centennial of Canadian independence was cause for issue of some of Canada's most beautiful and dignified wildlife coins. On the dollar, a majestic Canada goose is shown against stark open background. Unfortunately, the rising price of silver forced these coins out of circulation. Beginning in 1968, the 80 percent silver dollar was replaced by a smaller one of pure nickel.

In 1987, a radical new dollar coin was introduced to save the expense of producing perishable paper money. A small golden-bronze plated nickel dollar was introduced depicting a swimming loon. It was originally intended to use the standard Voyageur reverse, but the master dies were temporarily lost in transit! Today, this coin is popularly known as the "loonie."

With a long history of being used as a commemorative, one or more being struck every decade since its creation, it is natural that one dollar commemoratives would spearhead the modern aggressive collector coin program initiated during the 1970s. Most years a special cased silver alloy dollar is produced for the numismatic market. In many years a base metal commemorative is also issued, available in both circulation and collector's versions. Cased versions in either silver or base metal should always be kept in their cases of issue. Otherwise they are considered less salable.

Known Counterfeits: Any 1948 dollar should be examined by an expert.

George V 1935 1 Dollar

George VI 1951 1 Dollar

George VI 1949 1 Dollar

Elizabeth II 1958 1 Dollar

	XF	Unc.
1947 Blunt 7	85.00	110.00
1947 Maple leaf	150.00	225.00
1948	550.00	725.00
1949 Newfoundland	16.50	25.00
1950, 4 water lines	9.00	16.50
1950, Arnprior	12.50	30.00
1951, 4 water lines	7.00	10.00
1951, Arnprior	45.00	70.00
1952, 4 water lines	7.00	10.00
1952, Arnprior	20.00	50.00
1952, No water lines	8.00	16.50

GEORGE V

	XF	Unc.
1935 Jubilee	28.00	36.50
1936	16.50	35.00

GEORGE VI

	XF	Unc.
1937	12.50	25.00
1938	50.00	72.00
1939 Royal visit	8.00	11.50
1945	127.50	200.00
1946	31.00	65.00
1947 Pointed 7	100.00	275.00

ELIZABETH II

	XF	BU
1953 Wire rim, without shoulder strap	6.00	8.00
1953 Flat rim, with shoulder strap	6.00	8.00

Elizabeth II 1967 I Dollar

Elizabeth II 1987 1 Dollar

	XF	BU
1954	10.00	16.50
1955, 4 water lines	9.00	16.00
1955, Arnprior	50.00	80.00
1956	12.50	19.00
1957, 4 water lines	6.00	8.00
1957, Arnprior	7.50	10.00
1958 British Columbia	6.00	7.00
1959	—	6.00
1960	—	6.00
1961	—	6.00
1962	—	6.00
1963	—	6.00
1964 Charlottetown	—	6.00
1965	—	6.00
1966	—	6.00
1967 Centennial	—	6.00

Nickel, Voyageur reverse to 1987 unless noted

		BU
1968		1.25
1969		1.25
1970 Manitoba		2.00
1971 British Columbia		2.00
1971 British Columbia, Silver	PL	6.00
1972		1.50
1973 Pr. Edward Is.		2.00
1973 R.C.M.P., Silver	PL	6.00
1974 Winnipeg		2.00
1974 Winnipeg, Silver	PL	6.00
1975		1.50
1975 Calgary, Silver	PL	6.00
1976		1.50
1976 Library of Parliament, Silver	PL	6.00
1977		2.50
1977 Queen's Jubilee, Silver	PL	6.00

	XF	BU
1978		1.50
1978 Edmonton Games, Silver	PL	6.00
1979		1.50
1979 Sailing ship, Silver	PL	8.50
1980		2.00

	BU	PF
1980 Arctic Territories, Silver		17.50
1981	2.00	5.50
1981 Railroad, Silver	8.00	13.50
1982	1.50	5.25
1982 Constitution	2.50	6.00
1982 Regina, Silver	8.50	7.00
1983	1.50	6.50
1983 Edmonton Games, Silver	7.00	6.50
1984	1.50	6.00
1984 Cartier	2.25	6.00
1984 Toronto, Silver	14.75	6.00
1985	1.50	6.25
1985 National Parks, Silver	8.00	6.00
1986	2.25	8.00
1986 Vancouver, Silver	8.00	7.00
1987	*in sets only* 3.50	8.50
1987 Davis Strait, Silver	8.00	10.00

Loon Reverse: Aureate-bronze Plated Nickel, Other Reverses: Silver, unless noted

Note: Since 1988 uncirculated silver commemorative dollars have had a proof-like finish.

	BU	PF
1987 Loon	2.25	8.00
1988 Loon	2.25	6.75
1988 Ironworks	16.00	15.00
1989 Loon	2.25	6.75
1989 MacKenzie River	12.50	18.00
1990 Loon	1.75	7.00
1990 Kelsey	10.75	18.00

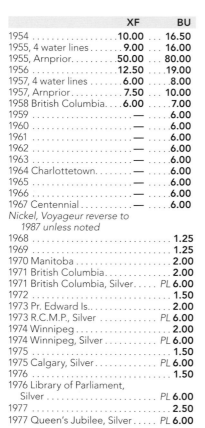

	BU	PF
1991 Loon	1.75	13.00
1991 S.S. Frontenac, Silver,	10.00	23.50
1992 "1867-1992" Loon	2.00	8.00
1992 "1867-1992" Parliament, Aureate-bronze plated nickel	2.25	9.00
1992 Stagecoach	10.75	12.50
1993 Loon	2.00	6.00
1993 Stanley Cup	8.50	12.50
1994 Loon	2.00	7.00
1994 War Memorial, Aureate-bronze plated nickel	2.25	10.00
1994 R.C.M.P. Dog Sled	15.00	24.50
1995 Loon	2.00	7.00
1995 Peacekeeping Monument, Aureate-bronze plated nickel	2.25	10.00
1995 Hudson's Bay Co.	10.00	16.00
1996 Loon	2.00	7.50
1996 McIntosh apple	11.00	19.00
1997 Loon . . . *in sets only*	5.00	8.00
1997 Loon flying	PL 18.00	
1997 Loon flying, Silver	—	65.00
1997 Hockey	10.00	24.00
1998 Loon . . . *in sets only*	2.50	10.00
1998W Loon	PL 5.00	
1998 R.C.M.P.	11.00	18.00
1999 Loon . . . *in sets only*	2.00	8.00
1999 Year of Old Persons	—	28.00
1999 Ship	11.00	22.00

	BU	PF
2000W Loon		PL 5.00
2000 Human and space shuttle	11.00	22.50
2001 Loon . . . *in sets only*	2.00	8.00
2001P	C$10	
2001 Ballet	10.00	22.00
2001 "1911-2001" Wreath	—	45.00
2002 "1952-2002" Loon	5.00	12.00
2002P Loon	—	5.00
2002 Loon family	—	15.00
2002 Loon with privy mark	—	35.00
2002 Queen in coach	12.00	20.00
2002 as above but gilt	—	21.50
2002 Queen Mother	—	145.00
2003 Loon, de Pedery portrait	5.00	12.00
2003 Cobalt	20.00	27.50
2003 Loon, bare portrait	—	12.00
2003P Loon	—	5.00
2003W Loon	—	6.00
2003 Voyageurs, young portrait	—	30.00
2003 Voyageurs, bare portrait	—	38.00
same, Gold		*unique*
(2003) Queen in Coach, bare portrait, Gold		*unique*
2004 Loon	1.00	12.00
2004WP Loon	—	5.00
2004 Loons flying	—	5.00
2004 Elusive Loon	—	15.00
2004 Ship	20.00	30.00

EUROPEAN COINS

Modern coinage as we know it began in Europe during the 1500s and spread throughout the world with the establishment of European colonies, or with the opening of European trade relations. Since this time, the manufacture of coinage has progressed from hand hammering, to screw press and roller dies, to steam-powered presses. Today's high tech, electronic minting machines, capable of striking thousands of coins per minute, are basically an improved version of the steam-powered ones first used in the late 1700s.

Many people collect European and other world coins by "type." This means one of each design, or of each design in each different alloy in which it is struck. Others collect one of each date and mint mark much as United States coins are collected. There is no right or wrong way to collect coins. The most important thing to remember is to enjoy the experience, and perhaps to learn by the process. There is no series more extensively documented in catalogues than the coinage of modern Europe, so whatever path the collector chooses, he need not do it in the dark. With the introduction of the Euro, the new pan-European currency, people are becoming more and more aware of the changes in European coinage, past, present, and future.

Because many colonial coins feature the name and symbolism of the colonizing power more prominently than any reference to the colony itself, such coins are included in this chapter. This should make it easier for the layman to find the type of coin he is trying to identify.

BOOKS ABOUT EUROPEAN COINS

While as in any field there are thousands of specialized books, a few very basic books will go a long way. Many collectors never feel the need to progress much further than the following volumes:

Bruce, Colin R., II. *Unusual World Coins*. Special listing of fantasies and non-circulating coins.

Krause, Chester, and Clifford Mishler. *Standard Catalog of World Coins, 1601-1700.*

Krause, Chester, and Clifford Mishler. *Standard Catalog of World Coins, 1701-1800.*

Krause, Chester, and Clifford Mishler. *Standard Catalog of World Coins, 1801-1900.*

Krause, Chester, and Clifford Mishler. *Standard Catalog of World Coins, 1901-2000*.

The above books are virtually an entire library in compact form. Coverage is extensive from the 1600s through the mid-1700s, and is virtually complete with individual date and mint listings from that time to the present.

Yeoman, R.S. *Current Coins of the World*.

Yeoman, R.S. *Modern World Coins, 1850-1964*.

COUNTERFEIT EUROPEAN COINS

While many individual counterfeits will be listed under each specific country, it is always important to remember that new counterfeits of the more expensive European coins appear every year. This also applies to many more common gold bullion issues.

As a general rule, Crown- and Thaler-sized coins are more prone to be counterfeited for the collector market. During the 19th and 20th centuries, tin or lead alloy circulation counterfeits of silver coins were likely to be of those coins 20 to 28 mm diameter. Recently, more and more circulation counterfeits of high denomination base-metal coins have been reported.

AUSTRIA

The modern coinage of Austria, until 1918, was used in a much larger area than is present day Austria. It circulated in the many lands of the Hapsburg dynasty, and of their dependent nobles. While modern coin production with the use of roller dies began before his reign, the later coinage of Leopold I the Hogmouth (1657-1705), took it to a new height of uniformity. Their excellent portraits are a perfect example of the Baroque style. Collectors should remember that coins struck with roller dies usually appear slightly curved and that this is not a flaw.

The standard design formula is an obverse portrait, and a double-headed eagle reverse. It continued through the 1890s, when a crown and values became the most common designs. A very few commemoratives were also struck during this time. Austria is one of three modern countries to have used the double-headed eagle. They are easily distinguished, as Austria's displays a Hapsburg shield on its breast. Russia's eagle has St. George slaying a dragon on its breast. Serbia's (later Yugoslavia's) eagle has a shield depicting a cross with C's in the angles. The later Yugoslav shield may be more complex, but still contains this element.

After World War I, Austria became a republic and was reduced to its present size. Its circulating coins and commemoratives both depict aspects of local history and culture, such as a Royal Lipizzaner stallion or fauna such as the edelweiss. During World War II, Austria was part of Germany, and Nazi coins with the mint mark B were struck in Vienna.

In January 2002, Austria replaced the schilling with coins denominated in Euros, the currency of the European Union. On the circulating denominations, 1 Cent through 2 Euros, one side carries an Austrian design, the other a common European design. On higher denomination commemoratives, both sides are distinctively Austrian.

During most of Austria's history, powerful nobles and bishops were allowed to strike their own coins. The Counts of Tyrol were the most prolific issuers of coins. Their three kreuzers are particularly common. The Archbishops of Salzburg also struck vast numbers of coins at several mints from 996 through 1806.

Additional Specialized Books:

Miller zu Aicholz. *Oesterreichische Munzpragungen, 1519-1938.*

Probszt, G. *Die Münzen Salzburgs.*

Known Counterfeits: All 1780 Maria Theresa thalers with mint marks SF are modern restrikes. The same is true for most 1915 gold 4 ducat, 1 ducat, 20 corona and 100 corona and 1892 8 florin and 4 florin.

	VF
Leopold I the Hogmouth, 1657-1705. 2 pfennig (S). Three shields/blank	**12.00**
___. 3 Kreuzer. Bust r./double-headed eagle	**25.00**
___. 15 Kreuzer. Similar	**35.00**
___. Thaler. Similar	**225.00**
___. Double Thaler. Bust r./one-headed eagle (for Tyrol)	**350.00**

EIGHTEENTH CENTURY

	F
1746 1/4 Kreuzer. Crowned eagle/blank	**20.00**
1761 Kreuzer. Bust of Maria Theresa r./cartouche (C)	**6.00**
1800 Kreuzer Bust of Francis II r./eagle (C)	**2.00**
1714 3 Kreuzer. Bust of Charles VI r./eagle (S)	**15.00**
1765 3 Kreuzer. Bust of Maria Theresa (Billon)	**15.00**
1754 10 Kreuzer. Bust of Francis I in wreath/eagle, 10 on altar (S)	**17.50**
1795 12 Kreuzer. Eagle/inscription (Billon)	**5.00**

	F
1778 20 Kreuzer. Bust of Joseph II in wreath/eagle (S)	**6.00**
1800 24 Kreuzer. Eagle/inscription (Billon)	**20.00**
1746 30 Kreuzer. Bust in diamond/eagle in diamond (S)	**40.00**
1751 2 Thaler. Bust of Francis I r./eagle (S)	**65.00**
1780 SF Thaler *restrike*. Bust of Maria Theresa/eagle	*Unc.* **7.50**
1798 Thaler. Bust of Francis II r./arms. (S)	**75.00**
1773 Ducat. Bust of Maria Theresa r./eagle (G)	**200.00**
1773 3 Ducat. Bust of Joseph II r./eagle (G)	**1,000.00**

NINETEENTH CENTURY TO 1920

	VF
1851 1/4 Kreuzer. Crowned eagle/value (C)	**1.00**
1816 Kreuzer. Crowned shield/inscription (C)	**2.00**
1885 Kreuzer. Crowned eagle/wreath (C)	**.50**

Austria 1893 10 Heller

Austria 1946 1 Schilling

Austria 1974 100 Schilling

	VF
1860 4 Kreuzer. Eagle/wreath (C)	**6.00**
1812 20 Kreuzer. Bust of Francis I in wreath/eagle (S)	**10.00**
1870 20 Kreuzer. Bust of Franz Josef/eagle (Billon)	**2.00**
1841 1/2 Thaler. Bust of Ferdinand I/eagle (S)	**90.00**
1857 2 Thaler. Bust of Franz Josef/tower between train and ship	**800.00**
1893 1 Heller. Eagle (C)	**.35**
1908 2 Heller. Eagle (C)	**.25**
1893 10 Heller. Eagle (N)	**.50**
1893 1 Corona. Head of Franz Josef/crown (S)	**3.00**
1900 5 Corona. Head of Franz Josef/double-headed eagle (S)	**12.50**
1897 20 Corona Head of Franz Josef/eagle (G)	**110.00**
1915 (restrike) Head of Franz Josef/eagle (G)	**100.00**

REPUBLIC COINAGE 1923 TO 1938

	XF
1924 100 Kronen. Eagle head/oak sprig (C)	**1.50**
1925 Schilling. Neo-classical building/shield (S)	**3.50**

	VF
1928 2 Schilling. Schubert/ten shields (S)	**10.00**
1935 5 Schilling. Madonna and child/eagle (S)	**28.00**
1926 25 Schilling. Eagle (G)	**125.00**

REPUBLIC COINAGE 1946 TO 2001

	BU
1972 2 Groschen. Eagle (AL)	**.20**
1946 Schilling. Sower (AL)	**1.50**
1957 10 Schilling. Shield/girl's head (S)	**6.00**
1974 10 Schilling. Eagle/girl's head (CN)	**1.75**
1996 20 Schilling. Anton Bruckner (ALB)	**4.00**
1956 25 Schilling. Mozart (S)	**4.50**
1974 100 Schilling. (S)	**9.00**
1982 500 Schilling. Printing press (S)	**50.00**

EURO COINAGE 2002 TO DATE

	BU
2002 1 Cent. Flower/globe. (C plated Steel)	**.35**
2002 5 Euro. Building and animals/circle of shield, in card (S)	**15.00**

BALKANS

The Ottoman conquest of the Balkan peninsula ended European-style coinage for most of the region, and it was not restored until the 1800s. The only surviving coinages were those of Transylvania, and the small Venetian and Ragusan settlements along the Adriatic coast. The former were all copper, the latter a variety of metals.

The first country to regain its independence from the Ottoman Turks was Greece. Its first coinage was very distinctive, and portrayed the mythological Phoenix bird reborn from its ashes, alluding to the rebirth of the Greek nation. After very few years, its coinage took on the less creative forms popular elsewhere in Europe: shields, royal portraits and a denomination within a wreath. The coinages of the two Greek republics, 1925-1935 and 1974 to date, are also distinctive in their harking back to ancient times for their inspiration.

Soon Serbia (1868), Romania (1867), Bulgaria (1881), and Montenegro (1906) struck their first modern coinages, on much the same European pattern as mentioned above. Albania lagged behind until 1926. After the first World War, Montenegro and the former Austrian territories of Slovenia, Croatia and Bosnia-Herzogovina were joined under the king of Serbia to form Yugoslavia. Following World War II these kingdoms were all overthrown by Communists. Most Communist coins follow the typical pattern of a state seal on the obverse and a value or a symbol of agricultural or industrial labor on the reverse. As a result of the Yugoslav Civil War, Slovenia, Croatia, Macedonia, and Bosnia-Herzegovina were established as independent states. Moldova came into being as a result of the break-up of the Soviet Union.

Post-Communist Balkan coinage varies from monotonous bank monograms, to exquisite depictions of flora and fauna. Some of these new governments have even chosen to use the same heraldic motifs that were found on their coinages during the 1930s. During the last few years, all these countries have struck collectors' coins. Some, such as Bosnia's, have been actively marketed in North America. Others such as Romania's have been very scantily distributed.

Because the alphabets and languages used may seem unusual to North American readers, it is useful here to give some Balkan country names in their native forms:

Albania.......	**SHQIPNI or SHQIPERI**	Macedonia	**МАКЕΔОНИЈА**
Bulgaria	**БЪЛГАРИЯ**	Montenegro	**цРНА гОРА**
Croatia	**HRVATSKA**	Serbia........	**СРБИЈА or СРПИЈА**
Greece.................	**ΕΛΛΑΣ**	Yugoslavia	**ЈУГОСΛАВИЈА**

Additional Specialized Books: see general European listings.

Known Counterfeits: Albanian gold and dollar-sized silver coins of the 1920s and 1930s, particularly the 1938 gold. Modern-style counterfeits exist of the 1600s Venetian coppers for Dalmatia and Albania.

Albania 1964 1 Lek

ALBANIA

	XF
1935 Qindar Ar. Eagle (C)	**10.00**
1926 2 Lek. Two headed eagle/man fighting lion (N)	**14.00**
1935 Frang Ar. Head of King Zog/arms (S)	**25.00**
1926 100 Franga Ar. Head of Amet Zogu/ chariot (G)	**800.00**
1941 0.20 Lek. King of Italy in helmet/ eagle between fasces (Steel)	**4.00**
1939 10 Lek. King of Italy/similar (S)	**120.00**
1947 2 Lek. Eagle (Z)	**1.50**
1964 1 Lek. Eagle (AL)	**2.00**

	BU
1988 5 Lek. Train/train (CN)	**12.00**
1996 50 Lek. Ancient horseman (CN)	**2.00**

BOSNIA-HERZEGOVINA

1994 500 Dinara. Arms over bridge/wolf (CN)	**8.50**

	BU
1998 10 fennig. Triangle/map (C plated Steel)	**1.00**
2000 2 Convertible Marks. Dove (CN in NB, bimetallic)	**11.50**

BULGARIA

	VF
1912 2 Stotinki. Arms/wreath (C)	**1.00**
1881 5 Stotinki. Similar (C)	**5.00**
1883 50 Stotinki. Similar (S)	**3.00**
1925 1 Lev. Similar (CN)	**.50**

Bulgaria 1979 10 Leva

	VF
1882 2 Leva. Similar (S)	**7.00**
1943 5 Leva. Medieval horseman r./wreath (Nickel Clad Steel)	**1.00**
1894 20 Leva. Head of Ferdinand I I./arms (G)	**100.00**
1934 100 Leva. Head of Boris III/Art Deco wreath (S)	**5.50**

POSTWAR ISSUES

	BU
1951 1 Stotinka. Arms/grain (ALB)	**.25**
1977 50 Stotinki. Runner/arms (CN)	**2.00**
1976 1 Lev. Gun and knife/lion (C)	**5.00**
1979 10 Leva. Arms/children (S) *PF* **22.50**
1992 10 Leva. Madara horseman(CN)	**2.50**
1996 1,000 Leva. Sailing ship/wreath (S)	*proof only* **45.00**

CROATIA

	VF
Ragusa, 1626-1761. Grosetto. Christ standing amid stars/St. Blasius stg. (AR)	**30.00**

	Unc.
1941 2 Kune. Shield (Z)	**30.00**
1993 1 Lipa. Corn (AL)	**.20**
1994 100 Kune. St. Blaza church/ altar (ii) (S)	*PF* **75.00**

Croatia 1994 100 Kuna

Greece 1994 50 Drachmes

	Unc.
1995 2 Kune. Tuna (CN)	1.75
1994 5 Kune. Bear (CN)	3.00
1998 25 Kune. Sailboat (Brass in CN bimetallic)	10.00

GREECE

	VF
Venetian Morea. 1688-90s Gazetta. Bust of winged lion, II below/ARMATA ET MOREA (C)	90.00
1828 1 Lepton. Phoenix/wreath (C)	120.00
1851 2 Lepta. Crowned shield/wreath (C)	40.00
1869 5 Lepta. Head of George/wreath (C)	6.00
1895 10 Lepta. Crown/wreath (CN)	5.00
1922 10 Lepta. Crown/branch (AL)	2.50
1831 20 Lepta. Phoenix/wreath (C)	125.00
1926 50 Lepta. Head. of Athena (CN)	1.00
1833 Drachma. Head of Otto/arms (S)	65.00
1911 2 Drachmai. Head of George/Thetis std. on hippocamp (S)	25.00
1875 5 Drachmai. Head of George/arms (S)	70.00
1884 20 Drachmai. Similar (G)	120.00

	BU
1954 5 Lepta. Crowned wreath/wheat (AL, holed)	2.00
1971 50 Lepta. Head of Constantine II/ Phoenix and soldier	2.00

	BU
1988 1 Drachma. Bouboulina/ship (C)	.50
1973 20 Drachmai. Phoenix/bust of Athena (CN)	2.00
1964 30 Drachmai. Busts of King and Queen/double-headed eagle (S)	7.00
1994 50 Drachmes. Kallergis/ Pariiament (Brass)	3.00
1998 100 Drachmes. Basketball players (ALB)	4.00
1991 500 Drachmes. Cartoon fish/flags (S)	proof only 60.00
2000 500 Drachmes. Woman handing torch to athlete/Olympic symbols (CN)	4.50
2002 10 Euro Cent. Bust of Feriaou/map (B)	1.25
2002 1 Euro. Owl on Athenian coin/map. (CN clad N in NB, bimetallic)	3.50

MACEDONIA

	BU
1993 50 Deni. Sea gull (Brass)	.50
1993 1 Denar. Dog. (Brass)	.75
2000 1 Denar. Elaborate cross/Byzantine coin (Brass)	1.75
1995 2 Denari. Fish/FAO symbol (Brass)	1.00

MOLDOVA

	BU
1993 25 Bani. Arms/wreath (AL)	.50
1993 5 Lei. Arms. (CN)	3.50

MONTENEGRO

	VF
1906 2 Pare	8.00

Macedonia 1993 1 Denar

Moldova 1993 25 Bani

Montenegro 1906 2 Pare

Romania 1867 5 Bani

	VF
1913 2 Pare. Eagle (C)	**7.50**
1908 20 Pare. Eagle (N)	**7.00**
1912 1 Perper. Head of Nicholas/arms (S)	**14.00**
1910 2 Perpera. Similar (S)	**30.00**
1910 10 Perpera. Similar (G)	**250.00**

ROMANIA

	VF
1900 1 Ban. Head of Carol I/arms (C)	**2.25**
1867 5 Bani. Arms/wreath (C)	**5.00**
1900 10 Bani. Crown in wreath (CN)	**2.00**
1921 25 Bani. Eagle (AL)	**1.00**
1939 1 Leu. Crown/corn (Brass)	**.50**
1924 2 Lei. Arms (CN)	**1.75**
1880 5 Lei. Head of Carol I/arms (S)	**35.00**
1930 10 Lei. Head of Carol II/eagle (Brass)	**3.00**
1942 20 Lei. Crown/wreath (Z)	**1.50**
1935 250 Lei. Head of Carol II/arms on eagle (S)	**16.00**
1946 2,000 Lei. Head of Michael/arms (Brass)	**1.00**
1946 10,000 Lei. Head of Michael/woman releasing dove (S)	**8.00**

	Unc.
1952 1 Ban. Arms (Brass)	**2.00**
1963 5 Bani. Arms (N clad Steel)	**2.00**
1966 3 Lei. Arms/factory (N clad Steel)	**2.50**
1993 1 Leu. Arms (C clad Steel)	**1.00**
1996 10 Lei. Arms/sailboat (N clad Steel)	**6.50**
1993 20 Lei. Bust of King Stefan (Brass clad Steel)	**1.75**
1999 500 Lei. Solar Eclipse (AL)	**3.00**
2003 5,000 Lei. Arms (AL)	**.50**

SERBIA

	VF
1868 1 Para. Head of Obrenovich III/ wreath (C)	**12.50**
1912 5 Para. Denom/Arms (Unc.)	**12.00**
1884 10 Pare. Eagle (CN)	**1.75**
1915 1 Dinar. Head of Petar I/wreath (S)	**4.00**
1897 2 Dinara. Head of Alexander I/ wreath (S)	**12.50**
1879 5 Dinara. Head of Milan I l./wreath (S)	**60.00**
1882 10 Dinara. Head of Milan I r./wreath (G)	**125.00**
1943 10 Dinara. Eagle/wreath (Z)	**2.50**

SLOVENIA

	BU
1992 10 Stotinov. Salamander (AL)	**.25**
1996 50 Stotinov. Bee (AL)	**.35**

Romania 1966 3 Lei

Yugoslavia 1980 1,000 Dinar

Slovenia 2000 10 Tolarjev

Yugoslavia 1992 1 Dinar

Yugoslavia 1925 50 Para

Yugoslavia 1993 10 Dinar

	BU
1996 5 Tolarjev. Locomotive (Brass). .	**1.65**
1994 500 Tolarjev. Quill pen (S).	*proof only* **28.50**
1993 5,000 Tolarjev. Bees around hive (G)	*proof only* **275.00**
2000 10 Tolarjev. Horse (CN).	**4.00**

YUGOSLAVIA

	VF
1925 50 Para. Head of Alexander I/wreath (CN).	**1.00**
1925 1 Dinar. Head of Alexander I/wreath (CN).	**2.00**
1938 2 Dinara. Crown (ALB).	**1.00**
1932 50 Dinara. Head of Alexander I/ eagle. (S).	**22.00**

	VF
1945 Dinar. Arms. (Z).	**1.00**
	BU
1953 50 Para. Arms (AL)	.25
1981 10 Dinar. Arms (B).	.25
1983 500 Dinara. Olympic symbols/skier (S).	*proof only* **17.50**
1980 1,000 Dinar	**27.50**
1990 1 Dinara. Arms (CNZ)	.25
1992 1 Dinar. Bank monogram (Brass)	.60
1993 10 Dinara. Bank monogram (CNZ)	**1.00**
1996 1 New Dinar. Eagle shield (Brass)	**1.25**
1996 20 New Dinar. Eagle shield/Bust of Nikola Tesla (CNZ) . .	*proof only* **16.00**

BALTIC STATES

The regions that are today Estonia, Latvia, Lithuania and Finland were until 1918 submerged under the domination of Russia, Poland, Germany and Sweden in various combinations. Usually these greater powers would permit certain cities such as Riga, or certain nobles, to strike their own coins. These were somewhat common in the 1600s, but by the 1700s they ceased to be significant. During the 1800s, virtually none of these states were permitted their own coinage besides Finland, which was a semi-autonomous Grand Duchy under Russia.

The collapse of the great European empires during World War I liberated these countries from Russia, the most recent power to dominate the area. The coats of arms of these newly independent states were used on one side or the other of virtually every coin struck between the wars. While in most cases the other side was a monotonous indication of value, certain other pieces were exceptionally attractive. Most notable are beautiful renditions of the personification of Latvia. Lithuania also struck interesting commemoratives.

With the exception of Finland, all these countries were conquered by the Soviet Union in 1940. They re-emerged with the break-up of the Soviet empire in 1989. It is almost shocking how closely some of the new post-Soviet Baltic coins resemble the coins struck by these countries in the 1930s. The exception of course is Finland, whose coinage had the opportunity to evolve naturally during its longer independence. Since 1951, its modernistic commemoratives have been released in quantity to the world collector market.

In January 2002, Finland replaced the Markka with coins denominated in Euros, the currency of the European Union. Some coins were struck years in advance, and held until 2002. On the circulating denominations, 1 Cent through 2 Euros, one side carries a Finnish design, the other a common European design. On higher denomination commemoratives both sides are distinctively Finnish.

Additional Specialized Books: See general European listings.

Known Counterfeits: Known Finnish counterfeits include the 1951 500 Markkaa and possibly the 1918 Red Government 5 penniä.

Estonia 1998 100 Krouni

Finland 1943 10 Penniä

Finland 2002 10 Euro

ESTONIA

	F
Reval, 1663-67. 1 Rundstück. Crowned shield/MON NOV CIVITA REVAL (AR)	**40.00**

	VF
1922 3 Marka. Three lions (CN)	**4.50**
1926 5 Marka. Shield in wreath(CN)	**150.00**
1929 1 Sent. Three lions/oak leaves (C)	**1.00**
1935 20 Senti. Shield (CN)	**2.00**
1934 1 Kroon. Shield in wreath/Viking ship (ALB)	**7.00**
1930 2 Krooni. Shield in wreath/castle (S)	**7.00**
1932 2 Krooni. Shield in wreath/university building (S)	**20.00**
1991 5 Senti. Three lions (Brass)	**.25**

	BU
1993 5 Krooni. Doe (Brass)	**2.50**
1992 100 Krooni. Three lions/three swallows (S)	*proof only* **30.00**
1998 100 Krouni. Man on eagle head design, (S)	*PF* **50.00**

FINLAND

	VF
1873 1 Penni. Crowned AII (C)	**8.00**
1913 1 Penni. Crowned NII (C)	**.65**
1889 5 Penniä. Crowned AIII (C)	**5.00**
1900 10 Penniä. Crowned NII (C)	**5.00**
1917 25 Penniä. Russian eagle (S)	**.75**

	VF
1917 25 Penniä. Eagle without crown. *Civil War issue* (S)	**.50**
1890 1 Markka. Russian Eagle (S)	**2.50**
1882 10 Markkaa. Russian Eagle (G)	**80.00**

	XF
1918 5 Penniä. Trumpets (C)	**55.00**
1919 1 Penni. Lion (C)	**1.75**

	BU
1943 10 Penniä	**3.00**
1986 50 Penniä. Lion/tree (ALB)	**.50**
1993 10 Markkaa. Capercaille bird/ branches (Brass in CN, bimetallic)	**4.50**
1956 100 Markkaa. Shield/trees (S)	**3.00**
1990 100 Markkaa. Lyre/owl (S)	**40.00**
1952 500 Markkaa. Olympic rings/wreath (S)	**38.00**
1999 2 Cent. Lion/globe (C plated Steel)	**2.00**
2002 1 Euro. Two swans flying/map (CN clad N in NB, bimetallic)	**3.00**
2002 10 Euro. Globe/coin (S)	**37.50**

LATVIA

	F
Riga, 1660-65. Schilling. CR monogram/ SOLIDVS CIVI RIG, crossed keys (Billon)	**30.00**

Latvia 2001 1 Lats

Lithuania 2002 5 Litai

REPUBLIC

	VF
1935 1 Santims. Shield (C)	**1.40**
1939 2 Santimi. Shield (C)	**2.00**
1922 5 Santimi. Shield (C)	**1.00**
1922 10 Santimu. Shield (N)	**1.00**
1922 50 Santimu. Shield/Latvia gazing from rudder of ship (N)	**3.00**
1924 1 Lats. Shield/wreath (S)	**3.00**
1925 2 Lati. Similar (S)	**3.00**
1931 5 Lati. Head of Latvia r./arms (S)	**11.50**

RESTORED REPUBLIC

	BU
1992 2 Santimi. Shield (C plated Steel)	**.50**
1992 1 Lats. Arms/fish (CN)	**3.75**
1992 2 Lati. Arms/cow (CN)	**7.00**
1995 10 Latu. Arms/schooner (S) *proof only*	**42.50**
1998 100 Latu. Arms/logo (G) *proof only*	**350.00**
2001 1 Lats. Hockey player (S) *proof only*	**50.00**

LITHUANIA

	F
John III Sobieski, 1674-1696. 1679, 6 Groszy. Bust r./knight riding (S)	**rare**
Augustus II, 1697-1704. 1706 6 Groszy. Crowned bust r./three shields (S)	**150.00**

REPUBLIC

	VF
1936 1 Centas. Knight riding l. (C)	**5.00**
1936 2 Centai. Similar. (C)	**8.00**
1925 10 Centu. Knight riding l./ear of grain. (Brass)	**3.00**
1925 50 Centu. Similar. (Brass)	**7.00**
1925 1 Litas. Similar/oak branch (S)	**3.00**
1925 2 Litu. Similar/wreath (S)	**5.50**
1925 5 Litai. Similar (S)	**8.00**
1936 5 Litai. Similar/bust l. (S)	**4.50**
1938 10 Litai. Stylized castle/bust l. (S)	**20.00**

RESTORED REPUBLIC

	BU
1991 5 Centai. Knight riding l. (AL)	**.40**
1997 50 Centai. Similar (Brass)	**.85**
1997 1 Litas. Bust/knight riding l. (CN)	**2.00**
1994 10 Litu. Two harps/similar (CN) *proof only*	**12.00**
1996 50 Litu. Basketball players/shield (S) *proof only*	**38.00**
2002 5 Litai. Knight/owl (S) *proof only*	**45.00**

LIVONIA & ESTONIA

	F
1757 2 Kopeks. Two Shields/double-headed eagle (base S)	**110.00**
1757 4 Kopeks. LIVO ESTHONICA, two shields/double-headed eagle (S)	**45.00**

BRITISH ISLES

Despite successful experiments with milled (screw press) coinage during the reign of Elizabeth I (1558-1603), this means of striking uniform, well-made coins was not finally adopted in England until the 1663, after the restoration of the monarchy. By this time there were a great many different denominations in silver, from the tiny silver penny, to the crown (60 pence) which had finally become common.

By the end of the century most of the silver denominations below six pence were being struck only for ceremonial distribution on Maundy Thursday, the Thursday before Easter. These silver coins were given to the poor, but usually passed into circulation. After the mid-1700s their value as collectibles was so established that almost all were immediately sold by their recipients to collectors, and today survive in high grade.

Another change was the replacement of puny, privately made royal contract farthings with officially struck regal farthings and halfpennies of good weight. For a while the government replaced these coppers with ones of tin, but this was soon abandoned due to their tendency to corrode.

The designs on British coins have usually been very conservative. The shield on a cross used before the Civil War was continued after it. New designs were often heraldic as well, sometimes showing one shield, other times showing arrangements of the shields of England, Scotland, Ireland and France. (England claimed France until the early 1800s.) The new copper coins show a seated female, Britannia, an allegory for Britain dating back to Roman days.

During the 1700s, the government failed to provide enough coins to satisfy Britain's growing industrial economy. The industrial Revolution also provided the answer to this dilemma. Merchants and miners took matters into their own hands and contracted with modern factories to strike their own money. These tokens, common from the late 1780s and 1790s as well as from 1811-15 depict a delightful array of scenes from Gothic cathedrals to the very machines of the Industrial Revolution.

Gradually the government responded. New steam-power struck coppers were introduced in 1797-99, including the first penny to be struck in copper instead of silver. A massive issue of machine struck silver and gold was released in 1816. Notable is the powerful Baroque-style depiction of St. George slaying the dragon by Benedetto Pistrucci, used on the crown and gold pieces.

During the reign of Queen Victoria (1837-1901) old designs were sometimes given a beautiful neo-Gothic interpretation. Another innovation on the practical side was the replacement of the copper coins with slightly smaller ones of bronze. These wore much better than pure copper.

The two world wars took their toll on British coinage. The purity of the silver was lowered from 92-1/2 percent to 50 percent in 1920 after the First World War. It was replaced completely by cupro-nickel in 1947 after the Second World War. From the Great Depression onward, gold ceased to circulate. The gold sovereigns struck from then until today were solely for bullion or collector purposes.

After 1,100 years of using a coinage derived from the penny of Charlemagne, and based on multiples of 12, Britain finally replaced the pound of 240 pence with one divided into 100 decimal new pence. The new seven-sided 50 pence introduced in 1969 proved so popular that since then, many countries have used this shape for their coinage.

During the second half of the twentieth century collectors' commemoratives were issued quite frequently. From the 1970s onward, new creative designs were used for these coins. Many were sold at a premium and were never placed in circulation.

Scotland

Scottish coins followed most of the same trends as on English coins quite closely. Where royal copper coins were needed, however, Britannia was not depicted. Instead a thistle, Scotland's national flower, or scepters were used. After 1707 Scotland and England were joined as the United Kingdom, and separate Scottish coinage was ended. However, from 1937 to 1970, special Scottish shillings were struck, good throughout the United Kingdom. The current five pence and several brass pound coins also honor Scotland.

Ireland

Irish coins continued longer, but were usually limited to base metal. From the Restoration until 1823, Ireland was usually provided with distinctive halfpennies, farthings, and ultimately pennies with a crowned harp as their reverse. The first machine-made ones were struck in 1805. There were two important exceptions. After James II was forced to flee

England in 1688, he managed to hold onto Ireland for several months. To help finance his war to keep the throne he struck high value coins in brass containing metal from melted cannon. These sixpences, shillings, half crowns, and crowns were dated to the exact month and are called "gun money." Another exception came in 1804-13 when the Bank of Ireland struck silver five, ten, and thirty pence, and six shilling tokens to ease the coinage shortage.

Ireland's first independent coinage was introduced in 1928, and this first year is the most commonly encountered for decades. The country name given on the coins was changed from SAORSTAT EIREANN (Irish Freestate) to EIRE (Ireland) in 1939 because Ireland changed from a dominion to a republic. It phased in decimal coins beginning in 1969.

In January 2002, Ireland replaced the Pound with coins denominated in Euros, the currency of the European Union. On the circulating denominations, 1 Cent through 2 Euros, one side carries an Irish harp, the other a common European design.

The Empire & Commonwealth

Colonial coins struck during the 1700s and early 1800s, less common than the later ones, were very similar in style to British issues. Ones struck for the thirteen colonies in America are discussed under the United States. One big exception is the coinage of the East India Company. Many of these are hardly distinguishable from local Indian states and Moghal Empire coins. Usually they are identified by certain symbols or their machine made fabric, but they were originally intended to circulate alongside local coins and their designs made this possible.

During the mid-1800s, colonial coins became increasingly more practical in their designs, and many have no other motif than a large number indicating the value. Beginning in the 1920s in most territories, somewhat earlier in a few others, local color and creativity entered into colonial coin design. Native plants and animals were depicted. Some larger values bore the coat of arms of the individual colony. Many of the designs were so pleasing that they continued in use for decades, even after independence. Like in the homeland, silver was phased out after World War II.

Many independent former colonies still recognize the British monarch as Queen. These British Commonwealth members often voluntarily depict the monarch on the obverse of their coins, as they did before independence. Most are listed here for convenience, except Canada which is covered in depth in its own section.

Additional Specialized Books:

Dalton and Hamer. *The Provincial Token-Coinage of the 18th Century.*

Jinks, David, ed. *British Coins Market Values.* Current updated values but minimal numismatic information.

Pridmore, F. *The Coins of the British Commonwealth of Nations.* 4 vols.

Spink & Son. *Coins of England and the United Kingdom.* The basic reference.

Known Counterfeits: Vast numbers of contemporary counterfeits of 1700s copper were made, both by striking and casting. Those made in America and those in middle grade are worth more than the real ones. Many brass counterfeits of 1811-1820 silver were made at the time and have some small numismatic value. Other circulation counterfeits include shilling 1916, florin 1900, 1918, 1942, half crown 1818, 3 shillings 1815, guinea 1798.

A great many sovereigns have been counterfeited, many originating in Lebanon. Some known examples include: 1887, 1910, 1911, 1913, 1918M, 1923SA (altered date), 1927SA. Some were even found in lots bought in the Middle East to issue to British troops during the First Gulf War. Despite their commonness, *all* sovereigns should be examined carefully.

Recently, base metal counterfeits of British trade dollars have been seen in abundance.

Collector counterfeits have been made of many coins with rare dates spanning the last 150 years. A partial list includes the 1905 half crown and 1847 Gothic crown.

ENGLAND

F

Charles II, 1660-85.
1672 Farthing. Bust l./Britannia std.
(C) **25.00**
1675 Halfpenny. Similar **35.00**
1670 Threepence. Bust r./three
interlocking C's (S) **20.00**
1681 Sixpence. Bust r./cross of shields, C's
in angles (S) **35.00**
1680 Crown. Same **125.00**
1676. Half Guinea. Bust r./cross of
shields, scepters in angles (G).. **225.00**

James II, 1685-88.
1686 Halfpenny. Bust r./Britannia std.
(Tin) **110.00**
1685 Shilling. Bust l./cross of shields
(S)............................. **85.00**
1686 Half Crown. Bust l./cross of shields
(S)............................. **100.00**
1688 Guinea. Bust l./cross of shields,
scepters in angles (G) **375.00**

William and Mary, 1688-94.
1690 Farthing. Two busts r./Britannia std.
l. (Tin) **85.00**
1694, similar but copper.......... **35.00**
1689 Twopence. Two busts r./crowned
2 (S) **30.00**
1693 Shilling. Two busts r./cross of shields,
monograms in angles (S) **40.00**
1689 Half Crown. Two busts r./crowned
shield (S)...................... **75.00**
1691 5 Guineas. Two busts r./crowned
shield (G) **1,500.00**

William III, 1694-1702.
1699 Halfpenny. Bust r./Britannia std.
l............................... **30.00**
1696 Sixpence. Bust r./cross of shields
(S)............................. **25.00**
1697 Shilling. Similar (S) **30.00**
1700 Half crown. Bust r./cross of shields
(S)............................. **50.00**
1695 Crown. Bust r./cross of shields.
(S)............................ **100.00**

Great Britain 1711 Half Crown

Great Britain 1723 1 Shilling

GREAT BRITAIN

F

Anne, 1702-14.
1714 Farthing. Bust l./Britannia std.
(C) **225.00**
1708 Shilling. Bust l./cross of shields
(S)............................. **30.00**
1708 Half Crown. Similar (S)........ **60.00**
1712 Guinea. Bust l./cross of shields,
scepters in angles (G) **225.00**

George I, 1714-27.
1719 Farthing. Bust r./Britannia std.
(C) **20.00**
1720 Halfpenny. Similar (C) **25.00**
1722 Shilling. Bust r./cross of shields, roses
and plumes in angles (S)........ **30.00**
1723 Shilling...................... **55.00**
1716 Crown. Similar. (S)........... **210.00**
1718 Quarter Guinea. Bust r./cross of
shields, scepters in angles (G).. **100.00**

George II, 1727-60.
1754 Farthing. Bust l./Britannia std.
(C) **6.00**
1749 Halfpenny. Similar (C) **8.00**
1757 Sixpence. Bust l./cross of shields
(S)............................. **10.00**

Great Britain 1750 Shilling

	F
1750 Shilling..	30.00
1758 Shilling. Similar (S)	15.00
1759 Guinea. Bust l /"Rose" shield (G)	175.00

George III, 1760-1820.
1773 Farthing. Bust r./Britannia std. (C)	9.00
1806 Farthing (reduced size) Bust r./ Britannia std. (C)	2.00
1797 Twopence. Bust r./Britannia std, heavy borders (C)	25.00

The above usually comes with heavy rim bruises.

1763 Three pence. Bust r./crowned 3 (S)	10.00
1787 Sixpence. Bust r./cross of shields, crowns in angles (S)	6.00
1798 Guinea. Bust r./"Spade" shield (G)	175.00

MACHINE-MADE COINAGE
	VF
1799 Farthing. Bust r./Britannia std. (C)	5.00
1797 Twopence. Similar but broad border (C, 2 ounces!)	35.00
1817 Shilling. Bust r./arms within garter (S)	15.00
1817 Half Crown. Similar.	35.00

George IV, 1820-30.
1826 Halfpenny. Bust l./Britannia std. (C)	7.00
1826 Sixpence. Bust l./lion on crown (S)	12.00
1824 Shilling. Bust l./arms (S)	20.00

	VF
1826 Sovereign. Bust l./crowned shield (G)	200.00
1826 5 Pounds. Bust l./crowned arms (G)	rare

William IV, 1830-37.
1831 Farthing. Bust r./Britannia std. (C)	10.00
1837 Halfpenny. Similar (C)	9.00
1836 4 Pence. Similar (S).	5.25
1832 Sovereign. Bust r./crowned shield (G)	200.00

Victoria, 1837-1901.
1844 Half Farthing Young head/crown (C)	5.00
1858 Farthing. Young head l./Britannia std. (C).	5.00
1884 Farthing. Bust/similar (C)	1.50
1886 Halfpenny. Bust/similar (C)	2.75
1858 Penny. Young head l./similar (C)	6.00
1890 Penny. Bust/similar (C)	6.00
1900 Penny. Veiled bust/similar (C)	1.00
1881 3 Pence. Young head/crowned 3 (S)	3.25
1838 4 Pence. Young head/Britannia std. (S)	5.25
1887 6 Pence. Crowned bust/arms (S)	3.00
1893 Shilling. Veiled bust/three crowned shields (S)	5.50
1852 Florin. Crowned "Gothic" bust/cross of shields, flowers in angles (S)	32.00
1874 Half Crown. Young head/crowned shield (S).	25.00
1887 Double Florin. Crowned bust/cross of shields, scepters in angles (S)	17.50
1893 Crown. Veiled bust/St. George slaying dragon (S)	32.00
1880 Half Sovereign. Young head/ crowned shield (G)	75.00
1887 Sovereign. Crowned bust/St. George slaying dragon (G)	100.00
1893 2 Pounds. Veiled bust/similar (G)	325.00
1893 5 Pounds. Similar (G)	750.00

Edward VII, 1901-10.
1903 Farthing. Head r./Britannia std. (C)	1.75

Great Britain 1910 6 Pence

Great Britain 1943 1 Shilling

Great Britain 1940 1 Farthing

Great Britain 1967 1 Penny

	VF
1910 3 Pence. Head r./crowned 3 (S)	**2.00**
1910 6 Pence. Head r./crown (S)	**5.00**
1910 Florin. Head r./Britannia stg. (S)	**20.00**
1902 Crown. Head r./St. George slaying dragon (S)	**65.00**
1910 Sovereign. Similar (G)	**120.00**

George V, 1910-36.

1917 Farthing. Head l./Britannia std. (C)	**.35**
1928 Halfpenny. Similar (C)	**.75**
1935 Penny. Similar (C)	**.50**
1929 Sixpence. Head l./six acorns (S)	**1.00**
1926 Shilling. Head l./lion on crown (S)	**2.50**
1928 Florin. Head l./cross of shields, scepters in angles (S)	**2.50**
1935 Half Crown. Head l./shield (S)	**4.00**
1935 Crown. Head l./crown in wreath (S)	**80.00**
1935 Crown. Head l./St. George, armored, slaying dragon (S)	**15.00**
1911 Half Sovereign. Similar but saint nude (G)	**60.00**
1932 Maundy set. 1, 2, 3, 4 Pence. Head l./crown over value (S) . . . . . Unc.	**75.00**

George VI, 1936-52.

1940 Farthing. Head l./wren (C)	**.25**
1943 Farthing. Head l./wren (C)	**.30**

	VF
1942 Halfpenny. Head l./ship (C)	**.60**
1944 Penny. Head l./Britannia std. (C)	**.25**
1937 3 Pence. Head l./thrift plant (Brass)	**1.00**
1946 6 Pence. Head l./crowned GRI (S)	**1.00**
1943 Shilling. Head l./Scottish crest (lion std. on crown) (S)	**1.50**
1950 Half Crown. Head l./shield (CN)	**1.50**
1951 Crown. Head l./St. George slaying dragon (CN)	**6.00**

Elizabeth II, 1952C.

	BU
1954 Farthing. Young bust/wren	**2.00**
1962 Penny. Young bust/Britannia std. (C)	**.15**
1967 Penny. Similar	**.30**
1966 3 Pence. Young bust/Portcullis (castle gate) (Brass)	**.25**
1963 Shilling. Young bust/crowned shield (CN)	**.60**
1967 Florin. Young bust/rose within border (CN)	**1.50**

Great Britain 2000 50 Pence

	BU
1965 Crown. Young bust/bust of Churchill (CN)	**1.00**
1958 Sovereign. Young bust/St. George slaying dragon (G)	**125.00**

DECIMAL COINAGE

	BU
1971 1 New Penny. Bust in tiara/Portcullis (C)	**.25**
1987 5 Pence. Bust in crown/crowned thistle (CN)	**.30**
1990 20 Pence. Bust in crown/crowned rose (CN, heptagonal)	**.75**
1981 25 Pence. Bust in tiara/heads of Charles and Diana (CN)	**1.75**
1973 50 Pence. Bust in tiara/wreath of hands (CN, heptagonal)	**2.00**
2000 50 Pence. Older head in tiara/ Britannia (CN, heptagonal)	**2.00**
2000 50 Pence. Older head in tiara/book and library (CN, heptagonal)	**2.75**
1995 Pound. Bust in tiara/Welsh dragon (Brass)	**3.50**
1988 50 Pounds. Bust in tiara/Britannia stg. (G, 2 ounce)	**250.00**

BRITISH TOKENS

	VF
1667 Farthing. Shield with castle and lion/ NORWICH FARTHING (C)	**35.00**
1792 Halfpenny. Elephant with castle on back/Lady Godiva on horse (C)	**12.00**

	VF
1791 Penny. Hooded head of Druid/ monogram (C)	**12.00**
1813 Penny. Birmingham Work House/ shield (C)	**10.00**
c.1980s R&W London/I (Brass)	**.10.00**

SCOTLAND

	F
Charles II, 1649-85. 1677 Bawbee. Bust l./ crowned thistle (C)	**40.00**
1669 Merk. Bust r./cross of shields, C's in angles (S)	**70.00**
James II, 1685-89. 1687 10 Shillings. Bust r., 10 below/shields in angle of X	**135.00**
1687 40 Shillings. Bust r., 40 below/ crowned shield (S)	**140.00**
William and Mary, 1689-94. 1691 Bawbee. Two busts l./crowned thistle (C)	**75.00**
1693 20 Shillings. Two busts l., 20 below/ crowned shield (S)	**150.00**
1692 40 Shillings. Two busts l., 40 below/ crowned shield (S)	**135.00**
William III, 1694-1702. 1695 Turner. Crowned sword and scepter/thistle (C)	**37.00**
1697 5 Shillings. Bust l./three thistles (S)	**45.00**
1696 40 Shillings. Bust l./crowned shield (S)	**125.00**
Anne, 1702-14. 1705 5 Shillings. Bust l., 5 below/three thistles (S)	**38.00**
1705 10 Shillings. Bust l., 10 below/ crowned shield (S)	**100.00**

IRELAND

	F
Charles II, 1660-1685. 1682 Halfpenny. Bust r./crowned Harp (C)	**35.00**
James II, 1685-91. 1686 Halfpenny. Bust l./ crowned Harp (C)	**35.00**
1689 Shilling. Bust l./XII over crown (C)	**45.00**
William and Mary, 1688-94. 1693 Halfpenny. Two busts r./crowned Harp (C)	**40.00**
William III, 1694-1702. 1696 Halfpenny. Bust r./crowned Harp (C)	**40.00**

Irish Free State 1937 1 Penny

Irish Republic 1964 3 Pence

Irish Republic 1971 1 Penny

Irish Republic 2003 10 Euro

	F
George I, 1714-27. 1723 Farthing. Bust r./ Hibernia std. with harp (C)	**35.00**
George II, 1727-60. 1760 Halfpenny. Bust l./crowned Harp (C)	**25.00**
George III, 1760-1820. 1806 Farthing. Bust r./crowned Harp (C)	**4.50**
1805 Halfpenny. Similar (C)	**6.00**
1805 5 Pence Bank Token. Bust r./ inscription (S)	**15.00**
George IV, 1820-30. 1822 Halfpenny. Bust l./crowned Harp (C)	**8.00**

Irish Free State

	VF
1928 Farthing. Harp/woodcock (C)	**1.50**
1935 Penny. Harp/hen and chicks (C)	**1.00**
1937 Penny. Similar	**1.00**
1928 6 Pence. Harp/wolfhound (N)	**1.00**
1928 Shilling. Harp/bull (S)	**5.00**
1928 Florin. Harp/salmon (S)	**7.00**

IRISH REPUBLIC

	XF
1953 Halfpenny. Harp/pig and piglets (C)	**.25**

	XF
1964 3 Pence. Harp/hare (CN)	**.25**
1939 Shilling. Harp/bull (S)	**4.50**
1962 Shilling. Similar (CN)	**1.00**
1963 Half Crown. Harp/horse (CN)	**2.00**
1966 10 Shillings. Bust of Pearse/statue of Cuchulainn (S)	**9.00**

DECIMAL COINAGE

	BU
1971 1 Penny. Harp/Celtic bird (C)	**.20**
1986 20 Pence. Harp/horse (Brass)	**1.50**
1988 50 Pence. Harp/arms of Dublin (CN)	**2.50**
1990 Pound. Harp/stag (CN)	**6.00**

EURO COINAGE 2002 TO DATE

	BU
2002 20 Cent. Harp/map (B)	**1.25**
2002 2 Euro. Harp/map (NB clad N in CN, bimetallic)	**4.00**
2003 10 Euro. Harp/Games Logo (S) *PF*	**40.00**

Australia 1937 1 Crown

Australia 1993 2 Dollars

BRITISH COLONIES & COMMONWEALTH

AUSTRALIA

	VF
1813 5 Shillings. NEW SOUTH WALES counterstamped on Spanish colonial 8 Reales with large central hole (S)	16,000.00
1927 Halfpenny. Bust of George V (C)	.75
1949 Penny. Head of George VI/kangaroo (C)	.25
1910 3 Pence. Bust of Edward VII/arms (S)	5.00
1936 6 Pence. Bust of George V/arms (S)	4.50
1943 6 Pence. Head of George VI/arms (S)	.75
1942 Shilling. Similar/Ram's head (S)	1.50
1910 Florin. Bust of Edward VII/arms (S)	150.00
1927 Florin. Bust of George V/Parliament (S)	7.50
1937 Crown. Head of George VI/crown (S)	11.00
1918 Sovereign. Head of George V/St. George slaying dragon (G)	100.00

Elizabeth II

1961 Penny. Young bust/kangaroo (C)	.40

Australia 1999 30 Dollars

	XF
1964 3 Pence. Young head/wheat (S)	.50
1954 6 Pence. Young bust/arms (S)	2.25
1961 Shilling. Young bust/ram's head (S)	.75
1960 Florin. Young bust/arms (S)	3.50

DECIMAL COINAGE

	BU
1981 1 Cent. Bust in tiara/ring-tailed opossum	.50
1966 2 Cents. Bust in tiara/frilled lizard (C)	.50

	BU
1966 50 Cents. Bust in tiara/arms (S).	**6.50**

1988 2 Dollars. Bust in crown/aboriginal
man (B) **4.00**
1993 2 Dollars. Bust in crown/kookabura r.
(S, 2 oz.) **115.00**
1996 5 Dollars. Similar/Bust of Donald
Bradman (ALB in Steel, bimetallic)
. . . . **12.50**
1999 30 Dollars. Bust in tiara/rabbit r. (S. 1
kilo.) **400.00**
1995 40 Dollars. Bust in crown/emu
(Palladium) **450.00**

BAHAMAS

	BU

1806 Penny. Bust of George III/ship
(C) . . . . *F* **36.00**
1971 1 Cent. Starfish (C) . . . . **.25**
1966 10 Cents. Two fish (CN,
scalloped) . . . . **.25**
1974 15 Cents. Hibiscus (CN) . . . . **.50**
1972 25 Cents. Sloop (N) . . . . **.50**
1966 1 Dollar. Conch shell (S) **5.00**
1971 2 Dollars. Two flamingos (S) **9.00**
1967 20 Dollars. Lighthouse (G) . . . **140.00**

BARBADOS

	F

1788 Penny. Slave head wearing prince of
Wales crown/pineapple (C) **25.00**
1792 Penny. Similar/king in chariot of
hippocamps (C) **50.00**

BELIZE

	BU

1973 1 Cent. Crowned bust (C) . . . . **.25**
1979 50 Cents. Similar (CN) **1.75**
1990 1 Dollar. Bust in tiara/Columbus'
ships (Brass, decagonal) **2.25**
1990 2 Dollars. Similar/EE monogram
(CN) **6.00**

BERMUDA

	F

c.1616 12 Pence. SOMMER ILANDS, Boar/
ship (C) **6,500.00**

Bermuda 1996 2 Dollars

	F
1793 Penny. Bust of George III/ship(C)	**35.00**
	BU

1964 Crown Crowned bust/arms (S) . **5.00**
1970 1 Cent. Bust in tiara/boar (C) . . . . **.20**
1996 2 Dollars. Crowned bust/horse
carriage (S) . . . . *PF* **35.00**
1996 60 Dollars. Bust in tiara/map above
ship (G, curved triangle)
. . . . *proof only* **800.00**

BRITISH CARIBBEAN TERRITORIES

	BU

1964 1 Cent. Crowned bust/wreath (C) **.35**
1956 5 Cents. Similar/ship (Brass) . . . **1.00**
1964 10 Cents. Similar/ship (CN) . . . . . **.65**
1955 50 Cents. Similar/queen stg. over
arms of islands (CN) **3.50**

BRITISH GUIANA

	VF

1813 Half Stiver. Bust of George III/
crowned wreath (C) **15.00**

British Honduras 1972 1 Cent

British North Borneo 1928 5 Cent

	VF
1891 4 Pence. Bust of Victoria/similar (S)	**4.50**
1936 4 Pence. Bust of George V/similar (S)	**2.50**
1945 4 Pence. Head of George VI/similar (S)	**2.00**

BRITISH HONDURAS

	VF
1888 1 Cent. Head of Victoria (C)	**8.50**
1972 1 Cent. Head of Elizabeth II (C, scallopped)	**.40**
1907 5 Cents. Bust of Edward VII (CN)	**50.00**
1936 10 Cents. Bust of George V (S)	**12.00**
1952 25 Cents. Head of George VI	**3.50**
1964 50 Cents. Bust of Elizabeth II (CN)	**.50**

The above are usually found worn.

BRITISH NORTH BORNEO

	VF
1891 1/2 Cent. Arms/wreath (C)	**12.00**
1886 1 Cent. Arms with supporters/wreath (C)	**7.00**
1928 5 Cent. Arms (CN)	**5.00**

British West Africa 1908 1/10 Penny

BRITISH VIRGIN ISLANDS

	BU
1983 10 Cents. Bust in tiara/kingfisher (CN)	**1.00**
1973 25 Cents. Similar/cuckoo (CN)	**1.50**
1985 20 Dollars. Similar/Spanish colonial cob coin (S)	*proof only* **16.50**
1975 100 Dollars. Similar/tern (G)	**110.00**

BRITISH WEST AFRICA

	VF
1908 1/10 Penny. Titles of Edward VII/six-pointed star (AL)	**3.00**
1908 similar (CN)	**.50**
1920 2 Penny. Titles of George V/six-pointed star (CN)	**2.00**
1936 Penny. Titles of Edward VIII/similar (CN)	**.75**
1956 Penny. Titles of Elizabeth II/similar (C)	**.60**
1940 3 Pence. Head of George VI/wreath (Brass)	**.60**
1913 6 Pence. Bust of George V/wreath (S)	**5.00**
1938 Shilling. Head of George VI/palm tree (Brass)	**1.00**
1938 2 Shillings. Similar (Brass)	**2.00**

BRITISH WEST INDIES

	VF
1822 1/16th Dollar. Rose-shaped arms/crowned anchor (S)	**15.00**
1822 1/8th Dollar. Similar (S)	**18.00**
1822 1/2 Dollar. Similar (S)	**175.00**

CAYMAN ISLANDS

	BU
1972 10 Cents. Elizabeth II/green turtle (CN)	**.50**

Ceylon 1911 25 Cents

BU

1992 1 Dollar Elizabeth II/iguana
 (S). . . . . *proof only* **50.00**
1975 100 Dollars. Elizabeth II/five queens
 (G) **195.00**

CEYLON

VF

1803 1/12th Rix Dollar. Large 12/elephant
 l. (C). **40.00**
1821 Rix Dollar. Bust of George IV/
 elephant l. (S). **28.00**
1891 1 Cent. Head of Victoria/palm tree
 (C) **4.00**
1910 5 Cents. Bust of Edward VII (CN,
 square) **2.00**
1911 25 Cents. George V/palm
 tree (S). **6.00**
1929 50 Cents. Bust of George V/palm
 tree (S). **5.00**
1951 50 Cents. Head of George VI
 (Brass). . . . .**.35**
1957 2 Cents. Elizabeth II (Brass,
 scalloped). . . . .**.15**

CYPRUS

VF

1881 ¼ Piastre. Victoria (C) **22.00**
1908 ½ Piastre. Edward VII (C) **200.00**
1931 1 Piastre. George V (C) **50.00**
1934 1 Piastre. Similar. (CN,
 scalloped). **2.50**
1901 3 Piastres. Bust of Victoria/crowned
 3 (S) **25.00**
1921 9 Piastres. Bust of George
 V/crowned shield (S) **13.00**
1947 Shilling. Head of George VI/two lions
 (CN). **3.00**

Unc.

1955 3 Mils. Bust of Elizabeth II/fish (C).**25**

Cyprus 1974 5 Mils

East Caribbean States 1996 10 Dollars

Unc.

1974 5 Mils. Arms/ship (C) . . . .**.35**
1955 50 Mils. Similar/ferns (CN) **1.00**

EAST AFRICA

VF

1898 1 Pice. Head of Victoria (C) . . .**10.00**
1908 ½ Cent. Titles of Edward
 VII/tusks (AL) **25.00**
1923 1 Cent. Titles of George
 V/tusks (C) . . . .**.50**
1956 1 Cent. Titles of Elizabeth II/tusks (C)
 . . . .**.30**
1936 5 Cents. Titles of Edward VIII/tusks
 (C) . . . .**.50**
1913 25 Cents. Bust of George V/lion
 (S). **7.50**
1963 50 Cents. Bust of Elizabeth II/lion
 (CN). . . . .**.25**
1946 Shilling. Head of George VI/lion
 (Billon). **2.00**

Fiji 1996 10 Dollars

Gibraltar 2000 1 Crown

EAST CARIBBEAN STATES

	BU
1981 1 Cent. Bust in tiara/wreath (AL) .	**.20**
1989 1 Dollar. Similar/ship (CN, 10-sided)	**2.00**
1994 10 Dollars. Mature bust/soccer ball and Manhattan buildings (S). . . . . *proof only* **45.00**	
1996 10 Dollars. Similar/yacht (S) *PF* **50.00**	

FIJI

	VF
1934 Halfpenny. Titles of George V (CN, holed) **3.00**	
1936 Penny. Titles of Edward VIII (CN, holed) **1.00**	
1950 3 Pence. Head of George VI/hut (Brass) **1.00**	
1965 6 Pence. Bust of Elizabeth II/sea turtle (CN) . . . . **.30**	
1934 Shilling. Bust of George V/outrigger (S) **5.00**	
1943 Florin. Head of George VI/shield (S) **2.50**	

	BU
1976 1 Cent. Bust of Elizabeth II/dish (C) . . . . **.35**	
1987 50 Cents. Similar/sailing canoe (CN, 12-sided). **1.75**	

	BU
1995 1 Dollar. Similar/rattle (Brass) . .	**3.50**
1986 10 Dollars. Similar/Fijian ground frog (S). . . . . *proof only* **40.00**	
1978 250 Dollars. Similar/banded iguana (G) **500.00**	
1996 10 Dollars. Similar/dancer (S) *PF* **15.00**	

GIBRALTAR

	VF
1813 1 Quarto. Lion holding key/crowned wreath (C). **30.00**	
1810 2 Quartos. Similar/castle (C) . . **17.50**	
1842 1/2 Quart. Head of Victoria/castle (C) **15.00**	

	BU
1967 Crown. Bust of Elizabeth II/castle (CN). **1.50**	
1988 5 Pence. Similar/Barbary ape(CN).**75**	
1990 50 Pence. Similar/five dolphins (CN, 7-sided). **3.50**	
1996 Crown. Similar/Audrey Hepburn (CN). **7.50**	
1989 5 Sovereigns. Similar/Una and lion (G) . . . . *proof only* **1,100.00**	
2000 1 Crown. Similar/jumper and kangaroo (CN). **8.00**	

Hong Kong 1937 5 Cents

Guernsey 1996 5 Pounds

Hong Kong 1960 1 Dollar

GOLD COAST

	XF
1818 1/2 Ackey. George III/arms (S)	**225.00**
1818 Ackey. Similar (S)	**450.00**

GUERNSEY

	VF
1903 Double. Shield (C)	**.30**
1929 2 Doubles. Shield (C)	**1.25**
	XF
1889 4 Doubles. Shield (C)	**1.25**
1834 8 Doubles. Shield in wreath/wreath (C)	**10.00**
	BU
1959 8 Doubles. Shield/three lilies (C)	**1.25**
1966 10 Shillings. Elizabeth II/William the Conqueror (CN, square)	**1.75**
1971 2 New Pence. Shield/windmill (C)	**.35**
1983 Pound. Shield/sailing ship (Brass)	**3.50**
1994 25 Pounds. Elizabeth II/Normandy invasion (G)	**185.00**
1996 5 Pounds. Elizabeth II/Elizabeth the Queen Mother (S)	*Proof* **45.00**

HONG KONG

	VF
1865 1 Mil. Crown/Chinese inscription (C, holed)	**15.00**
1905 1 Cent. Edward VII/Chinese inscription (C)	**4.50**
1932 5 Cents. George V/similar (S)	**1.50**
1937 5 Cents. George VI/similar (N)	**1.25**
1885 10 Cents. Victoria/similar (S)	**3.00**
1948 10 Cents. George VI/similar (Brass)	**.50**
1902 20 Cents. Edward VII/similar (S)	**40.00**
1866 1/2 Dollar. Victoria/ornament (S)	**550.00**
1891 50 Cents. Victoria/value (S)	**60.00**
1866 Dollar. Victoria/ornament (S)	**330.00**

Recent counterfeits of this coin are known.

	BU
1975 20 Cents. Elizabeth II/similar (Brass)	**.35**
1960 1 Dollar. Elizabeth II/lion (CN)	**5.00**
1993 2 Dollars. Bauhinia flower (CN, scalloped)	**1.25**
1994 10 Dollars. Similar (Brass in CN, *bimetallic*)	**5.00**

Hong Kong 2002 50 Dollars

India-East India Company 1857 1/4 Anna

India-Regal Coinage 1946 1/2 Anna

BU

1977 1,000 Dollars. Elizabeth II/snake
(G) **365.00**
1987 1,000 Dollars. Elizabeth II/rabbit
(G) **285.00**
2002 50 Dollars. Bauhinia flower/windmills
(A and S, bimetallic) . . . . *PF* **60.00**

INDIA—EAST INDIA CO.

F

1704-16 Pice. Crown/AUSPICIO REGIS ET
SENATUS ANGLIA (C) **45.00**
1741 Pice. Similar, BOMB below crown
(Tin) **40.00**
1179 AH (1765) Rupee. Arabic inscriptions
and ornament (S) **15.00**
1835 1/12th Anna. Arms/wreath (C) . . . .**.75**
1857 1/4 Anna. Similar (C) . . . .**.85**
1858 1/4 Anna. Similar (C) . . . .**.85**
1835 1/4 Rupee. William IV/wreath (S)**4.50**
1840 Rupee. Victoria/wreath (S) **3.00**
1841 1 Mohur. Victoria/lion and palm tree
(G) **150.00**

INDIA—REGAL COINAGE

VF

1862 1/12th Anna. Victoria as queen/
wreath (C) **1.25**

VF

1906 1/12th Anna. Edward VII/wreath
(C) **1.50**
1916 1/12th Anna. George V/wreath
(C) . . . .**.50**
1939 1/12th Anna. George VI/wreath
(C) . . . .**.50**
1895 1/2 Pice. Victoria as empress/wreath
(C) **1.75**
1862 1/4 Anna. Victoria as queen/wreath
(C) **1.50**
1880 1/4 Anna. Victoria as empress/
wreath (C) . . . .**.75**
1906 1/4 Anna. Edward VII/wreath (C)
. . . . **1.25**
1920 1/4 Anna. George V/wreath (C) . . .**.40**
1942 1/4 Anna. George VI/wreath (C) . .**.35**
1943 1 Pice. Crown/wreath (C) . . . .**.35**
1862 1/2 Anna. Victoria as queen/wreath
(C) **20.00**
1946 1/2 Anna. George VI (CN) . . . .**.30**
1936 1 Anna. George V (CN) . . . .**.35**
1945 1 Anna. George VI (Brass) . . . .**.25**
1901 2 Annas. Victoria as empress/wreath
(S) **2.50**

India-Regal Coinage 1946 1/4 Rupee

India-Princely States 1943 1/8 Kori

VF

1918 2 Annas. George V (CN, square)
. . . . **1.75**
1940 2 Annas. George VI (CN, square)
. . . .**30**
1919 4 Annas. George V (CN) **5.00**
1862 1/4 Rupee. Victoria as queen/wreath
(S). **5.00**
1892 1/4 Rupee. Victoria as empress/
wreath (S) **3.00**
1904 1/4 Rupee. Edward VII/flowers (S)
. . . . **3.00**
1936 1/4 Rupee. George V/wreath (S)
. . . . **2.25**
1945 1/4 Rupee. George VI/wreath (S) **.85**
1946 1/4 Rupee. George VI/tiger (N). . . **.75**
1919 8 Annas. George V (CN) **7.50**
1899 1/2 Rupee. Victoria as empress/
wreath (S) **5.00**
1885 Rupee. Similar (S) **8.00**
1903 Rupee. Edward VII/flowers (S). . **8.00**
1914 Rupee. George V/wreath (S) . . . **8.00**
1945 Rupee. George VI/wreath (S). . . **3.00**
1947 Rupee. George VI/tiger (N) **2.50**
1870 5 Rupees. Victoria as queen/wreath
(G) **175.00**
1870 10 Rupees. Similar (G) **275.00**
1881 Mohur. Victoria as empress/wreath
(G) **200.00**
1918 15 Rupees. George V/wreath
(G) **165.00**
1918 Sovereign. George V/St. George
slaying dragon, mint mark "I" on
ground (G) **135.00**

INDIA—PRINCELY STATES

VF

Alwar. 1891 Rupee. Victoria/Arabic
inscription (S). **10.00**
Bharatpur. 1910 VS (1858) Rupee. Victoria/
Arabic inscription (S) **85.00**

VF

Bikanir. 1895 1/4 Anna. Victoria/inscription
(C) **10.00**
Bundi. 1989 VS (1932) Rupee. EMPEROR
GEORGE V, Dagger/Hindi inscription
(S). **13.50**
Dewas, Junior Branch. 1888 1/12th Anna.
Victoria/wreath (C) **20.00**
Dewas, Senior Branch. 1888 1/12th Anna.
Victoria/wreath (C) **12.00**
Dhar. 1887 1/2 Pice. Victoria/inscription
(C) **5.00**
Kutch. 1936 5 Kori. Titles of Edward VIII
(S). **7.00**
1943 1/8 Kori. Titles of George VI (C,
holed) **40**
Sailana. 1912 1/4 Anna. George V/
inscription (C) **7.50**
*For princely states coins not struck in
name of British sovereign see India.*

IONIAN ISLANDS

F

1814 50 Paras. Bust of George III and 50
counterstamped on Spanish 2 Reales
(S). **300.00**
1834 Lepton. Lion/Britannia std. (C)
. . . . **5.00**

ISLE OF MAN

VF

1733 Penny. Eagle on cap/three legs
(C) **28.00**
1758 Penny. Crowned DA monogram/
three legs (C). **38.00**
1786 1/2 Penny. George III/three legs
(C) **38.00**
1839 Farthing. Victoria/three legs (C)
. . . . **9.00**

Isle of Man 1988 1 Crown

Isle of Man 2000 1 Crown

Jamaica 1937 Halfpenny

	BU
1971 1 New Penny. Elizabeth II/Celtic cross (C)	.35
1980 10 Pence. Elizabeth II/falcon(CN)	.85
1990 1/5th Crown. Elizabeth II/alley cat (G)	70.00
1976 Crown. Elizabeth II/George Washington (CN)	2.50
Same (S).	8.00
1983 Crown. Elizabeth II/1783 balloon (CN)	3.75
1988 Crown. Elizabeth II/Manx cat (S)	PF 15.00
1985 1 Angel. Elizabeth II/Archangel Michael slaying demon (G, 1 ounce)	450.00
2000 1 Crown. Elizabeth II/Willem Barents (CN)	8.00

JAMAICA

	VF
1882 Farthing. Victoria/shield (CN)	1.75
1928 Farthing. George V/shield (CN)	2.00

	VF
1950 Farthing. George VI/shield (Brass)	.25
1869 Halfpenny. Victoria/shield (CN)	2.50
1907 Halfpenny. Edward VII/shield (CN)	1.50
1937 Halfpenny.	1.00
1940 Halfpenny. George VI/shield (Brass)	.75
1910 Penny. Edward VII/shield (CN)	2.50
1920 Penny. George V/shield (CN)	2.50
1937 Penny. George VI in high relief/shield (Brass)	1.75
1950 Penny. George VI in low relief/shield (Brass)	.35

Jamaica 1953 1 Penny

Mauritius 1949 2 Cents

Malaya 1958 1 Cent

Mauritius 1934 1 Rupee

	VF
1953 Penny.	**.20**
1958 Penny. Elizabeth II/arms (Brass)	**.25**

	BU
1964 Halfpenny. Elizabeth II/arms (Brass)	**.15**
1966 5 Shillings. Crown in chain/arms (CN)	**5.00**

JERSEY

	VF
1813 18 Pence. Shield/wreath (S)	**80.00**
1841 1/52 Shilling. Victoria/shield (C)	**30.00**
1909 1/24 Shilling. Edward VII/shield (C)	**2.50**
1937 1/24 Shilling. George VI/shield (C)	**1.00**
1877 1/12 Shilling. Victoria/shield (C)	**2.00**
1931 1/12 Shilling. George V/shield (C)	**1.00**

	BU
1964 1/12 Shilling. Elizabeth II/shield (C)	**1.00**
1981 Penny. Elizabeth II/shield (C)	**.15**
1983 10 Pence. Elizabeth II/prehistoric stone structure (CN)	**1.00**

	BU
1972 2 Pounds 50 Pence. Elizabeth II/ lobster (S)	**20.00**

MALAYA

	VF
1943 1 Cent. George VI (C, square)	**.20**
1958 1 Cent. Elizabeth II (C, square)	**.20**

MAURITIUS

	VF
(1822) 25 Sous. REÇU au TRESOR/pour 25 Sous (S)	**50.00**
1969 1 Cent. Elizabeth II (C)	**.10**
1949 2 Cents. George VI (C)	**1.25**
1917 5 Cents. George V (C)	**4.50**
1886 10 Cents. Victoria (S)	**5.00**
1975 ¼ Rupee. Elizabeth II/crown and flowers (CN)	**.30**
1950 ½ Rupee. George VI/stag (CN)	**1.00**
1934 1 Rupee. George V/shield (S)	**8.00**
1975 25 Rupees. Elizabeth II/butterfly (S)	*BU* **15.00**

NEW GUINEA

	XF
1929 ½ Penny. Crown and scepters (CN, holed)	**350.00**

New Guinea 1936 1 Penny

New Zealand 1933 3 Pence

New Zealand 1943 6 Pence

New Zealand 1951 Half Crown

New Zealand 1949 1 Crown

	XF
1936 Penny. Crown and *ERI* (C, holed)	**2.00**
1944 Penny. Crown and GRI (C, holed)	**5.00**
1944 3 Pence. Similar (CN, holed)	**8.50**
1935 Shilling. Titles of George V, crown and scepters (S, holed)	**3.00**
1938 Shilling. Similar but George VI (S, holed)	**3.00**

NEW ZEALAND

	VF
1940 Halfpenny. George VI/Tiki idol (C)	**.65**
1950 Penny. George VI/Tui bird (C)	**.50**
1933 3 Pence. George V/crossed clubs (S)	**.75**
1952 3 Pence. George VI/similar (CN)	**.70**
1943 6 Pence. George VI/Huia bird (S)	**1.00**
1952 Shilling. George VI/Maori warrior (CN)	**3.00**

	VF
1935 Florin. George V/Kiwi bird (S)	**4.00**
1940 Florin. George VI/Maori and two views of Aukland (S)	**4.00**
1943 Half Crown. George VI/arms (S)	**3.50**
1951 Half Crown. Similar (CN)	**1.00**
1935 Crown. George V/Maori chief and British naval officer shaking hands (S)	**1,500.00**

	BU
1949 Crown. George VI/fern leaf (S)	**12.00**
1965 Halfpenny. Elizabeth II wearing wreath/Tiki idol (C)	**1.00**
1965 Penny. Similar/Tui bird (C)	**2.00**

New Zealand 1967 2 Cents

New Zealand 1990 1 Dollar

New Zealand 2003 5 Dollars

Nigeria 2003 1 Kobo

	BU
1960 3 Pence. George VI/crossed clubs (CN)	**1.00**
1956 6 Pence. Similar/Huia bird (S)	**5.00**
1964 Shilling. Similar/Maori warrior (CN)	**1.50**
1965 Florin. Similar/Kiwi bird (S)	**1.75**
1953 Crown. Similar/crowned monogram (CN)	**5.00**
1987 1 Cent. Crowned bust of Elizabeth II/ fern leaf (C)	**.50**
1967 2 Cents. Bust of Elizabeth II wearing tiara/Kowhai plant (C)	**.25**
1967 5 Cents. Bust of Elizabeth II wearing tiara/Tuatata lizard (CN)	**.25**
1988 10 Cents. Similar/Maori mask (CN)	**.25**
1993 50 Cents. Similar/H.M.S. Endeavor (CN)	**1.50**
1994 50 Cents. Similar (ALB in CN, bimetallic)	**22.00**
1967 Dollar. Bust of Elizabeth II wearing tiara/shield between branches (CN)	**1.50**
1990 Dollar. Similar/Kiwi bird (ALB)	**1.25**
1996 5 Dollars. Similar/Kaka parrot (CN)	**10.00**
similar (S)	*proof only* **25.00**
2003 5 Dollars. Similar/fish (CN)	**20.00**

NIGERIA

	BU
1959 ½ Penny. Crown/six-pointed star (C)	**.75**
1962 Shilling. Elizabeth II/palm branches (CN)	**3.50**
1959 2 Shillings. Elizabeth II/peanut plant (CN)	**6.00**
2003 1 Kobo. Arms/monkey (brass)	**.50**

RHODESIA

	BU
1974 1 Cent. Arns (C)	**1.00**
1964 6 Pence - 5 Cents. Elizabeth II wearing tiara/flame lily (CN)	**1.25**
1964 2 Shillings—20 Cents. Similar/ ancient bird sculpture (CN)	**3.00**
1966 Pound. Similar/Lion holding tusk (G)	*proof only* **200.00**

Rhodesia 1974 1 Cent

Rhodesia & Nyasaland 1957 1 Shilling

Seychelles 1995 25 Rupees

Union of South Africa 1943 3 Pence

RHODESIA & NYASALAND

BU

1964 1/2 Penny. Giraffes (C, holed) . . **1.50**
1957 1 Shilling. Eliz. II/Antelope (CN) **10.00**
1957 2 Shillings. Elizabeth II/African fish
    eagle holding fish (CN) **12.00**

SEYCHELLES

VF

1948 2 Cents. George VI (C) . . . . **.35**
1944 25 Cents. Similar (S) **3.50**

BU

1959 2 Cents. Elizabeth II (C) **2.50**
1972 5 Cents. Elizabeth II/cabbage(AL)**.25**
1974 1/2 Rupee. Elizabeth II (CN) **1.00**
1972 5 Rupees. Elizabeth II/beach scene
    with tree and turtle (CN) **5.00**
Similar (S) **25.00**
1995 25 Rupees. Arms/daGama (S) PF**37.50**

SOLOMON ISLANDS

BU

1977 2 Cents. Elizabeth II/eagle spirit
    (C) . . . . **.25**
1988 10 Cents. Elizabeth II/sea spirit
    (CN) . . . . **.50**

BU

1996 50 Cents. Elizabeth II/arms (CN,
    12-sided) **2.50**
1992 10 Dollars. Elizabeth II/crocodile
    (S) . . . . proof only **42.50**

SOUTH AFRICA, UNION OF

VF

1931 1/4 Penny. George V/two sparrows
    (C) **1.50**
1942 1/4 Penny. George VI/two sparrows
    (C) . . . . **.50**
1953 2-1/2 Penny. Elizabeth II/ship (C). **.35**
1929 2-1/2 Penny. George V/ship (C) . **5.00**
1952 Penny. George VI/ship (C) . . . . . . **.50**
1953 Penny. Elizabeth II/ship (C) . . . . . . **.35**
1927 3 Pence. George V/Protea plant
    within three bundles of sticks (S). . **2.50**
1943 3 Pence. George VI/similar (S) . . **1.00**
1927 6 Pence. George V/wreath (S) . **12.50**
1927 6 Pence. George V/Protea plant
    within six bundles of sticks (S) **4.00**

Union of South Africa 1958 5 Shillings

Southern Rhodesia 1932 2 Shillings

Straits Settlements 1916 1/4 Cent

	VF
1957 6 Pence. Elizabeth II/similar (S)	.75
1943 Shilling. George VI/allegory of Cape of Good Hope (S)	2.50
1953 Shilling. Elizabeth II/similar (S)	1.25
1932 2 Shillings. George V/shield (S)	6.00
1942 2 Shillings. George VI/shield (S)	3.00
1932 2-1/2 Shillings. George V/crowned shield (S)	6.00
1955 2-1/2 Shillings. Elizabeth II/similar (S)	3.00
1952 5 Shillings. George VI/ship (S)	4.50
1953 5 Shillings. Eliz. II/Springbok (S)	5.00
1958 5 Shillings. Similar	5.00

SOUTHERN RHODESIA

	VF
1936 Penny. Crowned rose (CN)	1.25
1942 6 Pence. George VI/two hatchets (S)	2.00
197 Shilling. George VI/stone bird (CN)	1.50
1932 2 Shillings. George V/antelope	20.00
1951 2 Shillings. George VI/antelope (CN)	3.00
1954 2 Shillings. Elizabeth II/antelope (CN)	75.00
1932 Half Crown. George V/crowned shield (S)	8.00

Straits Settlements 1908 1 Cent

	VF
1953 Crown. Elizabeth II/Cecil Rhodes (S)	Unc. 15.00

STRAITS SETTLEMENTS

	VF
1916 1/4 Cent. George V (C)	5.00
1908 1 Cent. Edward VII (C)	6.00
1926 1 Cent. George V (C, square)	.75
1901 5 Cents. Victoria (S)	2.50
1927 10 Cents. George V (S)	.75
1910 20 Cents. Edward VII (S)	3.50
1920 50 Cents. George V (S)	3.50
1920 Dollar. George V/ornamental design containing Chinese and Malay inscription (S)	20.00

CAUCASUS

The first modern, European-style coins struck in this region are the copper and silver issues struck by Georgia (1804-1833) while under Czarist Russian influence. It was not until the break-up of the Soviet Union that local coinage of the Caucasus region was again placed in circulation. The first coins were Azerbaijani and Armenian coins all struck in aluminum. Both were of fairly plain design. Well made coins with attractive reverse designs were introduced by Georgia in 1993. A limited number of collector issues have been struck by Georgia and Armenia.

Nagorno Karabakh is an ethnically Armenian area of Azerbaijan that broke away and declared its independence.

Known Counterfeits: None.

Armenia 1996 100 Drams

Azerbaijan 1999 50 Manat

ARMENIA

	BU
1994 10 Luma. Arms (AL)	.25
1994 3 Drams. Arms (AL)	.85
1996 100 Drams. Bagramian/Arms (S)	PF **300.00**
1996 100 Drams. Stork with chess board/arms (CN)	**7.00**
1997 25,000 Drams. Anahit (G)	PF **100.00**

AZERBAIJAN

	BU
1992 10 Qapik. Eight-pointed star (AL)	.50
1993 20 Qapik. Crescent and star (AL)	.75
1996 50 Manat. Romantic couple/ Mohammed Fuzuli (S) *Proof only*	**60.00**
1999 50 Manat.	PF **50.00**

Georgia 2000 10 Lari

Nagorno Karabakh 2004 1 Dram

GEORGIA

	BU

1827 2 Abazi. Masonry crown/inscription (S) . . . . *F* **30.00**

1993 20 Thetri. Emblem/stag (Steel) **1.50**

1995 500 Lari. Profiles of Stalin, Roosevelt, Churchill and DeGaulle (G) . . . . *proof only* **500.00**

2000 10 Lari. Eagle/lion (S) *proof only* **18.00**

NAGORNO KARABAKH

	BU

2004 1 Dram. Emblem / St. Gregory (AL) **1.00**

CZECHOSLOVAKIA

After four hundred years of Austrian rule, Czechoslovakia became an independent state in 1918, following the breakup of the Hapsburg empire. While most of the coins circulating here were regular coins of the empire, special copper pieces were struck for Bohemia in the late 1700s. Also common were the coins struck by the local bishops of Olmuetz.

Additional Specialized Books: Miller zu Aicholz. *Oesterreichische Münzpragungen, 1519-1938.* Despite the title, this is an excellent catalogue for later Bohemian coins.

Known Counterfeits: Few.

BOHEMIA

	F

1687 6 Kreuzer. Bust of Leopold I/double-headed eagle, double-tailed lion on chest (S) **40.00**

1699 Ducat. Similar (G) **250.00**

1782 Groeschl. Crowned shield (C) **12.00**

1943 1 Koruna. Double-tailed lion/ivy branches (Z) . . . . *VF* **.75**

OLMÜTZ

	F

1705 Kreuzer. Bust/arms (S) **15.00**

SCHLICK

	F

1638 3 Kreuzer. Madonna and child over arms/double-headed eagle (S) . . **25.00**

Czechoslavakia 1922 1 Koruna

Czechoslavakia 1981 100 Korun

CZECHOSLOVAKIA

VF

1925 10 Haleru. Double-tailed
lion/bridge. . . . .**.35**

1938 20 Haleru. Double-tailed lion/wheat
and scythe (CN) . . . .**.35**

1922 1 Koruna. Double-tailed lion/woman
with sheaf and scythe (C) . . . .**.50**

1934 20 Korun. Shield/three figures stg.
(S). **4.00**

BU

1949 50 Korun. Stalin/shield (S). **5.00**

1965 10 Korun. Shield/Jan Hus (S) . . **15.00**

1966 5 Haleru. Shield/wreath (AL) **25**

1980 2 Koruny. Shield/symbol (CN). . . .**75**

1991 5 Haleru. CSFR over shield/5h
(AL) . . . .**.25**

1981 100 Korun. Spaniel/arms (S). . . . **9.00**

1993 500 Korun. Shield/tennis player
(S). **35.00**

CZECH REPUBLIC

BU

1993 1 Koruna. Double-tailed lion/crown
(N clad Steel). . . . .**.60**

1993 50 Korun. Double-tailed lion/city
view (Steel, Brass, and Copper plated,
bimetallic). **7.50**

Czech Republic 2003 200 Korun

Slovakia 2001 500 Korun

BU

1994 200 Korun. Shield/cathedral (S)
. . . . **13.50**

2003 200 Korun. Vrehlicky/quill (S) . **17.00**

SLOVAKIA

VF

1939 10 Halierov. Shield/castle (C). . . **2.00**

1941 1 Koruna. Shield/wreath (CN) . . **1.00**

1944 10 Korun. Shield/King, bishop and
knight (S) **4.00**

BU

1993 10 Haliers. Shield/steeple (AL) . . .**35**

1993 10 Koruna. Shield/Medieval cross
(Brass). **2.50**

1993 100 Korun. Shield/three doves (S)**9.00**

1994 200 Korun. Logo/hockey player
(S). **18.00**

2001 500 Korun. Beetle cross/orchid (S)
. . . . **40.00**

FRANCE

After centuries of deterioration, French royal coinage began to stabilize somewhat by the 1600s. This coincides with the introduction of milled coinage of neat manufacture the same century. A silver-dollar-sized *ecu* and its fractions became common. Small values were struck in base silver and especially in copper. This included the old *denier tournois* which had survived since the 1200s. The gold *louis d'or* became so recognized for its stability that it saw wide circulation internationally. Most coins bore the king's portrait, with fleurs or a shield of arms on the reverse. Sometimes an elaborate cross or monogram would still be used, these being held over from the Renaissance. Despite the improved striking methods, imprecise means were used to manufacture blanks of exact weight, so many had to be adjusted with a file before striking to remove excess metal. The resultant "adjustment marks" are not damage, but if severe do reduce the coin's value.

Among the most important uses of coinage for the study of French history is the effect that the French Revolution had on the iconography. An entire new set of symbols replaced the traditional ones. Those reflecting new ideologies include one displaying a tablet inscribed "Men are equal before the law." An allegorical head, initially representing liberty was also quite popular. Even after Napoleon took the reins as emperor, he temporarily maintained the revolutionary name of the country as "French Republic" on the coinage. The Revolution's most lasting change on the coinage was the decimal system. This system, used the world over today, divides the monetary unit, the franc or the dollar, for example, into tenths or hundredths.

Most 19th century French coins were very conservative, depicting the monarch and a coat of arms or value. However, there was great artistic merit in the beautiful coins of the 1898 to 1920 period.

In this dawn of the new European currency, the Euro, it is all the more important to mention that French coinage was the basis of an earlier international currency, that of the Latin Monetary Union, from 1865 to 1920. During this period, the money of nations as diverse as Greece and Switzerland were struck on an international standard and held the same value.

The most common design to be used by the French republics is an allegorical female head or bust. This image, tracing its roots back to a 1790s allegory of liberty, is variously described today as the personification of the Republic, of France, and as Marie Anne (the personification's nickname).

Inflation again hit France after World War I and the currency did not finally stabilize until 1960. During this time most of the coins were of baser metals, including aluminum bronze and aluminum. Some denominations were distinguished with holes in their centers. Many mint marks were used on French coins before 1960 and some of the dates and mint marks can be valuable. Only common ones for the type are listed here. Coins before 1960, and some outmoded ones struck afterwards have no legal tender status.

In January 2002, France replaced the franc with coins denominated in Euros, the currency of the European Union. Some coins were struck as early as 1999 and held until 2002. On the circulating denominations, 1 Cent through 2 Euros, one side carries a French design, the other a common European design. On higher denomination commemoratives both sides are distinctively French.

In recent years, a phenomenal amount of collector issues has been struck, sometimes in odd sizes and at a rate of one every few weeks!

During and immediately after World War I, many municipal chambers of commerce throughout France struck small denomination emergency tokens to facilitate commerce. Their designs run from utilitarian to breathtaking.

Colonial coins from India are the earliest common French colonials. Many of these are hardly distinguishable from local Indian States coins. Usually they are identified by certain symbols, such as a fleur or a cock. They were originally intended to circulate alongside crude local coins and their designs and crudeness made this possible.

Other colonial coins were struck occasionally from the 1890s through the 1930s, but were not abundant except in Indo-China. During World War I, and especially right after, however, they were struck in abundant quantities in base metals. Usually one side bore a female head representing an allegory of France. The reverse would allude to the individual colony. Since 1948, virtually all French colonial coins can be easily collected in mint state.

Additional Specialized Books:
Duplessy, Jean. *Les Monnaies Francaises Royales*, vol. II.
Known Counterfeits:
Contemporary counterfeits of French coins have always been common. The gold 20 and 50 franc pieces should be examined with care. Counterfeits of smaller denominations are slightly less dangerous. A sampling of counterfeit French coins includes 1 Franc 1867BB and 1915, and 5 Francs 1875A, 1960 and 1975, but hundreds of others exist.

KINGDOM

Louis XIV, 1643-1715.

F

1696 Double denier. Bust r./crown and three fleurs
(C) **20.00**
1655 Liard. Crowned bust r./LIARD DE FRANCE, fleurs (C). **18.00**
1675 4 Sols. Bust r./four fleurs around mint mark (S)....................... **25.00**
1707 10 Sols =1/8 Ecu. Old bust r./crown over crossed scepters (S) **28.00**
1644 Quarter Ecu. Young bust r./crowned shield (S)...................... **125.00**
1690 Ecu. Old bust r./cross of 8 L's (S).......................... **100.00**
1694 Louis d'or. Old bust r./L's and crowned fleurs around mint mark (G) **300.00**
1709 Louis d'or. Old bust r./eight crowned L's in form of cross, fleurs in angles (G) **400.00**

Louis XV, 1715-74.

F

1720 1/2 Sol. Young bust r./crowned shield (C) **20.00**
1770 Sol. Bust r./crowned shield (C) . **7.00**
1750 2 Sols. Crowned L/crowned crossed floral L's (Billon)................. **6.00**
1744 6 Sols = 1/20 Ecu. Old bust l./ crowned shield in wreath (S) **13.50**
1729 24 Sols = 1/5 Ecu. Young bust l./ similar (S) **18.00**
1741 Ecu. Bust l./similar (S)......... **40.00**
1745 2 Louis d'or. Head l./crowned shields of France and Navarre (G) **400.00**

Louis XVI, 1774-93.

F

1786 Liard. Head l./crowned shield (C) **8.00**
1791 Liard. Head l./crowned shield (C) **8.00**
1792 3 Deniers. Bust l./fasces (C)... **20.00**
1791 12 Deniers. Similar (C)......... **8.00**
1793 2 Sols. Similar (C) **15.00**
1783 6 Sols ' 1/20 Ecu. Bust l./crowned shield in wreath (S)............. **30.00**
1791 30 Sols ' 1/4 Ecu. Bust l./angel writing on tablet (S) **40.00**

F

1783 1/2 Ecu. Bust l./crowned shield in wreath (S)..................... **40.00**
1792 Ecu. Similar (S) **90.00**
1786 Louis d'or. Bust l./crowned shields of France and Navarre (G)....... **200.00**

Republic, 1793-1804.

F

1793 24 Livres. Angel writing on tablet/ wreath (G). **1,250.00**
1793 6 Livres. Similar (S) **125.00**
1793 1 Sol. Tablet below eye/wreath on scales (C) **32.50**
L'An 2 (1793-94) 2 Sols. Similar, no AD date **100.00**
1792 5 Sols. Soldiers swearing oath (C). *Common token of the time* **12.00**
L'An 6 (1797-98) 1 Centime. Bust of Liberty (C) **2.00**
L'An 7 (1798-99) 5 Centimes. Similar/ wreath (C)...................... **8.00**
L'An 8 (1799-1800) 1 Decime. Similar/ wreath (C)..................... **10.00**
L'An 4 (1795-96) 2 Decimes. Similar/wreath (C) **65.00**
L'An 7 (1798-99) 5 Francs. Liberty, Hercules and Equality (S)................ **40.00**

Napoleon I, 1799-1815.

F

1808 5 Centimes. N in wreath, raised border (C)................... **100.00**
1810 10 Centimes. Crowned N in wreath, raised border (Billon)........... **7.00**
1814 1 Decime. Crowned N in wreath/ value in wreath (C) **15.00**
L'An 12 (1803-04) 1/4 Franc. Bust as Premier Consul/QUART in wreath (S) **32.50**
L'An 12 (1803-04) 1/2 Franc. Bust as Premier Consul/DEMI FRANC in wreath (S)..................... **13.50**
1809 1/2 Franc. Bust as Emperor/same (S)............................. **10.00**
1809 1 Franc. Similar (S) **16.00**
L'An 11 (1802-03) 5 Francs. Bust as Premier Consul/wreath (S).............. **50.00**
1811 5 Francs. Bust as Emperor/similar (S)............................. **30.00**
1812 20 Francs. Similar (G)........ **100.00**

Louis XVIII, 1814-1825.

F

1815 Decime. Crowned L in wreath/wreath
(C) **7.50**
1817 1/4 Franc. Bust l./crowned shield
(S) **10.00**
1822 1 Franc. Bust l./crowned shield in
wreath (S) **12.00**
1824 5 Francs. Similar (S) **20.00**
1816 20 Francs. Similar (G) **100.00**

Charles X, 1824-30.

F

1827 1/4 Franc. Bust l./crowned shield
(S) **6.00**
1827 1/2 Franc. Bust l./crowned shield
(S) **10.00**
1825 1 Franc. Bust l./crowned shield in
wreath (S) **20.00**
1830 40 Francs. Bust r./similar (G) . **200.00**

Louis Philippe, 1830-48.

F

1847 25 Centimes. Head r./wreath (S)
. . . . **6.00**
1840 1/2 Franc. Similar (S) **5.00**
1846 1 Franc. Similar (S) **8.00**
1834 2 Francs. Same (S) **20.00**
1848 5 Francs. Head r./wreath (S) **9.00**
1831 20 Francs. Bust l./wreath (G) . **100.00**

Second Republic, 1848-52.

VF

1849 1 Centime. Liberty head (C) . . . **5.00**
1849 1 Franc. Ceres head/wreath (S) **45.00**
1852 1 Franc. Head of Louis Napoleon/
wreath (S) **80.00**
1849 5 Francs. Liberty, Hercules and
Equality (S) **15.00**
1851 10 Francs. Ceres head/wreath
(G) **65.00**

Napoleon III, 1852-70.

VF

1862 1 Centime. Barehead/eagle (C) **1.00**
1854 2 Centimes. Similar (C) **2.00**
1861 2 Centimes. Head with wreath/eagle
(C) **1.50**
1855 5 Centimes. Barehead/eagle
(C) **4.00**

France 1862 10 Centimes

France 1922 10 Centimes

VF

1862 10 Centimes. Head with wreath/
eagle (C) **10.00**
1867 20 Centimes. Head l./crown (S). **4.00**
1867 50 Centimes. Similar (S) **6.00**
1858 1 Franc. Barehead/wreath (S) . **25.00**
1867 1 Franc. Head with wreath/arms
(S) **12.00**
1856 2 Francs. Barehead/wreath
(S) **275.00**
1866 2 Francs. Head with wreath/arms
(S) **25.00**
1868 5 Francs. Similar (S) **15.00**
1862 10 Francs. Head r./wreath (G) . **55.00**
1868 20 Francs. Head r./wreath
(G) **100.00**
1869 100 Francs. Similar (G) **500.00**

Restored Republic, 1871-1958.

VF

1895 1 Centime. Ceres head (C). **2.50**
1908 2 Centimes. Republic head (C) . **1.00**
1916 5 Centimes. Similar/allegorical group
(C) **1.00**
1897 10 Centimes. Ceres head (C). . . **3.00**
1916 10 Centimes. Head r./allegorical
scene (C). . . . . **.75**
1922 10 Centimes. Cap & RF (CN) . . . . **.75**

France 1904 25 Centimes

France 1952 10 Francs

France 1946 50 Centimes

France 1968 1 Centime

France 1943 1 Franc

France 1970 1 Franc

	VF
1931 10 Centimes. Cap and RF (CN, holed)	.35
1945 20 Centimes. Similar (Z)	5.00
1904 25 Centimes. Republic head/fasces (N)	.75
1916 50 Centimes. Sower (S)	1.00
1939 50 Centimes. Head l. (ALB)	.50
1946 50 Centimes. Head l. (AL)	.25
1872 1 Franc. Ceres head/wreath (S)	4.00
1943 1 Franc. Axe (AL)	.25
1947 1 Franc. Head l./cornucopia (AL)	.25
1915 2 Francs. Sower (S)	2.00
1921 2 Francs. Mercury std. (ALB)	2.00
1873 5 Francs. Liberty, Hercules and Equality (S)	9.00
1945 5 Francs. Head l./wreath (AL)	.35
1901 10 Francs. Head l./cock l. (G)	55.00
1952 10 Francs. Head l./cock and branch (ALB)	.35

	VF
1933 20 Francs. Head l./two ears of grain (S)	5.00
1953 50 Francs. Head l./cock and branch (ALB)	2.00
1909 100 Francs. Winged genius (G)	375.00
1955 100 Francs. Bust with torch/branches (CN)	1.00

Vichy France.

	VF
1941 20 Centimes. VINGT over oak leaves (Z)	2.00
1941 20 Centimes. 20 over oak leaves (Z)	.75
1943 1 Franc. Ax between wheat ears (AL)	.25
1941 5 Francs. Philippe Petain/ax (CN)	100.00

France 1964 5 Francs

France 1986 100 Francs

France 2004 1-1/2 Euro

Euro Coinage 2002 to date.

	BU
1999 20 Euro Cent. Sower/map (B, notched)	1.00
2001 1 Euro. Stylized tree/map (CN clad N in NB, bimetallic)	3.00
2004 1-1/2 Euro. Napoleon (S)	45.00

FRENCH COLONIAL

ALGERIA

	VF
1956 20 Francs. Head r./two wheat ears (CN)	1.00
1949 50 Francs. Similar (CN)	3.00
1952 100 Francs. Similar (CN)	4.00

CAMEROON

	VF
1943 50 Centimes. Cock/double cross (C)	3.50
1926 1 Franc. Head l./palm branches (ALB)	2.00
1948 1 Franc. Antelope head (AL)	.25
1924 2 Francs. Head l./palm branches (ALB)	15.00

COMOROS

	BU
1964 1 Franc. Head l./palm trees (AL)	1.25
1964 5 Francs. Similar (AL)	2.00
1964 10 Francs. Shells and Coelacanth fish (ALB)	3.00

Fifth Republic, 1959-date.

	BU
1968 1 Centime. Wheat ear (Steel)	.25
1987 5 Centimes. Bust l. (ALB)	.10
1967 20 Centimes. Bust l. (ALB)	.15
1976 1/2 Franc. Sower (N)	.30
1970 1 Franc. Sower (N)	.40
1979 2 Francs. Modernistic sower (N)	.65
1974 10 Francs. Map/girders (B)	2.00
1989 10 Francs. Winged genius (Steel in ALB, bimetallic)	7.50
1989 10 Francs. Montesquieu (Steel in ALB, bimetallic)	17.50
1986 100 Francs. Statue of Liberty (S)	16.50
1987 100 Francs. LaFayette (S)	20.00
1996 100 Francs. Clovis (S)	32.50
1990 500 Francs = 70 Ecu. Charlemagne (G)	*proof only* 450.00

French Cochin China 1879 1 Cent

French Equatorial Africa 1948 1 Franc

FRENCH AFARS & ISSAS

	BU
1975 2 Francs. Antelope head (AL)	**5.00**
1975 5 Francs. Similar (AL)	**4.00**
1975 20 Francs. Ocean liner and small sailing ship (ALB)	**7.00**
1975 50 Francs. Head l./two camels (CN)	**12.50**

FRENCH COCHIN CHINA

	VF
1879 1 Cent. Seated figure. (C)	**15.00**
1879 Sapeque. French inscription/Chinese inscription (C, holed)	**6.00**
1879 10 Cents. Seated figure (S)	**35.00**
1885 Piastre. Similar (S)	*rare*

FRENCH COLONIES

	F
1721 9 Deniers. Crowned crossed Ls/inscription (C)	**35.00**
1779 Stampee. Crowned C/blank (C)	**12.00**
1825 5 Centimes. Bust of Charles X (C)	**6.00**
1841 10 Centimes. Bust of Louis Philippe (C)	**10.00**

FRENCH EQUATORIAL AFRICA

	XF
1943 5 Centimes. Cap over RF (ALB, holed)	**275.00**
1943 50 Centimes. Cock/double cross (C)	**7.00**
1942 1 Franc. Similar (Brass)	**10.00**
1948 1 Franc. Head l./antelope head (AL)	**.50**
1948 2 Francs. Similar (AL)	**1.50**

FRENCH GUIANA

	F
1789 2 Sous. Crown/CAYENNE (Billon)	**5.00**
1818 10 Centimes. LL monogram (Billon)	**18.00**

FRENCH INDIA

	F
(1723) 1/2 Fanon. Crown/field of fleurs (C)	**100.00**
1720-1835 Doudou. Fleur/inscription (C)	**6.00**
1753 Biche. Five fleurs/1753 (C)	**20.00**
1776 1/5 Rupee. Arabic inscription, P on rev. (S)	**20.00**

FRENCH INDO-CHINA

	VF
1887 1 Sapeque. French inscription/Chinese inscription (C, holed)	**4.00**
1885 1 Cent. Std. figure/Chinese inscription in rectangle (C)	**4.00**
1899 1 Cent. Allegories of France and French Indo-China std. (C)	**2.00**
1888 10 Cents. Figure std. (S)	**10.00**
1921 10 Cents. Similar (S)	**3.00**
1899 20 Cents. Similar (S)	**20.00**
1894 50 Cents. Similar (S)	**100.00**

French Indo-China 1941 20 Cents

French Polynesia 1982 100 Francs

French Oceania 1949 2 Francs

French Somalia 1959 1 Franc

	VF
1886 Piastre. Similar (S).	**20.00**
1926 Piastre. Similar (S).	**17.50**

	XF
1942 1/4 Cent. (Z).	**40.00**
1935 1/2 Cent. Cap over RF (C)	**2.00**
1943 1 Cent. Ears of grain (AL)	**1.00**
1939 5 Cents. Head above two cornucopiae (CN, holed)	**1.00**
1946 5 Cents. Bust with olive branch (AL)	**1.00**
1941 10 Cents. Similar (CN)	**.75**
1941 20 Cents. Similar (CN)	**1.00**
1936 50 Cents. Figure std. (S)	**6.00**
1931 Piastre. Head l. (S)	**15.00**
1947 Piastre. Bust with olive branch (CN)	**2.00**

FRENCH OCEANIA

	XF
1949 50 Centimes. Republic std./beach scene (AL).	**1.50**
1949 2 Francs. Similar (AL)	**1.50**

FRENCH POLYNESIA

	BU
1965 50 Centimes. Republic std./beach scene (AL).	**1.50**
1987 1 Franc. Similar (AL).	**.45**
1965 2 Francs. Similar (AL)	**1.00**
1967 10 Francs. Carving (N).	**1.75**
1991 50 Francs. Beach huts below mountain (N)	**2.00**
1982 100 Francs. Similar (N-Brass).	**4.00**

FRENCH SOMALIA

	BU
1959 1 Franc.	**5.00**
1965 1 Franc. Antelope head (AL)	**4.00**
1959 2 Francs. Similar (AL)	**5.00**
1975 10 Francs. Ocean liner and small sailing ship (ALB)	**5.00**

FRENCH WEST AFRICA

	XF
1944 1 Franc. Head l./two cornucopiae (ALB)	**5.00**

French West Africa 1948 2 Francs

New Caledonia 1972 10 Francs

Madagascar 1948 2 Francs

New Caledonia 1972 50 Francs

	XF
1948 2 Francs. Head l./antelope head (AL)	.50
1956 10 Francs. Similar (ALB)	**1.50**
1957 25 Francs. Antelope head/root figure (ALB)	**2.00**

GUADELOUPE

	F
1921 50 Centimes. Carib Indian (CN)	**9.00**
1903 1 Franc. Carib Indian (CN)	**17.50**

MADAGASCAR

	XF
1943 50 Centimes. Cock/double cross (C)	**10.00**
1958 1 Franc. Three bull heads (AL)	.50
1948 2 Francs. Similar (AL)	.65
1953 20 Francs. Map (ALB)	**3.00**

MARTINIQUE

	F
1922 50 Centimes. Bust of contemporary woman (CN)	**20.00**
1897 1 Franc. Similar (CN)	**25.00**

NEW CALEDONIA

	BU
1949 50 Centimes. Republic std./Kagu bird (AL)	**3.50**
1994 1 Franc. Similar (AL)	.50
1949 2 Francs. Similar (AL)	**4.50**
1972 10 Francs. Small sailing ship (N)	**2.00**
1967 20 Francs. Busts of three bulls.	**5.00**
1972 50 Francs. Hut and trees (N)	**5.00**
1976 100 Francs. Similar (N-C)	**6.00**

NEW HEBRIDES

	BU
1970 1 Franc. Bird (N-Brass)	.75
1973 10 Francs. Carved head (N)	**1.25**
1966 100 Francs. Carving (S)	**15.00**

REUNION

	VF
1816 10 Centimes. LL monogram/ISLE DE BOURBON (Billon)	**85.00**
1896 50 Centimes. Bust of Mercury (CN)	**45.00**

New Hebrides 1973 10 Francs

Reunion 1948 1 Franc

St. Pierre & Miquelon 1948 1 Franc

Togo 1924 2 Francs

Tonkin 1905 1/600th Piastre

Tunisia 1938 5 Centimes

	BU
1948 1 Franc. Palm trees (AL)	**2.00**
1955 10 Francs. Shield (ALB)	**2.50**
1964 100 Francs. Shield (N)	**3.50**

SAINT PIERRE & MIQUELON

	BU
1948 1 Franc. Sailing ship (AL)	**4.00**
1948 2 Francs. Similar (AL)	**5.00**

TOGO

	VF
1924 50 Centimes. Palm branches (ALB)	**6.00**
1948 1 Franc. Antelope head (AL)	**6.00**
1924 2 Francs. Head/palm branches (ALB)	**15.00**
1925 2 Francs. Palm branches (ALB)	**18.00**

	VF
1956 5 Francs. Antelope head (ALB)	**3.00**

TONKIN

	XF
1905 1/600th Piastre. French inscription/Chinese inscription (Z)	**15.00**

TUNISIA

	VF
1938 5 Centimes. Arabic inscription/French inscription (CN, holed)	**2.00**
1945 50 Centimes. Wreath/wreath (ALB)	**.25**
1946 5 Francs. Arabic inscription/French inscription (ALB)	**1.50**
1939 20 Francs. Two branches/wreath (S)	**20.00**

GERMANY

The coinage of Germany is by far the most complex of the modern era. As more and more nobles and bishops were given the right to strike coins as a favor of the Holy Roman Emperor, the number of issuing authorities in greater Germany became almost bewildering. Certainly at its greatest, it ran into several hundred. Most struck coins solely in their own names, others such as cities cited their own authority on one side, but paid homage to the Holy Roman Emperor on the other. The local side of a coin would usually depict the bust or arms of the local prince, or a city's patron saint. Some depicted symbolic animals or a wildman (a giant wearing nothing but a loin-encircling bush.)

The Emperor was sometimes portrayed, but usually he was honored by inscribing his titles around a double-headed eagle. Usually the Emperor was the head of the Austrian house of Hapsburg, but not always.

Following the Napoleonic wars, many of the ecclesiastical territories were absorbed by the secular ones, the greater states began to take over the smaller ones, and the Holy Roman Empire ceased to exist. For the first time, the number of coin-issuing German states began to decline. This process continued until the German states were finally replaced by a republic in 1918.

While there were a great many local coinage standards, some basic ideas remained consistent. A thaler was a large, silver-dollar-sized coin. A ducat was made of gold and uniformly contained 11/100 troy ounce of that metal. Good silver coins were often valued in terms of how many went to make a thaler. Thus the inscription *6 einen thaler* meant that the coin was worth one sixth of a thaler. Guldens were not always used, but when they were, they usually resembled an American half dollar. The albus and groschen were small silver coins. Other small coins such as the pfennig, heller, or kreuzer, could be either copper or billon, but when they were created in the Middle Ages they were originally silver.

Almost fifty years before the German states passed into history, Germany became a unified nation. Each local prince retained his own territories and some aspect of local government, but after 1871 the national government fell to the hands of one German Emperor, who happened to be the hereditary King of Prussia, the most powerful of the German states. Throughout Germany, all copper and small silver coins (1 pfennig to 1 mark) were uniform. Larger silver and gold coins (2 through

20 marks) shared a common reverse design with the legend *Deutsches Reich*. The obverse bore the portrait of the local prince or the city arms.

During and immediately after World War I, hundreds of municipal governments and companies throughout Germany struck small denomination emergency tokens or *notgeld* to facilitate commerce. They were usually struck in zinc, iron, or aluminum, occasionally porcelain. Their designs run from traditionally heraldic to humorous to utilitarian.

The "Weimar" Republic of 1918 to 1933 struck minor coins of fairly bland agricultural designs, and a good number of exciting commemorative silver pieces. Its coins were replaced in the 1930s by ones bearing the notorious Nazi swastika held by an eagle. During World War II, like so many other countries, zinc replaced most coinage metals needed for the war effort.

From 1949 until 1990, there were two Germanies, the Federal Republic (West), and the smaller, Soviet dominated Democratic Republic (East). Each had its own coinage, the West with a traditional German eagle, the East, with typical Communist industrial symbolism. Both states struck numerous commemoratives often very similar in inspiration. With the fall of communism, East Germany chose to join West Germany, which then attempted to bail the smaller state out of the economic morass of communism.

In January 2002, Germany replaced the Mark with coins denominated in Euros, the currency of the European Union. On the circulating denominations, 1 Cent through 2 Euros, one side carries a German design, the other a common European design. On higher denomination commemoratives, both sides are distinctively German.

The German Empire struck coins for two colonies, and both are very popularly collected. The issues for German East Africa were struck in gold, silver, and bronze. The large silver pieces bear an exciting bust of Kaiser Wilhelm II wearing an elaborate griffin-topped helmet. The large silver pieces of German New Guinea display a detailed bird of paradise, considered by some to be among the most beautiful images of the entire European colonial series. All German New Guinea coins are scarce and in high demand.

Prices: In many specialized markets and in Europe, many German coins can sell for prices in excess of those listed below. Also, the prices shown here are for common dates. Rare date and mint combinations can be quite valuable.

Spelling: There are many spelling variations connected with German coins. Thaler is the earlier form of Taler. Kreuzer is the later form of kreutzer. Pfennig is a variant of pfenning. Also note that ü is a symbol for ue and both are quite common.

Additional Specialized Books: *Money Trend* magazine provides up-to-the-month pricing updates for this volatile market.

Known Counterfeits: A great many contemporary counterfeits exist of Prussian 1/24 and 1/12 Thalers of the 1700s. Some also exist of 1/3 Thalers, 1773A for example. Dangerous modern counterfeits exist of several 20 mark gold pieces. While rare patterns of Adolf Hitler portrait coins exist, virtually all those encountered are actually fantasy souvenirs made well after the war.

Some banks have restruck classic 17th and 18th century coins with new dies. These are easily distinguished from originals because of their brilliant proof finishes. Many also have a small date of restriking discretely placed on the coin.

Beware of damaged coins. Solder marks and other mount marks severely reduce the value of a coin. So does smoothing out an unpleasant surface by means of heavy polishing or scraping. This practice is particularly common on German coins. Early coins struck with roller dies will be slightly curved. This is not damage and is to be expected.

GERMAN STATES TO 1871

	F

Aachen. 1759 12 Heller. Eagle/inscription (C) **20.00**

Anhalt. 1862 2-1/2 Silber Groschen. Shield/inscription (Billon) **4.00**

Augsburg. 1715 Heller. Pine cone/cross with rose at center and leaves in angles (C) **6.00**

Baden. 1870 Kreuzer. Shield between griffins/wreath (C) **1.00**

Bavaria. 1750 12 Kreuzer. Bust r./crowned round arms (S) **12.00**

1760 Thaler. Bust r./Madonna and child (S) **30.00**

Many poor counterfeits of this Thaler have recently come onto the market.

___. 1846 1 Pfennig. Arms (C) **1.00**

Brandenburg-Anabach. 1766 Thaler. Bust/arms (S) **125.00**

___. 1855. 2 Gulden. Bust r./Madonna column (S) . . . . *VF* **30.00**

Brandenburg-Prussia. 1676 18 Groscher (¼ Thaler). Bust r. with sword/Eagle (S) **35.00**

Bremen. 1781 Schwaren. Key/inscription (C) **4.00**

Brunswick-Luneburg. 1679 Thaler. Shield/ wildman standing (S) **165.00**

Brunswick-Wolfenbuttel. 1823 1/24th Thaler. Horse leaping l./inscription (Billon) **3.00**

Camenz. 1822 3 Pfennig. Wing/inscription (C) **30.00**

Frankfurt. 1786 Pfennig. Eagle/inscription (C) **2.00**

Fulda. 1726 6 Pfennig. Arms/value (S) **15.00**

Hamburg. 1727 4 Schilling. Double-headed eagle/castle (S) **18.00**

Hesse-Darmstadt 1733 10 Kreuzer

Brandenburg Ansbach 1766 1 Thaler

Metz 1657 12 Groschen

Fulda 1726 6 Pfennig

Pfalz-Newberg 1724 1 Kreuzer

F

1861 Ducat. Knight stg./inscription (G)**175.00**
Hannover. 1834 Thaler. Head of William IV
  of England/crowned shield (S) . . **40.00**
__. 1855 6 Pfennig. Horse leaping
  (Billon). **2.00**
Hesse-Cassel. 1843 3 Heller. Shield/
  inscription (C) **2.00**
Hesse-Darmstadt. 1733 10 Kreuzer. Arms/
  values (S) **15.00**
Isenburg. (1847) "Snipe heller." AJ in
  wreath/snipe (C) **20.00**
Lindau. 1689 Pfennig. Linden tree/blank
  (C) **22.00**
Lippe-Detmold. 1685 Thaler. Bust Simon
  Heinrich r./arms (S). **600.00**
1860 Thaler. Bust of Paul F.E. Leopold r./
  arms (S). **40.00**
Lübeck. 1732 8 Schilling. Double-headed
  eagle/shield (S). **25.00**

F

Mainz. 1671 Ducat. Bust of Johann Philip
  r./shield (G) **275.00**
Metz. 165/ 12 Groschen. St. Steven/Arms**75.00**
Munster. 1735 3 Pfennig. CA monogram/
  inscription (C) **6.00**
Nassau. 1861 Kreuzer. Crowned shield/
  wreath (Billon) **1.00**
Nurnberg. (1700) 1/16 Ducat. Shield/lamb
  holding banner (G) square **90.00**
Oldenburg. 1858 Groschen. Crowned
  shield/inscription (Billon) **3.50**
Pfalz-Newberg. 1724 1 Kreuzer. (S). . **12.00**
Prussia. 1840 Pfenning. Crowned shield/
  inscription (C) **1.50**
1847 3 Pfenninge. Similar (C). **1.00**
1821 Silber Groschen. Head of Freidrich
  Wilhelm III r./inscription (Billon) . . **3.00**
1701 1/12 Thaler. Eagle surrounded by Fs
  and Rs/crowned scepter (S) **25.00**

Rostock 1729 3 Pfennig

Silesia 1808 1 Groschel

	F

Rostock. 1729 3 Pfennig. Griffin (C) . . **8.00**
Saxony. 1866 5 Pfennig. Crowned
   Baroque shield/inscription **1.50**
1668 1/24th Thaler. Arms/Royal orb
   (S) **15.00**
1776 Thaler. Bust of Friedrich August r./
   shield (S) **35.00**
Schwarzburg-Sondershausen. 1846
   Pfennig. Crowned shield/inscription
   (C) **1.50**
Silesia. 1808 1 Groschel. Monogram
   (Billon) **20.00**
Stolberg-Werningerode. 1768 Ducat. Bust
   of Christian Ernst/stag stg. l.(G) **400.00**
Trier. 1695 3 Petermenger. Crowned
   shield/bust of St. Peter (S) **14.00**
Westphalia. 1812 2 Centimes. HN
   monogram/inscription (C) **2.50**
1808 2 Franken. Bust of Jerome
   Napoleon/wreath (S) **400.00**
Württemberg. 1798 1/2 Kreuzer. Crowned
   FII 1/2 (Billon) **7.00**
1848 3 Kreuzer. Crowned shield/wreath
   . . . . **2.00**

GERMAN STATES 1873-1918

*(All reverses are the imperial eagle
unless noted.)*

	VF

Anhalt-Dessau. 1914 3 Mark. Heads of
   Duke and Duchess (S) **50.00**

	VF

Baden. 1908 3 Mark. Head of Friedrich II l.
   (S) **28.00**
Bavaria. 1876 2 Mark. Head of Ludwig II r.
   (S) **70.00**
__. 1909 3 Mark. Head of Otto l. (S). **18.00**
Bremen. 1904 2 Mark. Shield (S) **60.00**
Brunswick-Wolfenbuttel. 1915 3 Mark.
   Heads of Duke and Duchess r. (S)
   . . . . **120.00**
Hamburg. 1896 2 Mark. Shield between
   lions (S) **20.00**
Hesse-Darmstadt. 1904 2 Mark. Busts of
   Philipp and Ludwig l. (S) **50.00**
Lippe-Detmold. 1906 2 Mark. Bust of
   Leopold IV l. (S) **250.00**
Lübeck. 1908 3 Mark. Double headed
   eagle (S) **70.00**
Mecklenburg-Schwerin. 1904 2 Mark.
   Busts of Grand Duke and Grand
   Duchess l. (S) **40.00**
Mecklenburg-Strelitz. 1877 2 Mark. Bust
   of Friedrich Wilhelm l. (S) **250.00**
Oldenburg. 1901 2 Mark. Bust of Friedrich
   August l. (S) **225.00**
Prussia. 1913 2 Mark. Bust of Wilhelm II
   (S) **15.00**
1913 3 Mark. King on horse, surrounded
   by followers/Eagle grasping snake
   (S) **18.00**
1908 5 Mark. Wilhelm II (S) **17.00**
1872 10 Mark. Wilhelm I (G) **95.00**
1888 20 Mark. Friedrich III (G) **120.00**
Reuss-Greiz. 1899 2 Mark. Bust of Heinrich
   XXII (S) **200.00**
Reuss-Schleiz. 1884 2 Mark. Head of
   Heinrich XIV (S) **300.00**
Saxe-Altenburg. 1903 5 Mark. Bust of
   Ernst r. (S) **200.00**
Saxe-Coburg-Gotha. 1905 2 Mark. Head
   of Carl Eduard r. (S) **285.00**
Saxe-Meiningen. 1915 2 Mark. Bust of
   Georg II l. (S) **75.00**
Saxe-Weimar-Eisenach. 1910 3 Mark.
   Heads of Grand Duke and Grand
   Duchess (S) **40.00**
Saxony. 1913 3 Mark. Building (S). . . **18.00**
Schaumburg-Lippe. 1911 3 Mark. Bust of
   Georg l. (S) **65.00**

German Empire 1898 10 Pfennig

German Empire 1876 50 Pfennig

German Empire 1902 10 Pfennig

German Republic 1932 4 Reichspfennig

	VF
Schwarzburg-Rudolstadt. 1898 2 Mark. Bust of Günther l. (S)	**250.00**
Schwarzburg-Sondershausen. 1905 2 Mark. Head of Karl Günther r. (S)	**50.00**
Waldeck-Pyrmont. 1903 20 Mark. Head of Friedrich l. (G)	**2,750.00**
Württemberg. 1914 3 Mark. Bust of Wilhelm II r. (S)	**17.50**
__. 1904 10 Mark. Similar (G)	**120.00**

GERMAN EMPIRE 1873-1918

	VF
1915 1 Pfennig. Large eagle/inscription (C)	**.50**
1906 2 Pfennig. Similar (C)	**.25**
1874 5 Pfennig. Small eagle (CN)	**1.00**
1905 5 Pfennig. Large eagle (CN)	**.50**
1919 5 Pfennig. Similar (Iron)	**.20**
1898 10 Pfennig. Similar (CN)	**.25**
1902 10 Pfenning. Similar (CN)	**.25**
1905 10 Pfennig. Similar (CN)	**.25**
1875 20 Pfennig. Small eagle (S)	**8.00**
1888 20 Pfennig. Eagle in wreath/inscription (CN)	**18.50**
1909 25 Pfennig. Large eagle/wreath (N)	**7.00**
1876 50 Pfennig. Small eagle/inscription (S)	**12.00**

	VF
1918 ¼ Mark. Eagle in wreath/wreath (S)	**1.50**
1874 1 Mark. Small eagle/wreath (S)	**6.00**
1914 1 Mark. Large eagle/wreath (S)	**1.50**

NOTGELD

	VF
Aachen. 1920 10 Pfennig. Bear (Iron)	**3.00**
Coblenz. 1918 25 Pfennig. Arms (Iron)	**2.50**
Darmstadt. 1917 10 Pfennig. Crowned arms (Z)	**2.00**
Hamburg. 1923 5/100 Verrechnungsmarke. Arms (AL)	**4.00**
Leipzig. (1920) 20 Pfennig. Arms/Strassenbahn...(Iron)	**3.00**
similar but wooden	**5.00**
Westphalia. 1923 ¼ Million Mark. Von Stein/horse rearing (AL)	**6.00**

REPUBLIC 1919-1933

	VF
1923 1 Rentenpfennig. Sheaf of wheat (C)	**.50**
1925 2 Reichspfennig. Similar (C)	**.30**
1932 4 Reichspfennig. Eagle (C)	**12.00**

German Republic 1925 5 Reichspfennig

German Federal Republic 1950 1 Pfennig

German Federal Republic 1980 10 Pfennig

German Federal Republic 1976
5 Deutsche Mark

VF

1924 5 Reichspfennig. Stylized wheat (ALB) . . . . **.50**

1925 5 Reichspfennig. Similar (ALB). . . . **.50**

1929 10 Reichspfennig. Similar (ALB) . . **.50**

1924 50 Rentenpfennig. Similar (ALB) **10.00**

1931 50 Reichspfennig. Eagle (N). . . . **4.00**

1924 1 Mark. Eagle (S) **9.00**

1922 3 Mark. Eagle within legend (AL) **1.00**

1928 3 Mark. Eagle/Dinkelsbühl, man over city walls (S) **400.00**

1930 5 Mark. Eagle/Graf zeppelin (S). **110.00**

1931 5 Mark. Eagle/oak tree (S) **80.00**

NAZI STATE 1933-1945

VF

1937 1 Reichspfennig. Eagle holding swastika in wreath (C) . . . . **.25**

1940 5 Reichspfennig. Similar (Z) . . . . . . **.20**

1938 50 Reichspfennig. Similar (N). . **28.00**

1941 50 Reichspfennig. Similar (AL) . . **1.50**

1934 2 Reichsmark. Schiller (S) **70.00**

1936 5 Reichsmark. Hindenburg/eagle holding swastika in wreath (S) **6.00**

FEDERAL REPUBLIC

Unc.

1950 1 Pfennig. Oak sapling (C plated Steel) **1.00**

Unc.

1993 2 Pfennig. Oak sapling (C plated Steel) . . . . **.10**

1949 5 Pfennig. Oak sapling (Brass plated Steel) **30.00**

1980 10 Pfennig. Oak sapling (Brass plated Steel) . . . . **.20**

1950 50 Pfennig. Woman planting sapling (CN) **9.00**

1977 1 Deutsche Mark. Eagle/oak leaves (CN) **1.00**

1951 2 Deutsche Mark. Eagle/grapes and wheat (CN) **110.00**

1971 2 Deutsche Mark. Max Planck/eagle (CN) **3.00**

1952 5 Deutsche Mark. Museum, stylized eagle/eagle (S) **1,150.00**

1968 5 Deutsche Mark. Bust of Gutenberg/eagle (S) **12.50**

1970 5 Deutsche Mark. Eagle/inscription (S) **8.50**

1976 5 Deutsche Mark. Monster/ Eagle (S) **5.00**

1983 5 Deutsche Mark. Karl Marx/eagle (CN clad N) **5.00**

1972 10 Deutsche Mark. Olympic flame/ eagle (S) **8.50**

1990 10 Deutsche Mark. Friedrich Barbarossa/eagle (S) **8.00**

Germany 2002 10 Euro

German Democratic Republic (East Germany) 1988 10 Mark

German East Africa 1890 1 Pesa

Euro Coinage 2002 to date

	BU
2002 20 Cent. Brandenburg Gate/map (B, notched)	**1.00**
2002 1 Euro. Eagle/map (CN clad N in NB, bimetallic)	**3.00**
2002 10 Euro. Island (S)	**20.00**
2002 10 Euro. Eagle/map (S)	**20.00**

DEMOCRATIC REPUBLIC (EAST GERMANY)

	Unc.
1952 1 Pfennig. Hammer, compass and wheat (AL)	**6.00**
1948 5 Pfennig. Wheat on gear (AL)	**50.00**
1989 10 Pfennig. Hammer and compass within wheat (Al)	**.60**
1950 50 Pfennig. Three smoke stacks (ALB)	**32.50**
1982 2 Mark. Hammer and compass within wheat (AL)	**2.00**
1971. 5 Mark. Brandenburg Gate (CN)	**10.00**
1979 5 Mark. Albert Einstein (CN)	**65.00**
1972 10 Mark. Buchenwald Memorial (CN)	**7.50**
1988 10 Mark.Knight/Arms (S)	**85.00**
1988 20 Mark. Microscope (S)	**195.00**

GERMAN EAST AFRICA

	VF
1890 Pesa. Eagle/Arabic inscription (C)	**3.00**
1910 Heller. Crown/wreath (C)	**1.50**
1909 5 Heller. Similar (C)	**30.00**
1916 5 Heller. Crown over DOA/wreath (C)	**12.00**
1913 ¼ Rupie. Bust of Wilhelm II in griffin helmet/wreath (S)	**12.00**
1893 2 Rupien. Similar bust/arms (S)	**285.00**
1916 15 Rupien. Eagle/elephant (G)	**900.00**

GERMAN NEW GUINEA

	XF
1894 1 Pfennig. Inscription (C)	**90.00**
1894 5 Mark. Bird of paradise (S)	**1,250.00**
1895 20 Mark. Similar (G)	**8,750.00**

KIAO CHAU

	VF
1909 10 Cent. Eagle on anchor/Chinese Inscription (CN)	**55.00**

HUNGARY

The reign of Leopold I the Hogmouth (1657-1705) saw a far greater change for Hungarian coins than it did for the coinage of his Austrian dominions. Of course, as in Austria, modern coin production under Leopold, then using roller dies, was taken to a new height of uniformity. Their excellent portraits are a perfect example of the Baroque style. Collectors should be aware that coins struck with roller dies usually appear slightly curved and that this is not a flaw. But in Hungary before the mid-1600s, only three denominations, the small base silver denar, the big silver thaler, and the gold ducat were common in circulation. This period saw the increase in production of a whole range of middle denominations. For the most part, the Madonna and Child still dominated the reverse, with portraits on the obverse.

During the reign of Maria Theresa (1740-80) copper replaced base silver for the small denominations, and coats of arms became more common. The coppers in particular were ornamented with impressive, high relief portraits. Unfortunately, the poor condition of most surviving examples makes this difficult to appreciate today.

From 1892 until the Communist takeover, the Holy Crown of Saint Stephen, a relic of Hungary's patron saint, came to dominate the coinage, with the Madonna or a portrait to give diversity. The Communists replaced the old religious symbols with national heroes, architecture, and images idealizing industrial and agricultural labor. Interestingly, the new post-Communist republic combines both old and new imagery harmoniously, with a pleasant admixture of flora and fauna.

Additional Specialized Books: Huszar, L. *Münzkatalog Ungarn.*

Known Counterfeits: Many gold coins have been restruck in quantity. These include 1892 10 and 20 Korona, 1907 and 1908 100 Korona, and some 1895 pieces. Also note that all coins marked UP are restrikes, regardless of type or metal.

Leopold I Hogmouth, 1657-1705.

F

1662 Denar. Crowned shield/Madonna
and child (Billon). **6.00**
1703 Duarius. Crowned shield/small
Madonna and child over denomination
(Billon). **16.00**
1703 5 Ducat. Bust r./crowned imperial
eagle (G) . . . . *rare*
1627 3 Krajczar. Bust/Madonna and
chiild (S) **40.00**
1680 3 Krajczar. Bust r./Madonna and
child (S). **6.00**
1695 1/4 Thaler. Bust in diamond/
Madonna and child stg. in diamond (S)
. . . .**20.00**
1661 Thaler. Bust of Leopold, Hungarian
shield and Madonna and child in
margin/Double-headed eagle (S)
. . . .**150.00**
1694 Ducat. Leopold stg./Madonna and
child (G) **175.00**

Other Rulers, 1705-1848.

F

1707 Poltura. Shield/Madonna and child
(C) **8.00**
1711 Poltura. Joseph I/small Madonna and
child over denomination (S) **15.00**
1705 10 Poltura. Crowned shield/PRO
LIBERTATE X (C) **10.00**
1848 1 Krajczar. Crowned shield (C) . **2.00**
1849 6 Krajczar. Crowned shield (Billon)**5.00**
1778 20 Krajczar. Maria Theresa in wreath/
Madonna and child in wreath (S). . **8.00**
1839 20 Krajczar. Ferdinand I/Madonna
and child (S). **3.50**
1742 1/2 Thaler. Maria Theresa/similar
(S). **50.00**
1785 1/2 Thaler. Angels over arms/similar
(S). **25.00**
1833 Thaler. Francis I/similar (S) **80.00**

Hungary 1937 2 Filler

Francis Joseph, 1848-1916.

VF

1868 1 Krajczar. Angels over shield/wreath
(C) **1.00**
1870 10 Krajczar. Head r./crown of St.
Stephen (Billon) **7.50**
1879 1 Forint. Head r./crowned shield
(S). **8.00**
1909 2 Filler. Crown of St. Stephen
(C) **1.00**
1893 10 Filler. Crown of St. Stephen
(N) **50**
1915 Korona. Head r./crown of St. Stephen
(S). **3.00**
1908 5 Korona. Similar (S) **18.00**
1901 20 Korona Francis Joseph stg./arms
(G) **80.00**

Regency, 1920-45.

VF

1937 2 Filler. Crown of St. Stephen (C) **.25**
1938 2 Filler. Crown of St. Stephen (C) **.20**
1927 1 Pengo. Crowned shield (S) . . . **1.50**
1942 2 Pengo. Similar (AL) **30**
1938 5 Pengo. Bust of St. Stephen/arms
(S). **9.00**
1943 5 Pengo. Bust of Nicholas Horthy/
arms (AL) **1.00**

Republics, 1946-date

BU

1950 2 Filler. Wreath (AL, holed). **50**
1982 10 Filler. Dove (AL). **1.50**
1979 50 Filler. Bridge (AL) **1.50**
1979 200 Forint. IYC Logo (S) **10.00**

Hungary 2001 5 Forint

Hungary 1979 200 Forint

	BU
1949 1 Forint. Arms (AL)	**12.00**
1971 5 Forint. Kossuth/arms (CN)	**1.50**
1956 25 Forint. Parliament/arms and gear (S)	**20.00**
1985 100 Forint. Turtle (S)	**10.00**

	BU
1961 500 Forint. Bela Bartok (G)	**575.00**
1997 5 Forint. Egret (Brass)	**.75**
2001 5 Forint. Same	**1.00**
1996 100 Forint. Crowned shield (Steel, Brass plated center, *bimetallic*)	**5.00**
2000 200 Forint. Rhodin's Thinker and solar system/arms (ALB)	**5.00**
1992 500 Forint. Tellstar satellite (S)	**22.50**
same but Proof	**27.50**
2002 500 Forint. Rubik's Cube (CN)	**25.00**

ITALY

Much like Germany, Italy until 1861 was divided into a number of smaller independent countries. During most of the modern era, the south was unified as one kingdom, the Kingdom of Naples and Sicily (more properly called the Two Sicilies). While artistically creative in the 1600s and 1700s, its more mundane later coinage is more commonly encountered. The island of Sicily itself usually had separate coinage.

Central Italy was ruled by the Pope. Despite being one unified Papal State, many of the larger cities under papal rule did have special designs and sometimes even different coinage standards. This local variation ended by 1800. Unlike the other Italian states incorporated into the new unified Kingdom of Italy in 1860-61, the Pope was able to maintain his independence until 1870. After decades of dispute with Italy, the Papal State was restored its independence in 1929 as the much smaller State of the Vatican City. Since then Papal coins have been routinely struck and can occasionally be found circulating not only at the Vatican but in and around Rome. Most Vatican coins today are collected in mint sets.

Throughout this period, most papal and Vatican coins have depicted the Pope or his coat of arms, along with some religious iconography or a Latin saying reflecting some moral precept. There are three kinds of "special" coins. *Sede Vacante* coins are struck between Popes and have the arms of the Papal Secretary of State. Holy Year coins are struck to celebrate the Jubilee when pilgrims are encouraged to come to Rome. Lastly, Lateran coins were given to the crowds when the Pope took possession of the Cathedral of St. John Lateran in Rome. This is his church as Bishop of Rome, not St. Peter's Basilica.

Papal medals are quite common and are struck for commemorative purposes only. They should not be confused for coins. They are usually large and have very high relief. Most of those dated before 1775 are actually government restrikes struck from the original dies from the late 1700s and later. Those after 1550 that appear cast are unofficial replicas, but not necessarily worthless.

Northern Italy was much more complex. It was a variable mix of small states. Some such as Venice were international powers, others were controlled by petty princes. Ultimately a good number of them fell into the hands of foreign powers such as Spain, France, and Austria. The Duke of Savoy (who was also King of Sardinia) began to unify Italy by conquering these small states, and then moving south. One Italian state which has survived is San Marino. It has had coinage since 1864, but today most of its coins are sold to collectors. Like the Vatican's coins, they are struck to Italian standards and can be spent in Italy.

The first unified Italian coinage was struck to the standard of the international Latin Monetary Union (see France). Italian coins of the 20th century are usually of high artistic merit. After World War I, the *Lira* shrunk to one fifth of its previous value. Its value evaporated again after World War II, and many coins minted from the 1940s to the 1980s were made from aluminum or steel.

In January 2002, Italy replaced the Lira with coins denominated in Euros, the currency of the European Union. On the circulating denominations, 1 Cent through 2 Euros, one side carries an Italian design, the other a common European design. Because of their monetary unions with Italy, the Vatican and San Marino have Euro coins struck out of Italy's allotment of coinage.

The colonial coins of Italy are very popularly collected, and are in high demand. Most silver is found cleaned and most copper pitted, but despite this fact, collectors will often settle for these imperfect specimens.

Additional Specialized Books:

Berman, Allen G. *Papal Coins.*

Gill, Dennis. *Coinage of Ethiopia, Eritrea and Italian Somalia.*

Muntoni. *Le monete dei Papi e degli Stati Pontifici.*

Known Counterfeits: There are many contemporary counterfeits of Italian minors, including 1863M 1 Lira, 1863N and 1911 2 Lire, 1927 and 1930 5 Lire, 1958 500 lire. Vatican and papal pieces include 1736 1 Grosso, 1796 2 Carlini, 1797 5 Baiocchi and 1868 4 soldi. Naples include 1796 120 grana.

More dangerous counterfeits capable of fooling collectors are quite common. Mostly they are imitations of the old silver-dollar-size 5 and 20 Lire pieces. This is also true of similar Papal and San Marino 5 Lire pieces. The overwhelming majority of Eritrea 5 Lire and Talero pieces are counterfeit. Many Italian, Papal, and Vatican gold coins have also been counterfeited, but less commonly than the large silver. A partial list of counterfeits includes 2 lire 1895 and 1898, and 5 Lire 1914. Authentic common coins are sometimes found altered to rare dates.

The 20 Lire depicting Mussolini is not a coin, but a privately struck fantasy.

Gorizia 1733 1 Soldo

ITALIAN STATES

	F
Bologna. 1680 Quattrino. Lion with banner/BONONIA DOCET (C)	**18.00**
1769 5 Bolognini. City arms/cartouche (S)	**16.00**
Genoa. 1814 10 Soldi. Arms/John the Baptist (S)	**11.50**

	F
Gorizia. 1733 1 Soldo. Arms (S)	**6.50**
Gorizia. 1759 Soldo. Crowned arms/ cartouche (C)	**6.50**
Lombardy-Venetia. 1846 1 Centesimo. Two crowns (C)	**3.00**
Lucca. 1664 Quattrino. L/Holy Countenance (C)	**10.00**
Milan. 1665-1700 Quattrino. Charles II of Spain/crowned MLNI DVX in wreath (C)	**20.00**
Naples. 1788 Grano. Ferdinand IV/wreath (C)	**8.00**
1791 Piastra. King and Queen/band of zodiac over sun and earth (S)	**100.00**
1857 2 Tornesi. Head r./crown (C)	**2.50**
Napoleonic Kingdom. 1813 5 Soldi. Head r./crown (S)	**6.50**
Sardinia. 1794 5 Soldi	**7.00**

Sardinia 1794 5 Soldi

Italy 1908 20 Centesimi

Tuscany-Pisa 1710 3 Quattrino

	F
Savoy (as Kingdom of Sardinia). 1794 5 Soldi. Bust r./St. Mauritius stg. (C)	**12.00**
1830 1 Lira. Bust r./arms (S)	**20.00**
Sicily. 1737 Grano. Eagle/cartouche (C)	**20.00**
1793 Oncia. Bust r./Phoenix in flames (S)	**500.00**
Tuscany. 1692 Tallero. Cosimo III/Port of Livorno (S)	**175.00**
Tuscany-Pisa. 1710 3 Quattrino. Arms (S)	**7.00**
1859 2 Centesimi. Arms (C)	**4.00**
Venice. 1684-88 Soldo. S M V M A IVSTIN, Doge and lion/Christ (C)	**20.00**
1676-84 Zecchino (Ducat). ALOYSIVS CONT, Doge and St. Mark/Christ (G)	**80.00**
1722-32 Scudo. ALOYSIVS MOCENICO... VQ, Cross/bust of lion in shield (S)	**85.00**
1741-52 Soldo. S M V PET GRIM D, Doge and lion/Christ (C)	**15.00**

ITALY

	VF
Vittorio Emanuele II, 1861-78.	
1861 1 Centesimo. Head l./wreath (C)	**1.50**
1862 2 Centesimi. Similar (C)	**1.50**
1861 5 Centesimi. Similar (C)	**1.50**
1866 10 Centesimi. Similar (C)	**3.50**
1863 1 Lira. Head r./wreath (S)	**5.00**
1874 5 Lire. Head r./arms (S)	**17.50**
1863 20 Lire. Head l./arms (G)	**100.00**
Umberto II, 1878-1900.	
1897 2 Centesimi. Head l./wreath (C)	**1.50**
1895 5 Centesimi. Similar (C)	**25.00**
1893 10 Centesimi. Similar (C)	**3.50**
1889 50 Centesimi. Head r./arms (S)	**40.00**
1886 1 Lira. Similar (S)	**6.00**
1882 20 Lire. Head l./arms (G)	**90.00**
Vittorio Emanuele III, 1900-46.	
1915 2 Centesimi. Bust l./Italia on ship (C)	**1.30**
1921 10 Centesimi. Head l./bee (C)	**1.25**
1908 20 Centesimi. Head l/lady (N)	**3.00**
1940 20 Centesimi. Head l./allegorical head r. with fasces (Steel)	**.40**
1922 1 Lira. Italia std. (N)	**1.00**
1924 2 Lire. Bust r./fasces (N)	**2.00**
1914 5 Lire. Bust r./Italia in four-horse chariot (S)	**950.00**
1927 5 Lire. Head l./eagle (S)	**3.00**
1927 10 Lire. Head l./Italia in two-horse chariot (S)	**15.00**
1927 20 Lire. Head r./naked youth before std. Italia (S)	**90.00**
1943 20 Lire. Mussolini/fasces and lion head (Silvered brass). *This is a common post-war fantasy*	BU **6.00**
1912 50 Lire. Bust l./Italia and plow (G)	**650.00**

Republic, 1946-date

	BU
1954 1 Lira. Scales/cornucopia (AL)	**1.85**
1957 2 Lire. Bee (AL)	**2.50**
1969 5 Lire. Rudder/porpoise (AL)	**.75**
1950 10 Lire. Pegasus (AL)	**10.00**

Italy 1954 1 Lira

Italy 2004 2 Euro

Italy 1956 100 Lire

Italy 2002 1 Euro

	BU
1975 50 Lire. Vulcan at forge (Steel). . . .	.75
1956 100 Lire. Minerva presenting olive tree (Steel)	30.00
1974 100 Lire. Minerva presenting olive tree (Steel)	.85
1974 100 Lire. Marconi (Steel)	1.75
1959 500 Lire. Renaissance bust/ Columbus' ships (S)	8.00
1986 500 Lire. Donatello/Donatello's David (S)	65.00
1970 1,000 Lire. Concord/Campidoglio pattern (S)	15.00

Euro Coinage 2002 to date

	BU
2002 5 Euro Cent. Colusseum/globe (C plated Steel)	.75
2002 1 Euro. Da Vinci drawing of man/ map (CN clad N in NB, bimetallic)	3.50
2004 2 Euro. Logo (bimetallic)	5.75

ITALIAN COLONIES

	VF
Eritrea. 1890 50 Centesimi. Umberto II/ branches (S)	50.00
1890 2 Lire. Similar (S)	70.00
1918 Tallero. Female bust r./eagle (S)	60.00

	VF
Italian Somalia. 1909 1 Besa. Bust l. (C)	22.00
1919 1/2 Rupia. Head r./crown and wreath (S)	40.00
1925 5 Lire. Bust r./arms (S)	120.00

Note: The majority of the Tallero size coins of Eritrea and Italian Somalia found in the market are counterfeit.

SAN MARINO

	XF
1935 5 Centesimi. Arms (C)	3.00
1893 10 Centesimi. Arms (C)	25.00
1906 1 Lira. Arms/wreath (S)	40.00
	BU
1972 1 Lira. Bust of St. Marino (AL) . . .	.20
1974 20 Lire. Three towers/lobster (ALB)	.70
1974 Scudo. Arms/ Saint Standing.	60.00

BU

1992 100 Lire. Similar/Columbus' ship
(Steel) **1.25**
1982 500 Lire. Similar/Garibaldi (S) . **12.50**
1996 10,000 Lire. Arms/wolves
(S). . . . . *proof only* **40.00**
1979 5 Scudi. Three palm fronds/three
arms (G) **240.00**
2002 1 Euro. Arms/map (CN clad N in
NB, bimetallic). **25.00**

PAPAL STATE

F

Clement X, 1670-76. 1672 Piastra. Arms/
Port of Civitavecchia (S) **500.00**
. 1675 1-1/2 inch medal.
Bust/bricking up the Holy Door
(C) **125.00**
__. Same, restike **40.00**
Innocent XI, 1676-89 1/2 Grosso. Arms/
NOCET MINVS (S) **15.00**
Alexander VIII, 1689-91. 1690 Testone.
Bust r./two oxen plowing (S) . . . **165.00**
Innocent XII, 1691-1700. Quattrino. Arms/
St. Paul with sword (C). **12.00**
Clement XI, 1700-21. Grosso. Arms/DEDIT
PAVPERIBVS (S). **22.00**
Clement XII, 1730-40. 1738 Quattrino
Arms (C) **12.50**
Benedict XIV 1740-58. 1750 Grosso. Arms/
holy door (S) **22.00**
Clement XIII, 1758-69. 1766 Zecchino.
Arms/Church std. on cloud (G) . **135.00**
Pius VI, 1775-99. 1797 2-½ Baiocchi. Bust of
St. Peter (C) **18.00**
Pius VII, 1800-23. 1816 Quattrino. Arms
(C) **7.50**
Sede Vacante, 1830. 30 Baiocchi. Arms/
dove of Holy Spirit (S) **40.00**
Gregory XVI, 1831-46. 1839 1/2 Baiocco.
Arms/wreath (C) **4.00**
Pius IX, 1846-78. 1858 20 Baiocchi. Bust/
wreath (S) **4.00**
1866 1 Soldo. Bust (C) **1.75**
1868 10 Soldi. Bust/wreath (S) **2.50**
1868 20 Lire. Similar (G) **125.00**

VATICAN CITY

BU

1930 5 Centesimi. Arms/olive sprig
(C) **6.00**

Italy 2000 2,000 Lire

BU

1942 10 Centesimi. Pius XII/dove
(Brass) **55.00**
1934 20 Centesimi. Arms/St. Paul (N)
. . . . **6.00**
1941 50 Centesimi. Arms/Archangel
Michael (Steel). **5.00**
1931 1 Lira. Arms/Madonna stg. (N)
. . . . **6.00**
1942 2 Lire. Arms/Justice std. (Steel). **3.00**
1962 5 Lire. John XXIII/Dove of Holy Spirit
(AL) **1.50**
1973 10 Lire. Arms/fish (AL) **1.00**
1985 20 Lire. John Paul II/eagle
(ALB) **1.00**
1955 50 Lire. Pius XII/Hope (Steel) . . . **3.00**
1929 100 Lire. Pius XI/Christ stg.(G) **300.00**
1978 200 Lire. Arms/sermon on the mount
(ALB) **2.50**
1963 500 Lire. Sede Vacante, arms/dove
of Holy Spirit (S) **10.00**
1978 1,000 Lire. John Paul I/arms (S)
. . . . **25.00**
1990 1,000 Lire. John Paul II treading over
barbed wire/arms (S) **18.50**
2000 2,000 Lire. Pope/baby Jesus (S)
Proof **75.00**
1998 100,000 Lire. John Paul II/Basilica of
St. Mary Major (G) . . *proof only* **450.00**
2002 50 Euro Cent. John Paul II/map
(B). **50.00**
(1986-87) Official medal. John Paul II/St.
Francis of Assisi (S, 44mm) **110.00**
same but bronze **50.00**
1986 Unofficial medal. John Paul II/
Madonna and Child between saints (B,
50mm). **25.00**

LOW COUNTRIES

These countries are Belgium, the Netherlands, and Luxembourg. They are called this because most of their land is flat and hardly above sea level. They are sometimes also called "BeNeLux" after their customs and trade union. All three were controlled by the Spanish Hapsburgs until the late 1500s. At that time, the Netherlands became Protestant and declared its independence. The Spanish Hapsburgs continued to rule Belgium and Luxembourg until 1714 when they were transferred to the Austrian branch of the same dynasty. During the Napoleonic Wars, all three were part of the French Empire. After that, a newly independent Kingdom of the Netherlands was given all three territories, only to lose Belgium in 1830 in a revolt due to cultural and religious differences. In 1890, Luxembourg was lost when it was decided that the Queen of the Netherlands, as a woman, could not legally succeed to the Grand Duchy of Luxembourg.

In addition to royal portraits and heraldry, the coins of Belgium (called Spanish Netherlands and later Austrian Netherlands) and Luxembourg had a few distinctive motifs. This included an X-cross and some purely inscriptional types. A few small territories such as Liege had the arms of the local bishop or the bust of a patron saint. The new Kingdom of the Belgians used the international standard of the Latin Monetary Union (see France) until World War I. Interestingly most Belgian coins are struck in two different versions. Some have French and some have Flemish inscriptions, because both languages are commonly spoken.

The coins of the Netherlands have traditionally been struck by its constituent provinces. These almost always had a coat of arms on the copper. Some of the silver coins shared designs from province to province, such as arrows or a knight, but each individual province changed small details such as the shield and its name in the legend. Thus, they could circulate interchangeably throughout the Netherlands. The Lion Dalders are particularly common in this series. These are usually poorly struck on irregular blanks. Sea salvaged examples are worth less, unless accompanied by documentation.

After the new kingdom was founded in 1815, the national arms or the monarch's monogram or portrait were used on a more uniform national coinage. Since the 1500s, Dutch gold ducats with a standing knight have been particularly common in international commerce. The word BELGII on their reverse does not refer to Belgium, which did not exist when they were first struck but to the ancient name for the region.

Belgian and Netherlands zinc coins struck during World War II were issued under the Nazi occupation. Fully brilliant specimens of these are virtually nonexistent.

In January 2002, Belgium, Luxembourg and the Netherlands replaced the currencies with coins denominated in Euros, the currency of the European Union. Some coins were struck years in advance, and held until 2002. On the circulating denominations, 1 Cent through 2 Euros, one side carries a portrait of the monarch, the other has a common European design. On higher denomination commemoratives both sides are distinctively local.

Both Belgium and the Netherlands struck colonial coinages. The issues of the Belgian Congo (earlier called Congo Free State) are particularly attractive. Some are enormous copper coins, others depict a powerful elephant. Dutch colonials for the Netherlands Antilles are of homeland types, although some have a distinctive inscription. Coins for the Netherlands Indies (today Indonesia) are far more distinctive. They either appear European or East Asian depending on which side one examines. Dutch colonials from World War II were struck by United States Government mints, and bear their mint marks.

Additional Specialized Books: De Mey. *Les Monnaies des Souverains Luxembourgeois.*

De Mey and Van Keymeulen. *Les Monnaies de Brabant 1598-1790.*

Mevius, J. *De Nederlandse Munten van 1795 tot Heden.*

Zonnenbloem, U. *Catalogus van de Zilvern Munten.*

Known Counterfeits: Low Countries coins have not been as extensively counterfeited as many other countries. A Holland 1791 2 stuiver exists and an occasional counterfeit gold ducat may be encountered.

Belgium 1916 10 Centimes

Belgium 1955 50 Centimes

BELGIUM under Austria

	F
1789 Liard. Joseph II/AD USUM BELGII AUSTR (C)	**6.00**
1790 Liard. Lion holding hat on pole (C) *Insurrection*	**7.50**
1766 Kronenthaler. Cross, crowns in angles/double-headed eagle (S)	**40.00**
1750 1/2 Souverain d'or. Maria Theresa/ arms (G)	**300.00**

BELGIUM

	VF
1862 1 Centime. Crowned L/lion with tablets (C)	**5.00**
1876 2 Centimes. Similar (C)	**.75**
1919 2 Centimes. Crowned A/lion with tablets (C)	**.35**
1862 5 Centimes. Lion (CN)	**.25**
1832 10 Centimes. Crowned L/lion with tablets (C)	**100.00**
1916 10 Centimes (without dot after cent) Lion (Zinc)	**15.00**
1944 25 Centimes. Monogram/three shields (Z, holed)	**.20**
1844 1 Franc. Leopold I/wreath (S)	**140.00**
1887 1 Franc. Leopold II/arms (S)	**15.00**
1923 2 Francs. Belgium binding wound/ Caduceus (N)	**1.50**
1869 5 Francs. Similar (S)	**8.00**
1877 20 Francs. Similar (G)	**80.00**
1932 20 Francs. Albert/arms (N)	**45.00**
1934 20 Francs. Similar (S)	**2.50**
1935 50 Francs. Train station/Michael the Archangel (S)	**80.00**

Belgium 2002 10 Euro

Post-War Coinage

	BU
1971 25 Centimes. Crowned B (CN)	**.15**
1955 50 Centimes. Large Head (C)	**.35**
1986 5 Francs. King Baudouin (AB)	**.50**
1994 5 Francs. Albert II (AB)	**.50**
1960 50 Francs. King and Queen/crown over two shields (S)	**9.00**
1989 100 Ecu. Maria Theresa (G)	**500.00**

Euro Coinage

	BU
1999 1 Euro Cent. Albert II/globe (C plated Steel)	**.50**
2001 10 Euro Cent. Albert II/map (B)	**.75**
2002 10 Euro. Albert II/train (S)	*proof only* **40.00**

BELGIAN COLONIES

	VF
Congo Free State. 1888 1 Centime. Star (C)	**2.00**

Congo Free State 1888 1 Centime

Luxembourg 1970 25 Centimes

Luxembourg 1924 10 Centimes

Luxembourg 2004 2 Euro

	VF
1887 2 Francs. Leopold II/arms (S)	**45.00**
Belgian Congo. 1910 5 Centimes. Star (CN)	**1.50**
1955 50 Centimes. Crowned shield/palm tree (AL)	**.15**
1926 1 Franc. Albert I/palm tree (CN)	**2.75**
1943 2 Francs. Elephant (Brass, hexagonal)	**4.50**
1944 50 Francs. Elephant (S)	**50.00**
Rwanda-Burundi. 1961 1 Franc. Lion (Brass)	**.50**

LUXEMBOURG

	VF
1757 2 Liards. Maria Theresa/wreath (C)	**85.00**
1789 1/2 Liard. Crowned shield (C)	**15.00**
1854 2-1/2 Centimes. Arms (C)	**3.50**
1908 5 Centimes. William (CN)	**1.00**
1901 10 Centimes. Adolphe (CN)	**.75**
1924 10 Centimes. Monogram (CN)	**.50**
1924 2 Francs. Ch monogram/iron worker (N)	**2.25**
1929 5 Francs. Charlotte/arms at angle (S)	**3.00**

Postwar Coinage

	BU
1970 25 Centimes. Arms (AL)	**.10**
1957 1 Franc. Ch monogram/iron worker (CN)	**.40**
1946 100 Francs. Jean/knight riding (S)	**40.00**
1964 100 Francs. Jean/arms (S)	**12.00**

Euro Coinage 2002 to date

	BU
2002 2 Euro Cent. Henri/globe (C plated Steel)	**.50**
2002 2 Euro. Henri/map (NB clad N in CN, bimetallic)	**5.00**
2004 2 Euro. Same	**5.50**

NETHERLANDS (PROVINCES)

	F

Most coins below exist in several varieties with varying provincial shields and legends.

1794 Duit. Shield/D GEL RIE (C)	**6.00**
1681 1 Stuiver. Shield between I S/GRON ET OML (S)	**17.50**
1787 2 Stuivers. Shield between 2 S/TRA IEC TUM (S)	**6.00**
1764 1 Gulden. Crowned shield/woman stg. (S)	**22.00**
1642 Lion Daalder. Bust of knight over shield/lion (S)	**55.00**

Netherlands 1918 10 Cents

Netherlands 1939 10 Cents

Netherlands 1848 1 Gulden

	F
1698 Ducat. Knight stg., shield at feet/ crowned shield (S)	**100.00**
1673 Ducat. Knight stg./MON ORD PROVIN... (G)	**135.00**

NETHERLANDS (KINGDOM)

	VF
1823 1/2 Cent. Crowned w/crowned shield (C)	**28.00**
1884 1/2 Cent. Lion/wreath (C)	**4.00**
1876 1 Cent. Crowned shield (C)	**5.50**
1883 1 Cent. Lion/wreath (C)	**3.00**
1941 1 Cent. Similar (C)	**.75**
1942 1 Cent. Cross (Z)	**.50**
1877 2-1/2 Cents. Similar (C)	**5.00**
1941 2-1/2 Cents. Similar (C)	**2.00**
1827 5 Cents. Crowned w/crowned shield (S)	**50.00**
1850 5 Cents. Willem III/wreath (S)	**5.00**
1907 5 Cents. Crown (CN)	**6.00**
1913 5 Cents. Orange plant (CN, square)	**3.00**
1827 10 Cents. Crowned w/crowned shield (S)	**25.00**
1849 10 Cents. Willem II/wreath (S)	**30.00**
1897 10 Cents. Wilhelmina as child/wreath (S)	**12.00**
1918 10 Cents. Wilhelmina as adult/wreath (S)	**2.50**
1939 10 Cents. Wilhelmina/wreath (S)	**75**

	VF
1826 25 Cents. Crowned w/crowned shield (S)	**28.00**
1890 25 Cents. Willem III/wreath (S)	**150.00**
1943 25 Cents. Wilhelmina/wreath (S)	**1.25**
1942 25 Cents. Viking ship (Z)	**1.50**
1818 1/2 Gulden. Willem I/crowned shield (S)	**280.00**
1858 1/2 Gulden. Willem III/crowned shield (S)	**25.00**
1922 1/2 Gulden. Wilhelmina/crowned shield (S)	**1.50**
1840 1 Gulden. Willem I/crowned shield (S)	**110.00**
1848 1 Gulden. Willem II/crowned shield (S)	**25.00**
1892 1 Gulden. Wilhelmina as child/ crowned shield (S)	**20.00**
1929 1 Gulden. Wilhelmina as adult/ crowned shield (S)	**3.00**
1872 2-1/2 Gulden. Willem III/crowned shield (S)	**15.00**
1930 2-1/2 Gulden. Wilemina as adult/ crowned shield (S)	**7.50**
1831 3 Gulden. Willem I/crowned shield (S)	**450.00**
1827 5 Gulden. Similar (G)	**200.00**
1823 10 Gulden. Similar (G)	**275.00**
1875 10 Gulden. Willem III/crowned shield (S)	**75.00**
1927 Ducat. Knight stg./MO AUR REG BELGII... (G)	*XF* **50.00**

Netherlands 1982 50 Gulden

Netherlands 2005 5 Euro

Postwar Coinage

	Unc.
1948 1 Cent. Wilhelmina old (C)	**1.50**
1977 5 Cents. Juliana (C)	**.25**
1948 10 Cents. Wilhelmina old (N)	**1.00**
1951 25 Cents. Juliana (N)	**1.50**
1982 1 Gulden. Beatrix (N)	**1.00**
1815 2 Reales. Ferdinand VII/Shield (FIne)	**16.00**
1962 2-1/2 Gulden. Juliana (S)	**4.00**
1999 5 Gulden. Beatrix (B clad steel)	**3.50**
1997 10 Gulden. Beatrix/George Marshall (S)	**20.00**
1982 50 Gulden. Beatrix/lion and eagle (S)	**25.00**

Euro Coinage

	BU
2000 5 Euro Cent. Beatrix/globe (C plated Steel)	**.75**
2000 50 Euro Cent. Beatrix/map (B)	**1.25**
2003 5 Euro. Beatrix/Van Gogh (S)	**6.00**
2005 5 Euro. Beatrix (stylized) (S)	**12.00**

NETHERLANDS COLONIES

Aruba

	BU
1992 5 Cents. Arms (N clad Steel)	**.30**
1995 5 Florin. Beatrix/arms (N clad Steel, square)	**5.00**

	BU
1995 25 Florin. Beatrix/sea turtles (S)	**35.00**

Ceylon

	F.
1660-1720 2 Stuiver. IISt in wreath/same (C)	**20.00**
1791 1 Stuiver. T over Voc monogram/I over S T (C)	**35.00**

Curacao

	VF
1821 1 Real. Caduceus and branch (S)	**100.00**
1944 1 Cent. Lion/wreath (C)	**1.75**
1900 1/4 Gulden. Wilemina as adolescent/ crowned shield (S)	**20.00**
1944 1 Gulden. Wilemina as adult/ crowned shield (S)	**5.00**

Netherlands Antilles

	BU
1965 1 Cent. Lion/wreath (C)	**1.50**
1978 25 Cents. Shield (N)	**.75**
1985 2-1/2 Gulden. Beatrix/arms (N)	**4.00**
1977 25 Gulden. Juliana/Peter Stuyvesant (S)	**160.00**
1978 100 Gulden. Juliana/Willem I (G)	**95.00**

Netherlands Antilles 1979 25 Gulden

	BU
1979 25 Gulden. Children (S)	80.00

Netherlands East Indies

	VF
1789 Duit. Shield/VoC monogram (C)	4.00

	BU
1807 Duit. 5 1/16 G, Shield/INDIA BATAV (C)	2.00
1802 1/4 Gulden. Crowned shield/ship (S)	60.00
1859 1/2 Cent. Crowned shield/ Indonesian inscription (C)	4.00
1945 1 Cent. Rice plant (C, holed)	.25
1899 2-1/2 Cents. Crowned shield/ Indonesian inscription (C)	10.00
1913 5 Cents. Crown (CN, holed)	1.25
1857 1/10 Gulden. Crowned shield/ Indonesian inscription (S)	3.00
1945 1/4 Gulden. Similar (S)	.50
1826 1/2 Gulden. Willem I/wreath (S)	35.00
1840 1 Gulden. Similar (S)	40.00

Surinam

	BU
1764 Duit. Plant/SOCIETEI VAN SURINAME (C)	F 30.00
1972 1 Cent. Arms (C)	1.00
1962 1 Gulden. Juliana/arms (S)	8.00

POLAND

Early modern Poland was mostly ruled by the royal House of Saxony, and its coins closely resembled the German States coins of the day. Mostly they were small coppers, small- to medium-sized coins of base silver, big, good silver thalers, and gold. Most bore a bust, some had monograms on the obverse, and the royal arms dominated the reverse. Some of the most creative designs were memorial issues for the death of the king. Some of these depicted a butterfly.

Poland may have been dissolved in 1795, but there were still Polish coins struck after that. The remnant state, the Grand Duchy of Warsaw, struck some heraldic types, though briefly. Krakow even more briefly did the same as an independent republic. Also the part of Poland under Russian rule had its own distinctive coinage from 1816 to 1850. Some of these bore a portrait of the Czar even when Russian coins did not. Others actually had the exchange rate on the reverse, giving values in both Polish and Russian currencies.

Polish independence was restored in 1918, and the crowned white eagle became a national symbol always depicted on the coins of the between-the-wars republic. Portraits of an idealized Polonia, an allegory of the nation, and the forceful bust of Marshall Pilsudski also were very common.

After World War II the Communist government removed the crown and changed most of the minor coins to aluminum. Initially monotonous, later Communist issues depict diverse national heroes and local animals. Post-Communist coins are very similar in style to late Communist issues, but with the crown replaced on the eagle's head.

Poland has produced collectors' issues in quantity since the mid 1960s. The moderately priced circulating 2 zlote commemoratives, issued every few months, have proven quite popular. There is also a strong market for coins depicting Pope John Paul II. Virtually unique among world coinage of the era, Poland has since then actually distributed quantities of rejected designs. These patterns, or *probas*, are usually far from rare like most other countries' patterns, and can usually be bought for $10 to $20 each!

Additional Specialized Books:
Gumowski, M. *Handbuch der Polnischen Numismatik.*
Kopicki, E. *Katalog podstawowych typow monet i banknotow Polski.*

Known Counterfeits: Polish coins have not been the victims of significant counterfeiting in the past, but may be slightly more so as a result of Eastern European counterfeiters. Counterfeits exist of the 1925 5 Zlotych and klippe (square) 1933 Sobieski 10 Zlotych. An older circulation counterfeit of the 1932 5 Zlotych is known.

KINGDOM

	F
1752 Solidus. August III/arms (C)	**9.00**
1780 Grosz. SR monogram/arms (C)	**9.50**
1755 Tympf. August III/arms, 18 below (Billon)	**29.50**
1767 1 Groschen. Monogram (Billon)	**25.00**
1733 16 Groschen. AR monogram, 16 gr below/butterfly (S)	XF **1,250.00**
1702 Thaler. Monograms around cross/arms (S)	**375.00**

Poland 1767 1 Groschen

	F
1775 Thaler. Stanislaus Augustus/arms (S)	**95.00**
1703 Ducat. August II/crown over three shields (G)	**450.00**

Poland 1962 5 Groszy

GRAND DUCHY OF WARSAW

	F
1813 3 Grosze. Arms (C)	**7.00**
1814 1/3 Talara. Friedrich August/arms (S)	**35.00**
1811 Ducat. Similar (G)	**400.00**

RUSSIAN RULE

	F
1817 1 Grosz. Polish arms on Russian eagle (C)	**4.00**
1840 10 Groszy. Russian arms (Billon)	**6.00**
1838 2 Zlote = 30 Kopeks. Similar (S)	**15.00**
1817 5 Zlotych. Alexander I/Polish arms on Russian eagle (S)	**45.00**

KRAKOW

	F
1835 5 Groszy. Eagle in crowned city gate (Billon)	**30.00**

2002 20 Zlotych

REPUBLIC

	VF
1923 10 Groszy. Eagle (N)	**.45**
Same, Nazi restrike (Z)	**.20**
1925 5 Zlotych. Eagle/Polonia and youth (S)	**300.00**
1934 5 Zlotych. Pilsudski/eagle (S)	**4.00**
1925 20 Zlotych. King Boleslaus/eagle (G)	*BU* **185.00**

Postwar Coinage

	BU
1949 5 Groszy. Eagle (C)	**1.00**
1958 5 Groszy. Eagle (AL)	**.20**
1962 5 Groszy. Eagle (AL)	**.15**
1960 5 Zlotych. Eagle/fisher (AL)	**5.00**

	BU
1967 10 Zlotych. Eagle/Marie Curie (CN)	**2.25**
1978 100 Zlotych. Moose/eagle (S)	*proof only* **22.00**
1991 20,000 Zlotych. SAR monogram/ eagle (CN in Brass, bimetallic)	**18.00**
1992 5 Groszy. Crowned eagle (Brass)	**.25**
1997 2 Zlotye. Beetle/crowned eagle (Brass)	**6.00**
2002 2 Zlotye. Turtles/crowned eagle (Brass)	**4.50**
1997 10 Zlotych. Pope with Eucharist/ similar (S)	*proof only* **28.00**
2002 20 Zlotych Matejko (S, rect.)	*PF***40.00**

PORTUGAL

Artistically, the coins of Portugal before the 20th century are distinctive in their consistent adherence to Baroque-style ornamentation generation after generation. They are also distinctive in their relative lack of portraiture, on silver and copper before the 1800s. The most common design is either a shield or a monogram. The reverse typically displays a cross or the denomination in Roman numerals.

Twentieth century Portuguese coinage, both circulating and commemorative, places a heavy emphasis on the country's nautical heritage.

In January 2002, Portugal replaced the escudo with coins denominated in Euros, the currency of the European Union. On the circulating denominations, 1 Cent through 2 Euros, one side carries a Portugese design, the other a common European design. On higher denomination commemoratives both sides are distinctively Portuguese.

During the 1600s, much Portuguese silver was revalued by the application of a countermark with a new value.

Portugal maintained its colonial empire longer than most European powers, and had an extensive colonial coinage. During the 1600s and 1700s, most of it was either of homeland types or bore a globe on the reverse. The coins of Portuguese India up to the 1800s is interesting in its very European designs combined with primitive methods of local manufacture. Early in the 20th century Portugal's colonial coinage was fairly uniform from colony to colony. By the 1930s, a distinctive formula was developed: One side bore an emblem of Portugal, the other a heraldic symbol of the colony itself. On smaller denominations, one of these was sometimes replaced by the value.

Additional Specialized Books:

Gomes. *Moedas Portuguesas*.

Vaz, J. *Book of the Coins of Portugal*.

Known Counterfeits: Contemporary counterfeits of Brazilian copper are not rare and considered desirable. 1700s and 1800s gold should be inspected with care. The Azores crowned GP countermarked silver has been subject to cast counterfeits. Some lack the flat spot that would naturally occur on the back side corresponding to the countermark.

Portugal 1891 20 Reis

Portugal 1916 50 Centavos

KINGDOM

F

Philip III, 1621-40. Tostao. PHILIPVS...,
Crowned Shield, L B at sides/cross
(S) **275.00**

John IV, 1640-56. 80 Reis. Crowned IoIIII
over LXXX/cross (S) **65.00**

Afonso VI, 1656-83. 40 Reis. Crowned
XXX/cross (S) **50.00**

Peter II, 1683-1706. 1699 5 Reis. Crowned
P∞II/V in wreath (C) **9.00**

John V, 1706-50. 1721 10 Reis. Crowned
JV/X in wreath (C). **12.00**

Joseph I, 1750-77. 1760 4 Escudos. Bust of
Joseph r./arms (G) **300.00**

Maria and Peter III, 1777-86. 200 Reis.
Crowned shield/cross (S) **20.00**

Maria alone, 1786-99. 1789 4 Escudos.
Bust of Maria r./arms (G). **280.00**

John, Regent 1799-1816. ½ Tostao.
Crowned XXXX/cross (S) **17.50**

John VI, 1816-1826. 1820 400 Reis.
Portuguese shield on crowned globe/
cross (S) **25.00**

Peter IV, 1826-28. 1828 40 Reis. Bust r./
crowned shield (C) **20.00**

Michael, 1828-34. 120 Reis. Crowned
shield/cross (S) **20.00**

Maria II, 1834-53. 1850 10 Reis. Crowned
arms/X in wreath (C) **3.00**

Peter V, 1853-61. 1860 5,000 Reis. Head r./
arms (G) **210.00**

Luiz I, 1861-89. 1884 20 Reis. Head l./
wreath (C). **2.00**

VF

Carlos I, 1889-1908.
1900 100 Reis. Crowned shield/value (CN)
. . . . **1.50**

1891 20 Reis Head r. (C) **2.00**

1892 500 Reis. Head r./crowned arms
(S). **5.50**

Manuel II, 1908-10. 1909 200 Reis. Head l./
crown in wreath (S). **4.50**

1910 500 Reis. Emanuel II/Winged Victory
(VF) **25.00**

REPUBLIC

XF

1918 2 Centavos. Arms (C). **1.50**

same but (Iron). **300.00**

1919 4 Centavos. Bust of young girl (CN)**1.50**

1916 50 Centavos. Bust/armellary sphere
(S). **9.00**

1910 Escudo. Bust with flag/arms (S) **85.00**

1933 5 Escudos. Ship/arms (S) **20.00**

1942 5 Escudos. Same **5.00**

1948 5 Escudos. Same **4.00**

1934 10 Escudos. Similar (S) **50.00**

BU

1968 20 Centavos. Cross of shields/XX (C)**1.50**

1983 2-½ Escudos. Corn ear/arms (CN)
. . . . **1.25**

1966 20 Escudos. Bridge/arms (S) . . . **4.50**

1986 50 Escudos. Ship/arms (CN) . . . **2.25**

1991 100 Escudos. de Quental (CN) . **3.00**

1997 200 Escudos. Francis Xavier/ship
(CN). **5.00**

Portugal 1942 5 Escudos

Portugal 2005 5 Euro

Portugal 1991 100 Escudos

Portuguese Colonies-Angola
1927 10 Centavos

Euro Coinage 2002 to date

	BU
2002 1 Cent. Royal signature/globe. (C plated Steel)	.50
2002 2 Euro. Royal cypher/map (NB clad N in CN, bimetallic)	4.50
2005 5 Euro. Pope John XXI (S)	30.00

PORTUGUESE COLONIES

Angola

	VF
1698 20 Reis. Crowned shield/XX (C)	25.00
1762 2 Macutas. Crowned shield/wreath (S)	25.00
1860 2 Macuta. Arms (C)	20.00
1921 1 Centavo. Arms (C)	12.50
1927 10 Centavos. Bust l./arms (CN)	4.00
1953 1 Escudo (C)	1.50
1952 10 Escudos. Portuguese arms/ Angolan arms (S)	2.50
1972 20 Escudos. Portuguese arms/ Angolan arms (N)	2.50

Azores

	VF
1750 5 Reis. Crowned II over V/crown over five shields within wreath (C)	45.00
1830 5 Reis. MARIA II, etc., arms (C)	15.00
1901 5 Reis. Arms/wreath (C)	3.50
1980 25 Escudos. Arms (CN)	BU 5.00

Brazil

	F
1695 320 Reis. Crowned shield/globe over cross (S)	27.00
1768 5 Reis. Crowned V/globe (C)	10.00
1819 20 Reis. Crowned XX/arms on globe (C)	8.00
1812/1 960 Reis. Arms/globe (S)	55.00
1821 960 Reis. Crown and wreath/arms on globe (S)	25.00
1810 4,000 Reis. Crowned shield/cross (G)	125.00

Cape Verde

	XF
1930 5 Centavos	3.50
1930 10 Centavos. Head l. (C)	4.00

Portuguese Colonies-Cape Verde
1930 5 Centavos

Portuguese Colonies-Macao
1952 5 Avos

Portuguese Colonies-Brazil
1812/1 960 Reis

	XF
1949 50 Arms (CN)	**2.50**
1967 2-½ Escudos. Portuguese arms/Cape Verde arms (CN)	**2.50**
1953 10 Escudos. Similar (S)	**6.00**

Portuguese Guinea

	XF
1933 10 Centavos. Head l. (C)	**500.00**
1946 50 Centavos. Arms (C)	**15.00**
1952 22 Escudos. Portuguese arms/ Guinea arms (CN)	**3.00**
1973 5 Escudos. Similar (CN)	**10.00**
1952 20 Escudos. Similar (S)	**45.00**

Portuguese India

	Crude F
1706-50 5 Bazarucos. Shield between G A/wheel (Tin, 5.3g.)	**50.00**
1769 10 Bazarucos. Shield between G A/ IO in wreath (Tin)	**60.00**
1854 4-½ Reis. Crowned shield/4-½ R (C)	**12.00**
1750-77 12 Reis. Crowned shield/doze rei in wreath (C)	**60.00**
1746 Pardao. John V/arms (S)	**150.00**
1650 2 Tangas. Shield between G A/St. John between S I (S)	**65.00**
1796 Rupia. Maria I/arms (S)	**30.00**
1857 Rupia. Peter V/wreath (S)	**55.00**
1776 12 Xerafins. Arms/12 X 17 76 in angles of cross (G)	**950.00**

Portuguese India, modern coinage

	VF
1871 3 Reis. Crowned shield/wreath (C)	**10.00**

	VF
1881 1/8 Tanga. Luiz I/crown (C)	**3.50**
1881 1/8 Rupia. Luiz I/arms (S)	**6.00**
1901 1/4 Tanga. Carlos I/arms (C)	**16.00**
1934 2 Tangas. Indian shield/Portuguese shield (CN)	**20.00**
1935 Rupia. Portuguese shield/Indian shield (S)	**15.00**
1961 10 Centavos. Arms (C)	**1.00**
1958 1 Escudo. Portuguese arms/Indian arms (CN)	**2.50**
1959 6 Escudos. Similar (CN)	**4.50**

Macao

	BU
1952 5 Avos. Arms (C)	**30.00**
1973 50 Avos. Portuguese arms/Macao arms (CN)	**3.00**
1952 1 Pataca. Similar (S)	**40.00**
1998 2 Patacas. (Brass, octagonal) Church and gateway	**5.50**
1992 5 Patacas. Junk passing cathedral (CN, 12-sided)	**6.50**
1989 100 Patacas. Arms/snake (S)	**47.50**

Madeira

	BU
1981 25 Escudos. Head of Zarco/arms (CN)	**6.00**

Mozambique

	VF
1853 1 Real. Arms/wreath (C)	**20.00**
1820 80 Reis. Crown/shield on globe (C)	**35.00**
1936 10 Centavos. Arms (C)	**10.00**

Portuguese Colonies-Macao
1992 5 Patacas

Portuguese Colonies-Mozambique
1970 10 Escudos

Portuguese Colonies-Madeira
1981 25 Escudos

Portuguese Colonies-St. Thomas
and Prince 1962 20 Centavos

Portuguese Colonies-Timor
1945 20 Avos

	VF
1945 50 Centavos. Arms (C)	**3.50**
1951 1 Escudo. Arms (CN)	**3.00**
1965 2-1/2 Escudos. Portuguese arms/ Mozambique arms (CN)	**.25**
1935 5 Escudos. Similar (S)	**22.50**
1960 5 Escudos. Similar (S)	**2.00**
1970 10 Escudos. Similar (CN)	**.70**
1955 20 Escudos. Similar (S)	**3.50**

St. Thomas and Prince

	VF
1971 10 Centavos. Arms (AL)	**.65**
1962 20 Centavos. Arms (C)	**1.25**
1951 50 Centavos. Arms (CN)	**3.50**
1948 1 Escudo. Arms (N-C)	**40.00**
1939 2-1/2 Escudos. Portuguese arms/ colonial arms (S)	**30.00**
1951 5 Escudos. Similar (S)	**6.00**
1951 10 Escudos. Similar (S)	**7.00**

	BU
1971 20 Escudos. Similar (N)	**13.50**
1970 50 Escudos. Two shields/cross of shields (S)	**8.00**

Timor

	XF
1951 10 Avos. Cross of shields (C)	**7.50**
1945 20 Avos. Bust r./arms (CN)	**70.00**
1951 50 Avos. Arms (S)	**8.50**
1970 20 Centavos. Arms (C)	**2.50**
1970 1 Escudo. Arms (C)	**9.00**
1970 2-1/2 Escudos. Portuguese arms/ Timor arms (CN)	**3.50**
1958 3 Escudos. Similar (S)	**10.00**
1970 5 Escudos. Similar (CN)	**8.00**
1958 6 Escudos (S). Similar (S)	**12.50**

RUSSIA

Russia has the dual distinction of being the last European country to abandon primitive medieval-hammered coinage and the first country with a modern decimal-based coinage. When the silver-dollar-sized ruble was introduced in 1704 it was valued at 100 of the old kopeks. Modern Russian coinage is attributable to the personal will of Peter the Great, who was determined to make Russia into a modern country in a single lifetime. Before his reign, portrait coins were virtually unheard of in Russia, and large silver or gold coins were generally imported foreign coins. He was also the first ruler since the 1400s to successfully circulate copper coinage.

The standards of copper coins changed several times in the 1700s and 1800s, and often new coins were struck over old ones. Specialized collectors consider these particularly desirable, but not everyone cares.

During the early and mid-1800s, portraiture was removed from silver coinage. It was replaced by a double-headed eagle. Throughout the century, the number of shields on its wings increased. Each shield represented an additional territory, such as Finland or Poland, that the Czar had incorporated into his empire.

One distinctive type of coin struck under Czarist Russia is the *novodel*. This is an official government "restrike" with new dies. Some *novodels* are actually new issues of old coins which were never actually struck. They can sometimes be identified by their unusually uniform quality, not representative of the earlier coins they resemble. They were generally struck for wealthy 19th century collectors, and today are considered rare and desirable.

From 1921-23, coins were struck in the name of the Russian Soviet Federated Socialist Republic. These pieces carried the Communist slogan "Workers of all countries unite!" and purely agricultural symbols. With the establishment of the Union of Soviet Socialist Republics and the addition of new territories, symbols of expansion began to appear. The new state symbol consisted of a hammer and sickle superimposed on a globe, with ribbons at its side. Each ribbon represented a republic added to the Soviet Union, much as the shields were added to the czarist eagle's wings. Among the most splendid depictions of Soviet iconography is the scene on the Soviet ruble of 1924. Nicknamed the "worker ruble" it shows an industrial worker pointing out the rising sun of Communism to a less enthusiastic agricultural worker. This relates clearly to the difficulties implicit in Russia, an agrarian nation, being the first one to implement Communism, a system intended for initial implementation in an industrial society.

During the 1970s and 1980s, a wide range of commemoratives were released. Some base metal pieces were widely distributed within the Soviet Union, others, mostly platinum or silver, were not even made available to the average Soviet citizen. Much of the commemorative coin program continued after the fall of Communism, but other changes occurred. Most of the low value circulating coins released over the last several years bear the double-headed eagle, former symbol of Czarist Russia, for the first time since 1918! Another post-Communist phenomenon was rapid inflation. This has caused a revaluation of the currency, followed by more inflation.

After the fall of Communism, the republics within the U.S.S.R. became independent nations. Among the most important, besides Russia proper, is the Ukraine. Ukrainian coins were released after years of being distributed unofficially in small quantities. Because of the initial difficulty in obtaining them, followed by abundant supplies, Ukrainian minor coinage has been the subject of one of the most precipitous drops in value in the recent world numismatic market. The trident symbol depicted on them goes back to the early coinage of Kievian Rus, virtually all of which are considered museum pieces.

Belarus, between Russia and Poland has yet to actively circulate coinage, but has made available some collectors' issues.

Additional Specialized Books:

Spassky, I.G. *Russian Monetary System*.

Uzdenikov, V. *Russian Coins, 1700-1917*.

Known Counterfeits: Many new counterfeits of czarist coins have been appearing recently. More copper and gold has recently been counterfeited than silver.

This includes Siberian coppers and many novodels. Know your dealer!

(Most of the massive quantities of 1700s copper coming onto the market recently are authentic however.)

Russia 1857 5 Kopeks

Russia 1884 1 Kopek

	F
Peter I, 1689-1725. 1706 Denga. Two-headed eagle (C)	30.00
1705 Kopek. Peter riding horse r. (C)	30.00
1725 Ruble. Bust r./Cross of four crowned П's (S)	175.00
Anna, 1730-40. 1734 Denga. Two-headed eagle cartouche (C)	7.50
Ivan IV, 1740-41. 1741 Grivennik (10 Kopeks). Bust r. as child/crown (S)	300.00
Elizabeth, 1741-61. 1758 5 Kopeks. Monogram in wreath/two-headed eagle (C)	35.00
1752 Ruble. Bust r./two-headed eagle (S)	150.00
1756 2 Rubles. Similar (G)	250.00
Peter III, 1761-62. 1762 4 Kopeks. St. George spearing dragon/drum, cannon and flags (C)	45.00
Catherine II the Great, 1762-1796. 1792 5 Kopeks. Monogram in wreath/two-headed eagle (C)	10.00
1783 15 Kopeks. Bust r./15 on two-headed eagle (S)	28.00
1769 Ruble. Bust r./two-headed eagle (S)	90.00
Paul I, 1796-1801. 1798 2 Kopeks. Crowned (C)	8.00

	F
1800 Poltina (=1/2 Ruble). Cross with four crowns/inscription in square (S)	75.00
1798 Ruble. Similar (S)	70.00
Alexander I, 1801-25. 1802 2 Kopeks. Two-headed eagle in thick border with two dots/inscription in similar border (C)	27.00
1812 2 Kopeks. Two-headed eagle without border/wreath (C)	2.50
1831 25 Kopeks. Two-headed eagle with wings down/wreath (S)	10.00
1820 Ruble. Two-headed eagle/wreath (S)	25.00
Nicholas I, 1825-55. 1835 Kopek. Two-headed eagle with wings down (C)	3.00
1844 Kopek. Crowned H (C)	3.00
1850 20 Kopeks. Two-headed eagle/wreath (S)	5.00

	VF
Alexander II, 1855-81. 1875 1/4 Kopek. Crowned AII monogram in wreath (C)	2.50
1855 Denga. Crowned AII monogram (C)	4.00
1857 5 Kopeks. Two-headed eagle (C)	4.00
1869 20 Kopeks. Two-headed eagle/wreath (S)	2.00
1877 Ruble. Similar (S)	30.00
Alexander III, 1881-94. 1889 1/2 Kopek. Crowned AIII monogram (C)	2.00
1884 1 Kopek. Two-headed eagle (C)	1.00
1893 3 Kopeks. Two-headed eagle in ornate border/wreath (C)	1.50
1894 50 Kopeks. Head r./two-headed eagle (S)	25.00
Nicholas II, 1894-1917. 1909 1/2 Kopek. Crowned NII monogram (C)	.50

Russia 1896 3 Kopeks

Russia 1965 15 Kopeks

Russia 1923 20 Kopeks

Russia 2000 2 Rubles

VF

1896 3 Kopeks. Two-headed eagle (C) **2.00**

1903 3 Kopeks. Two-headed eagle in
ornate border/wreath (C) **1.50**

1905 5 Kopeks. Two-headed eagle/wreath
(S). **2.00**

1896 50 Kopeks. Head l./two-headed
eagle (S) **8.00**

1899 Ruble. Similar (S) **25.00**

1902 5 Rubles. Similar (G) **65.00**

1902 37-1/2 Rubles. Similar (CN). . . . **12.50**

This is a restrike with original dies. Look
for the "P" added after 1902 Г. Beware:
some have been gold plated.

Communist Russia (РСФСР)

XF

1923 10 Kopeks. Hammer and sickle/
wreath (S) **2.00**

1923 20 Kopeks. Similar (S) **7.00**

1923 50 Kopeks. Similar/star (S) **7.00**

Soviet Union (CCCP)

1925 1/2 Kopek. CCCP (C) **14.50**

1931 1 Kopek. Arms/wreath (ALB) . . . **1.50**

1936 2 Kopeks. Similar (ALB). **2.00**

1943 3 Kopeks. Similar (ALB). **1.00**

1952 5 Kopeks. Similar (ALB). **1.00**

1957 10 Kopeks. Arms/octagon (CN) **2.00**

1965 15 Kopeks. Arms (CNZ). . . . . **.40**

1967 20 Kopeks. Arms/ship (CNZ) . . . . **.75**

XF

1991 50 Kopeks. Dome and tower (CN)
. . . . **.50**

1924 Ruble. Industrial worker leading
farmer towards sun/arms (S) **25.00**

BU

1981 Ruble. Cosmonaut/arms (CNZ)
. . . . **2.00**

1991 5 Rubles. Cathedral/arms (CN) . **5.00**

1979 150 Ruble. Wrestlers/arms
(Platinum). **450.00**

Russian Federation

BU

1992 1 Ruble. Two-headed eagle (Brass
clad Steel). . . . . **.75**

1994 50 Rubles. Flamingos/two-headed
eagle (CN in ALB, *bimetallic*) **2.50**

1995 100 Rubles. Ballerina/similar
(G) . . . . *proof only* **695.00**

2002 2 Rubles. Battle (CN) **1.50**

SIBERIA

F

*1768 Polushka (=1/4 Kopek). Crowned
E II monogram in wreath/cartouche
(C)* **75.00**

1770 2 Kopeks. Similar/value on shield
between sables (C) **35.00**

Ukraine 2001 10 Hryven

UKRAINE

	BU
1996 200,000 Karbovantsiv. Chernobyl memorial. Bell/arms (CN)	**5.50**
1993 2 Kopiyky. Arms/value (AL)	**1.00**
2000 5 Hryven. Christ, crowds in background/arms between two angels (CN)	**9.00**
2001 10 Hryven. Hockey player (S)	*Proof Only* **45.00**

SCANDINAVIA

Scandinavian coins first became common in the 1500s. By the 1600s, the small base-silver coins of Denmark were frequently found. During this period, the coins of both Sweden and Denmark follow a typical European pattern of portraits, monograms, crowns, and shields. Other features are distinctive. In both countries, standing figures of the monarch become more common than elsewhere in Europe. Monograms in Denmark are more likely to use modern than Roman numerals. In Sweden, the Divine name, the Tetragramaton, in Hebrew is often depicted.

The single most distinguishing feature of Scandinavian coinage is the abundant use of copper. Large copper coins struck on crudely made blanks were common particularly in 1600s Sweden. There also, large slabs of copper, called "plate money," were used instead of silver coins. Each piece, weighing up to several pounds, was usually stamped five times with circular dies: once in each corner to prevent clipping, with an additional stamp in the center. Most of the plate money on the market in recent years is from one shipwreck, the *Nicobar*, and is corroded. These are worth less than non-sea-salvaged pieces. By the late 1700s, plate money had ceased to be struck, but large copper continued to be common throughout Scandinavia.

During the 1800s, Scandinavian coins were decimalized, and in 1872 a common monetary union was formed with all Scandinavian countries striking distinctive coins on a common standard. During this time, most countries used portraits only on silver and gold, and monograms on copper.

Norway has been part of either the Danish (1397-1814) or the Swedish (1814-1905) monarchy through most of the modern era. In 1905 it elected a king of its own, Haakon VII. Modern Norwegian coins usually resemble that of the kingdom with which it was united, sometimes with the distinctive Norwegian arms, a lion with a battle ax, other times differentiated only by a small crossed hammers mint mark.

Iceland had no separate coinage until 1922, Greenland until 1926. Before then, Danish coins circulated on both islands. In 1941, Iceland became independent and royal symbols such as the crown were removed from above the arms. Many recent coins show the guardian spirits of Iceland, sometimes supporting the country's shield. After 1964, regular Danish coins were reintroduced to Greenland, and today it is an integral part of Denmark.

All these countries have issued plentiful silver commemoratives in the modern era, with some base metal ones more recently.

One convenient way to distinguish Swedish from other Scandinavian coins is that the word *ore* is spelled with ö in Swedish, ø in the others.

It is convenient to mention the names of the Scandinavian countries in their native languages:

Denmark	DANMARK
Greenland	GRØNLAND
Iceland	ISLAND
Norway	NORGE or NOREG
Sweden	SVERIGE

Denmark struck colonial coins for its possessions in the West Indies. They are generally artistic and not particularly rare. In 1913, Denmark sold these islands to the United States and they became the United States Virgin Islands. Today, these coins are popular with collectors not only of Danish coins, but with many U.S. collectors as well. The coins of Danish India are both scarcer and less popular.

Swedish issues for the West Indies are very rare. They consist only of countermarks on other countries' coins for local use.

Additional Specialized Books: Hobson, Burton. *Catalogue of Scandinavian Coins.*

Sømod, J. *Danmarks Mønter.* Also covers Norway 1481-1813.

Tonkin, Archie. *Myntboken.* Annual editions with up-to-date Swedish pricing.

Known Counterfeits: Contemporary counterfeits exist of some 17th and 18th century Danish minors. Swedish plate money has been the victim of dangerous counterfeits. The rare Danish 1776 2 skilling is known altered from 1778.

Denmark 1702 8 Skilling

DENMARK

	F
1702 8 Skilling. Bust/crown (S) **25.00**	
1719 ½ Skilling. Crowned double F4 monogram in wreath (C). **16.00**	
1771 1 Skilling. Crowned double C7 monogram (C). **8.00**	
1778 2 Skilling. Crowned C7 monogram/ crowned shield (Billon) **3.50**	
1764 4 Skilling. Crowned double F4 monogram (Billon) **10.00**	
1701 8 Skilling. Frederick IV/crown (S). **25.00**	
1732 24 Skilling. Christian VI/crowned shield (S). **100.00**	
1711 Krone. Frederick IV on horse r./arms (S). **125.00**	
1786 Daler. Large wild man with club supporting Danish arms/Norwegian arms (S). **550.00**	
1738 Ducat. Crowned double C6 monogram/fortress (G). **650.00**	

	VF
1869 1 Skilling. Crowned CIX in wreath (C) **4.50**	
1856 16 Skilling. Frederick VII/wreath (S). **7.75**	
1855 1 Rigsdaler (S). similar (S) **40.00**	
1846 1 Species Daler. Christian VIII/arms (S). **100.00**	
1899 1 Øre. Crowned CIX/dolphin and wheat ear (C). **1.25**	
1907 2 Øre. Crowned F8 monogram (C) **1.50**	
1919 5 Øre. Crowned Cx monogram (C) **5.00**	
1897 10 Øre. Christian IX/dolphin and wheat ear (Billon) **6.00**	

	VF
1924 25 Øre. Crowned CxR (CN, holed) **1.00**	
1942 similar (Z, holed). **1.50**	
1925 ½ Krone. Crowned CxC monogram/ crown (ALB) **6.50**	
1875 1 Krone. Christian IX/shield between dolphin and wheat ear (S). **25.00**	
1923 2 Kroner. King and Queen/arms (S). **8.00**	

	BU
1908 10 Kroner. Frederik VIII/arms (G) **80.00**	
1913 10 Kroner. Frederick VII/arms (G) **80.00**	
1873 20 Kroner. Christian IX/Dania std. l. (G). **200.00**	

Post-War Coinage

	BU
1962 1 Øre. Crowned FRIX monogram (Z). **1.25**	
1973 10 Øre. Crowned M2R monogram (CN). . . . . **.25**	
1957 1 Krone. Frederick XI/shield (ALB) **3.00**	
1968 10 Kroner. Frederick XI/Princess Benedikte (S). **11.50**	
1992 200 Kroner. Queen and Prince/ stylized house (S) **37.50**	

GREENLAND

	XF
1926 25 Øre. Crowned shield/bear (CN). **12.50**	
same but holed **65.00**	
1960 1 Krone. Crown over two shields/ wreath (CN) **10.00**	

ICELAND

	XF
1931 1 Eyrir. Crowned Cx (C). **6.00**	
1942 2 Aurar. Similar (C) **1.00**	
1963 5 Aurar. Shield in wreath (C) . . . . **.75**	
1981 10 Aurar. Ox/cuttle-fish (C) . . . . . . **.20**	
1922 25 Aurar. Crowned shield (CN) **4.00**	
1940 1 Krona. Similar (ALB) **2.00**	

Iceland 1995 100 Kronur

Norway 1876 5 Øre

	BU
1981 1 Krona. Giant/Cod (CN)	.50
1970 10 Kronur. Arms (CN)	.75
1974 500 Kronur. Four spirits/woman loading cow (S)	8.00
1987 50 Kronur. Four spirits/crab (CNZ)	3.00
1995 100 Kronur. Same/lumpfish (NB)	7.00
2000 1,000 Kronur. Leif Ericson (S)	Proof 55.00

This was sold in a two-piece set with the United States Leif Ericson commemorative.

NORWAY

	F
1643 Skilling. Lion with battle ax/I SKILLING DA (Billon)	45.00
1714 2 Skilling. Crowned double F4 monogram/lion with battle ax (Billon)	15.00
1778 4 Skilling Danske. Crowned C7 monogram/crowned arms, crossed hammers below (Billon)	20.00
1655 8 Skilling. Crowned F3 monogram/lion with battle ax (S)	90.00
1740 24 Skilling. Crowned C6 monogram/similar (S)	40.00
1763 24 Skilling. Crowned F5 monogram/similar (S)	25.00
1684 Mark. Crowned C5/lion with battle ax, in wreath (S)	250.00
1689 4 Mark. Crowned double C6 monogram/lion with battle ax, in wreath (S)	125.00
1673 1/2 Specie Daler. Christian V/crowned shield (S)	2,200.00
1749 1 Riksdaler. Frederick V/lion with battle ax, mountains behind (S)	275.00

Norway 1905 2 Kroner

	VF
1870 1 Skilling. Arms (C)	7.00
1825 8 Skilling. Carl XIV/arms (S)	40.00
1847 24 Skilling. Oscar I/arms (S)	20.00
1891 2 Øre. Arms, Ocr II at sides (C)	5.00
1876 5 Øre. Same (C)	10.00
1917 10 Øre. Crowned H7 monogram (Billon)	2.00
1939 50 Øre. Cross of monograms/crown (CN, holed)	.60
1906 2 Kroner. Arms/tree within border of hands (S)	15.00

Post-War Coinage

	Unc.
1957 1 Øre. Crowned H7 monogram (C)	1.50
1964 10 Øre. Crowned Ov monogram/Bee (CN)	1.00
1992 1 Krone. Harald V/crown (CN)	.75
1964 10 Kroner. Arms/building (S)	8.00
1993 100 Kroner. Harald V/figure skater (S)	60.00
2002 20 Kronor. Harald V/N.H. Abel (NB)	10.00

Norway 1964 10 Kroner

Norway 2002 20 Kroner

SWEDEN

	F
1666 1/6 Öre. C R S, three crowns/ crowned lion (C)	**12.00**
1720 1/2 Öre. F R S, three crowns/ crowned arrow shield (C)	**7.00**
1690 1 Öre. Crowned CXI/three crowns (Billon)	**12.00**
1748 2 Öre. FI SG V R, crowned shield/ crown over crossed arrows (C)	**6.00**
1759 2 Öre. AF SG V R, crowned shield/ crown over crossed arrows (C)	**6.00**
1669 4 Öre. Crowned C/three crowns (S)	**25.00**
1719 1 Mark. Ulrica Eleonora r./crowned shield (S)	**165.00**

	F
1676 2 Mark. Charles XI l./three crowns (S)	**55.00**
1753 4 Mark. Adolf Frederick r./arms (S)	**150.00**
1697 8 Mark. Charles XII r./crowned shield (S)	**550.00**
1778 1/24th Riksdaler. Crowned GIII/ crowned shield (Billon)	**15.00**
1779 1/12th Riksdaler. Similar (S)	**27.50**
1718 Daler. Jupiter and eagle (C)	**10.00**
1719 Daler. Hope (C)	**10.00**
1725 Riksdaler. Frederick I r./arms (S)	**225.00**
1781 Riksdaler. Gustav III r./arms(S)	**75.00**
1721 2 Daler "Plate money." Crowned FRS in each corner, 2 DALER SILF.MYNT in center (C)	**450.00**
1741 ½ Daler "Plate money." Crowned FRS in each corner, 2 DALER SILF.MYNT in center (C)	**250.00**
1709 Ducat. Carl XII r./crowned CC monogram (G)	**850.00**
1776 Ducat. Gustav III r./arms (G)	**525.00**

	VF
1821 ½ Skilling. Crowned CXIV/crossed arrows (C)	**5.00**
1848 1/16th Riksdaler. Oscar I/arms (S)	**8.00**
1721 Riksdaler, Anniv. of Liberation War, busts of Gustav Vasa and Gustav II Adolf	**400.00**
1806 Riksdaler. Gustav IV/arms (S)	**300.00**
1866 1 Öre. Carl XV/wreath (C)	**3.00**
1920 1 Öre. Crowned GvG monogram three crowns (C)	**.50**
1935 same (C)	**.30**
1890 2 Öre. Crowned OII monogram (C)	**2.00**
1917 2 Öre. Crowned GvG monogram/ three crowns (Iron)	**3.75**
1907 5 Öre. Crowned OII monogram (C)	**2.25**
1941 5 Öre. Crowned GvG monogram/ three crowns (C)	**.35**
1898 10 Öre. Crowned OII monogram (Billon)	**4.50**
1934 10 Öre. Crowned shield (Billon)	**.50**
1943 25 Öre. Crown (Billon)	**.50**
1856 25 Öre. Oscar I/wreath (S)	**12.00**

Sweden 1907 5 Öre

Sweden 1897 2 Kronor

Sweden 1967 2 Öre

Sweden 1979 5 Öre

Sweden 1956 25 Öre

Sweden 1972 10 Kronor

VF

1907 50 Öre. Crowned OII monogram/
    wreath (S) **6.00**
1938 50 Öre. Crowned shield (S) **1.25**
1940 50 Öre. Crowned Gv monogram/
    wreath (CN) **1.00**
1898 1 Krona. Oscar II/arms (S). **30.00**
1936 1 Krona. Gustav V/arms (S). **2.25**
1897 2 Kronor. Oscar II crowned/arms
    (S). **9.00**
1944 2 Kronor. Gustav V old/arms
    (Billon). **2.25**
1874 10 Kronor. Oscar II/arms (G). . . **85.00**

Unc.

1895 20 Kronor. Similar (G) **185.00**
1953 1 Öre. Crown/crown (C) **2.00**
1967 2 Öre. Similar (C) . . . . **.45**
1979 5 Öre. Crowned CXVIG monogram
    (C) . . . . **.25**
1988 10 Öre. Similar (CN). . . . . **.15**
1956 25 Öre. Crown (Billon). **3.00**
1968 50 Öre. Crowned GVIA monogram
    (CN). **1.00**
1979 1 Krona. Carl XVI/crowned shield
    (CN). . . . . **.60**
1964 2 Kronor. Gustav VI/crowned shield
    (Billon). **5.00**

Unc.

1952 5 Kronor. Gustav VI/crowned GVIA
    monogram (Billon) **32.50**
1972 10 Kronor. Gustav VI/signature
    (S). **9.00**
1976 50 Kronor. King and Queen/arms
    (S) **11.50**
1990 200 Kronor. Carl XVI/ship Vasa
    (S). **40.00**
1993 200 Kronor. 20th Anniv. Carl XVI
    (Unc.). **35.00**
1993 1,000 Kronor. Queen/arms (G)
    . . . . **175.00**

SPAIN

During the 1500s through early 1800s, Spanish coins were among the most important international trade coins in the world, particularly those struck at Spain's colonial mints in the Americas. They were so respected that they were the standard of value on which the original United States Dollar was based.

Spanish coinage until the mid-1800s was based on the *real* introduced by Ferdinand and Isabella. It was originally a silver coin larger than a quarter, although it had shrunk to the size of a nickel and was thinner by the 1600s. From then until the Napoleonic Wars it remained quite stable. During most of this period, it carried the coat of arms of Spain on the reverse, a portrait or variation of the arms on the obverse.

Gold coins were plentiful as well. They were denominated in *escudos*, worth 16 *reales*. They bore portraits more often than the silver did.

Copper coins were denominated in *maravedi*, 34 of which were worth one *real*. During most of this period, the copper coinage was poor. There was often a shortage of new copper, causing old worn out coins to continue in use long after they should have been replaced. Often these coins would be counterstamped to revalidate them. A number indicating a new value and sometimes a date would be impressed. When this was done repeatedly, the coins took on a mutilated appearance, and sometimes ceased to remain flat. This practice of making *resellados* ended in the 1700s, but the practice of forcing worn out copper into continued use persisted.

Spanish coins from the mid-1800s until recently have carried two dates. The large date is the year of authorization, but not when the coin was actually manufactured. The real date was usually indicated in tiny incuse numbers on the six-pointed star, which is a Madrid mint mark.

After a few monetary experiments in the mid-1800s, Spain joined many other European countries in 1869 in striking its coins according to the international standard of the Latin Monetary Union, and continued to do so until 1926. Most of the issues during this period uniformly bore the royal portrait and the coat of arms.

The final years of the monarchy and the period of the Civil War not only saw a deterioration of the value of the coinage, but also an opening up of the designs to new ideas under all three governments. Despite the extremely modernistic eagle supporting the shield, Franco's later coinage, mostly of base metal, was fairly conservative in pattern.

The restoration of the monarchy not only promised a progressive government for Spain, but also changes in the coinage. Since the 1980s, new shapes have been used to distinguish denominations, and a plethora of designs have been used to promote the recognition of various cultural sights and events throughout Spain. There have also been a vast number of collector issues sold at a premium. These too have had unusual and progressive designs.

In January 2002, Spain replaced the peseta with coins denominated in Euros, the currency of the European Union. Some coins were struck years in advance and held until 2002. On the circulating denominations, 1 Cent through 2 Euros, one side carries a Spanish design, the other a common European design. On higher denomination commemoratives, both sides are distinctively Spanish.

COLONIAL COINAGE

The *real* issued in the New World was struck to the same standards as in European Spain, but the designs often varied. The first issues of the early 1500s displayed the Pillars of Hercules and a coat of arms. In terms of style, they seemed no different than European coins. The first copper coins struck in the New World, minted in Santo Domingo, featured monograms, but they were far more carelessly made.

When the quantities of silver and gold being mined and shipped back to Spain became so great that they could not be struck into nicely finished coins, a rough, improvised coin was devised. Called "cobs" by modern collectors, these coins were struck to the same exacting weight standards, but the designs were only hastily impressed, with no entire image being found on any one coin. The blanks on which they were struck were neither round nor flat. Originally it was intended that these be shipped back to Europe and remelted, but the pressing needs for money in the Spanish American colonies caused them to be pressed into service as regular coinage.

While dates were engraved on the dies of these cobs, they are usually not clear on the coins. Specialized references sometimes permit the dating of these pieces by the correlation of mint marks and assayers' initials, which are more often legible than the dates.

Many of the cobs on the market are recovered from shipwrecks or found on beaches near shipwrecks. Generally sea salvaged coins are either pitted or covered with black compounds called horn silver. This is bonded to the metal and cannot be removed without removing part of the coin. Such corroded coins are worth far less than other cobs and Spanish colonial coins. The exception is for those coins with pedigrees to known shipwrecks. If satisfactorily documented, the novelty value of their history can far exceed their value as low-grade Spanish Colonial coins. Be careful of false documentation and made-to-order pedigrees. When possible, documentation from the original salvers is desirable.

From 1732 onward, more careful methods of manufacture were implemented. Initially the improved silver carried the crowned shield of Spain on one side, two globes between the Pillars of Hercules on the other. In 1760, the designs were changed to bear the king's portrait and a Spanish shield. The face value of each silver coin was indicated in numbers of reales indicated as 8R through 1R, with the half real simply as "R" without a numeral. The improved gold had carried a similar design since the 1730s. Copper in the Spanish colonies was not common, and at most mints not struck at all.

Despite the vast expanse covered by the Spanish colonies in the Americas, most of the coins struck were of similar design from mint to mint. Some mints, however, are far scarcer than others, so it is important to recognize their marks. Usually the mint mark is incorporated into the reverse legend. The Colonial Listings below follow a large representation of the mint mark which appears on the coins listed. Later Spanish colonial coins of the Philippines and Puerto Rico resemble Spanish coins of the turn of the century. On these the name of the colony is clearly indicated.

Additional Specialized Books:

Cayon. *Las Monedas Españolas del Tremis al Euro.*

Sedwick, D. and F. *The Practical Book of Cobs*, 3rd ed.

Known Counterfeits: Gold coins of Isabella II have been counterfeited. So have many 19th century, silver-dollar-sized coins. These include among others: 20 reales 1852, 5 peseta 1870 (69), 1871 (73), 1897, 1899. The "star" dates are the ones in parentheses. Many are not silver, but a nickel alloy. Other gold coins of Alfonso XII and XIII have been restruck by the Spanish mint but they bear the accurate "secret" dates of (19)61 and (19)62.

Counterfeits of Spanish colonial cobs are plentiful in both gold and silver. Examine any example for casting seams, raised pimples or a cloudy appearance. This is different from the graininess found on authentic sea-salvaged coins. Also note that no two cobs are precisely identical, so if you have a pair of identical coins, there is a good chance both are counterfeit. Many of the two globes and portrait pieces have also been counterfeited, both at the time of issue and recently. Most of the recent counterfeits are poor quality metal and will not ring correctly.

Be careful not to accidentally purchase Puerto Rican coins with solder marks on the edges.

EUROPEAN COINAGE

Carlos II, 1665-1700.

Spain 1833 2 Maravedis

	F
1682 2 Reales. Arms in octolobe/crowned CAROLVSII monogram (C)	**35.00**
1685 4 Reales. Crowned shield/arms in octolobe (S)	**275.00**
1687 4 Reales. Similar/cross over MA monogram (S)	**550.00**

Carlos III Pretender, 1701-13.

| 1711 2 Reales. Similar/crowned CAROLVSIII monogram (S) | **32.00** |

Philip V, 1700-46.

1719 4 Maravedi. Crowned shield/lion holding globes (C)	**12.00**
1707 1 Real Crowned shield/floral monogram (S)	**25.00**
1726 1 Real. Crowned shield/arms in octolobe (S)	**20.00**
1734 4 Reales. Similar (S)	**200.00**
1743 2 Escudo. Bust r./crowned shield (G)	**80.00**

Louis, 1724.

| 1724 2 Reales. Crowned shield/arms in octolobe (S) | **45.00** |

Ferdinand VI, 1746-59.

| 1757 2 Reales. Crowned shield/arms in octolobe (S) | **30.00** |
| 1747 1/2 Escudo. Bust r./crowned shield (G) | **75.00** |

Carlos III, 1759-88.

1780 8 Maravedis. Bust r./castles and lions in angles of cross (C)	**15.00**
1788 2 Reales. Bust r./crowned shield (S)	**25.00**
1786 4 Escudo. Bust r./crowned shield in collar (G)	**250.00**

Carlos, IV, 1788-1808.

| 1800 4 Maravedis. Bust r./castles and lions in angles of cross (C) | **12.00** |
| 1793 1 Real. Bust r./crowned shield (S) | **15.00** |

Joseph Napoleon, 1808-13.

| 1810 4 Reales. Bust l./crowned shield (S) | **12.50** |

Ferdinand VII, 1808-33.

	F
1824 2 Maravedis. Bust r./castles and lions in angles of cross (C)	**6.00**
1833 2 Maravedis. Same (C)	**2.00**
1809 4 Reales. Bust r./crowned shield (S)	**125.00**

Isabel II, 1833-68.

1846 2 Maravedis. Bust r./castles and lions in angles of cross (C)	**7.50**
1837 4 Reales. Bust r./crowned shield in collar (S)	**25.00**
1868 2-1/2 Centimos. Bust r./crowned shield (C)	**4.50**
1868 Escudo. Bust r./crowned shield between pillars (S)	**10.00**

Latin Monetary Union Standard

	VF
1870 2 Centimos. Hispania std./lion holding shield (C)	**2.00**
1879 5 Centimos. Alfonso XII/arms (C)	**4.00**
1900 50 Centimos. Alfonso XIII as child/arms (S)	**3.00**
1891 1 Peseta. Alfonso XIII as baby/arms (S)	**25.00**
1871 5 Pesetas. Amadeo l/arms (S)	**15.00**
1883 5 Pesetas. Alfonso XII/arms (S)	**12.00**
1878 25 Pesetas. Alfonso XII/arms (G)	**135.00**

Republic & Civil War

1938 10 Centimos. Arms (Iron)	**650.00**
1937 25 Centimos. Yoke and arrows/crowned shield (CN, holed)	**.40**
1937 1 Peseta. Head l./grapes (Brass)	**1.00**

Franco Regency

	BU
1953 10 Centimos. Horseman/arms (AL)	**3.00**

Spain 1959 10 Centimos

Spain 1983 1 Peseta

Spain 2002 10 Euros

Spain 1999 2,000 Pesetas

	BU
1989 5,000 Pesetas. Arms/ship Santa Maria (S)	**45.00**
1999 2,000 Pesetas. Train (S) *Proof*	**32.50**
Euro Coinage	
1999 20 Euro Cent. Cervantes/map (B, notched)	**.85**
2000 1 Euro. Juan Carlos/map. (CN clad N in NB, bimetallic)	**4.00**
2002 10 Euro. King & queen (S). *PF*	**50.00**

COLONIAL COINAGE

F

SANTO DOMINGO, HISPANIOLA
1506-1516 and later. 4 Maravedis. Crowned Y/crowned pillars (C) . . **40.00**

C

CARTAGENA, COLOMBIA
1634 8 Reales cob. Crowned shield/pillars over waves (S) **2,500.00**

C or CA

CHIHUAHUA, MEXICO
1812 8 Reales. Ferdinand VII/arms (cast S) **60.00**

	BU
1959 10 Centimos. Franco (AL)	**.10**
1964 1 Peseta. Franco/arms (ALB)	**.75**
1949 5 Pesetas. Similar (N)	**2.00**
1975 25 Pesetas. Franco/eagle holding arms (CN)	**.75**
1966 100 Pesetas. Franco/arms in octolobe (S)	**6.00**
Kingdom Restored	
1983 1 Peseta. Juan Carlos/arms (AL)	**.20**
1990 50 Pesetas. Juan Carlos/globe (CN, notched)	**1.50**
1994 100 Pesetas. Juan Carlos/Prado Museum (ALB)	**3.00**

D

DURANGO, MEXICO

1814 1/8th Real. Crowned FoV monogram
(C) **27.00**

                                    F

1814 1 Real. Ferdinad VII/arms (S) . **450.00**
1821 8 Reales. same (S) **50.00**

GA

GUADALAJARA, MEXICO

1821 8 Reales. Ferdinand VII/arms
(S) **45.00**
1821 8 Escudos. Similar (G) **2,500.00**

G

GUANAJUATO, MEXICO

                                    F

1822 8 Reales. Ferdinand VII/arms
(S) **45.00**

ME

LIMA, PERU

                                    F

1689 1 Real cob. Pillars over waves/castles
and lions in angles of cross (S) . . **50.00**
1740 2 Reales cob. Similar (S) **45.00**
1697 4 Reales cob. Similar (S) **270.00**
1746 8 Reales cob. Similar (S) **100.00**
1696 8 Escudos cob. Similar (G) . **2,250.00**
1754 1/2 Real. Crowned shield/two globes
between pillars (S) **15.00**
1761 4 Reales. Similar (S) **125.00**
1772 4 Reales. Similar (S) **90.00**
1769 8 Reales. Similar (S) **150.00**
1796 1/4 Real. Castle/lion (S) **15.00**
1812 1/2 Real. Ferdinand VII/arms (S)
. . . . **7.00**
1793 2 Reales. Charles IV/arms (S) . . **20.00**
1805 4 Reales. Similar (S) **40.00**
1782 8 Reales. Charles III/arms (S) . . **35.00**
1821 2 Escudos. Ferdinand VII/arms
(G) **350.00**
1775 8 Escudos. Carlos III/arms (G)
. . . . **500.00**

Spain 1780 8 Reales

M

Mexico City, Mexico

                                    F

1653 1/2 Real cob. CAROLVS monogram/
arms in octolobe (S) **120.00**
1714 1 Real cob. Crowned shield/arms in
octolobe (S) **57.50**
1613 2 Reales cob. Similar (S) **150.00**
1733 4 Reales cob. Similar (S) **185.00**
1664 8 Reales cob. Similar (S) **225.00**
1688 4 Escudos cob. Cross, fleurs in
angles (G) **1,400.00**
1755 1/2 Real. Crowned shield/two globes
between pillars (S) **15.00**
1736 2 Reales. Similar (S) **30.00**
1768 4 Reales. Similar (S) **100.00**
1769 8 Reales. Similar (S) **100.00**
1780 1/2 Real. Carlos III/arms (S) **10.00**
1817 1 Real. Ferdinand VII/arms (S) . . **7.50**
1/88 2 Reales. Carlos III/arms (S) . . . **20.00**
1805 4 Reales. Carlos IV/arms (S) . . . **40.00**
1780 8 Reales. Carlos III/arms (S) . . . **45.00**
1791 8 Reales. Similar (S) **40.00**
1808 1 Escudo. Similar (G) **165.00**
1736 4 Escudos. Philip V/arms (G)
. . . . **1,000.00**

NG or G

NUEVA GUATEMALA, GUATEMALA

                                    F

1743 1/2 Real cob. Crowned shield/two
globes between pillars (S) **40.00**
1752 8 Reales cob. Similar (S) **110.00**
1758 2 Reales. Similar (S) **60.00**
1772 2 Reales. Carlos III/arms (S) . . . **30.00**
1812 2 Reales. Ferdinand VII/arms (S)
. . . . **25.00**

NR or SF

NUEVO REINO/SANTA FE DE BOGOTÁ COLOMBIA

	F
1652 2 Reales cob. Crowned shield/pillars over waves (S)	**525.00**
1663 2 Escudos cob. Crowned shield/ cross, fleurs in angles (G)	**1,000.00**
1795 1 Real. Carlos IV/arms (S)	**25.00**
1777 1 Escudo. Carlos III/arms (G)	**90.00**

P

POPAYAN, COLOMBIA

	F
1810 1/2 Real. Ferdinand VII/arms (S)	**25.00**
1772 1 Real. Carlos III/arms (S)	**150.00**
1776 8 Escudos. Similar (G)	**475.00**
1814 8 Escudos. Ferdinand VII/arms (G)	**425.00**

 or P

POTOSI, BOLIVIA

	F
1662 1/2 Real cob. PHILIPVS monogram/ castles and lions in angles of cross (S)	**95.00**
1749 2 Reales cob. Pillars over waves/ cross, castles and lions in angles (S)	**45.00**
1648 8 Reales cob. Crowned shield/arms in octolobe (S)	**150.00**
1761 8 Reales cob. Pillars over waves/ cross, castles and lions in angles (S)	**135.00**
1770 1 Real. Two globes between pillars/ arms (S)	**27.50**
1770 8 Reales. Similar (S)	**150.00**
1799 1/4 Real. Lion/castle (S)	**15.00**
1808 1 Real. Carlos IV/arms (S)	**9.00**
1776 2 Reales. Charles III/arms (S)	**12.50**
1823 4 Reales. Ferdinand VII/arms (S)	**30.00**

	F
1795 8 Reales. Charles IV/arms (S)	**35.00**
1822 1 Escudo. Ferdinand VII/arms (G)	**300.00**
1784 2 Escudos. Charles III/arms (G)	**350.00**
1822 8 Escudos. Ferdinand VII/arms (G)	**550.00**

§

SANTIAGO, CHILE

	F
1792 1/4 Real. Carlos IV/castles and lions in angles of floral cross (S)	**17.50**
1810 2 Reales. Imaginary bust of Ferdinand VII/arms (S)	**35.00**
1797 8 Reales. Carlos III/arms (S)	**100.00**
1749 2 Escudos. Ferdinand VI/arms (G)	**1,000.00**
1810 2 Escudos. Bust of Carlos III with titles of Ferdinand VII/arms (G)	**400.00**

Z or ZS

ZACATECAS, MEXICO

	F
1820 1 Real. Ferdinand VII/arms (S)	**15.00**
1821 8 Reales.	**40.00**

PHILIPPINES

	F
1805 Octavo. Crowned shield/lion with two globes (C)	**55.00**

	VF
1868 10 Centavos. Isabel II/arms (S)	**12.00**
1864 20 Centavos. Similar (S)	**65.00**
1868 50 Centavos. Similar (S)	**15.00**
1868 2 Pesos. Similar (G)	**65.00**
1880 10 Centavos. Alfonso XII/arms (S)	**325.00**
1885 20 Centavos. Similar (S)	**8.00**
1885 50 Centavos. Similar (S)	**7.50**
1882 4 Pesos. Similar (G)	**750.00**
1897 Peso. Alfonso XIII/arms (S)	**30.00**

PUERTO RICO

	VF
(1884) 1/2 Dollar. Fleur-de-lis countermark on United States Liberty Seated half dollar (S)	*F* **250.00**

	VF		VF
1896 5 Centavos. Arms (S)	**45.00**	Hacienda Vega Redonda. 1890s 2 Almud token (Brass) *This is the most common of the many different Puerto Rican hacienda tokens. Most others are far scarcer.*	*EF* **16.00**
1896 10 Centavos. Alfonso XIII/arms (S)	**55.00**		
1895 20 Centavos. Similar (S)	**65.00**		
1896 40 Centavos. Similar (S)	**300.00**		
1895 Peso. Similar (S)	**325.00**		

SWITZERLAND

While the Swiss cantons (provinces) gradually formed a union during the 13th through 15th centuries, each one maintained its own coinage. During the early modern period, most had a range of small silver denominations, with some striking silver-dollar sized talers and gold. Copper was not generally favored, so very small denominations were usually struck in billon, a very base silver-copper alloy.

During the Napoleonic era, a Swiss Republic was established (1798-1803), and even after its demise, the various cantons maintained similar standards. After a new Swiss Confederation was founded, a uniform national coinage was created, replacing the issues of the cantons in 1850. It was based on the French franc, which became an international standard under the Latin Monetary Union.

Shooting competitions have for centuries been major events in Switzerland. Many of these festivities were commemorated, especially in the 19th century, by special silver talers and later 5 Franc pieces of very high artistic merit. These are much prized by collectors and should be examined carefully for signs of cleaning, which reduces their value.

The regular coinage of Switzerland is perhaps the most conservative in the world, reflecting its extreme stability and resistance to inflation. Bearing a female representation of Helvetia, the allegory of the nation, or the Swiss cross, the designs of many denominations have not changed in over 125 years. Like most countries, Switzerland moved from silver to base metal in 1968. Interestingly, Swiss coins rarely bear any language spoken in Switzerland. Because of the awkwardness of inscribing the coins in the four different languages spoken there, most coins are inscribed only in Latin. Switzerland in Latin is *Helvetia,* Swiss is *Helvetica.*

Additional Specialized Books: Meier, Albert. *HMZ Katalog.*

Known Counterfeits: Pre-1850 coins of Switzerland are not often counterfeited. Gold 20 Francs of the late 19th and 20th centuries should be examined with reasonable care. A partial list of years counterfeited include 1897, 1900, 1902-04, 1911, 1912, 1915, 1919, 1922, 1927, 1930, 1931, 1933, 1935, all with the B mint mark. The 1935 with the LB mint mark is an official restrike from 1945-47.

Zurich ca. 1628 3 Haller

Switzerland 1920 20 Rappen

CANTONAL ISSUES

	F

Aargau. 1811 5 Batzen. Shield/wreath (S)............................**12.50**

Appenzell. 1808 1 Batzen. Shield/wreath (Billon)........................**20.00**

Basel. 1749 1/4 Thaler. City view/Basilisk (S)............................**100.00**

Bern. 1809 1 Batzen. Shield/wreath (Billon)......................... **9.00**

Freiburg. 1830 5 Rappen. Shield/cross, C at center (Billon) **6.00**

Geneva. 1791 3 Sols. Shield/cross in quatrilobe (Billon)............... **8.50**

1840 1 Centime. Arms (C) **2.50**

Glarus. 1808 1 Schilling. Shield/wreath (Billon)........................**35.00**

Graubunden. 1842 1/6 Batzen. Three oval shields/wreath (Billon)........... **6.00**

Luzern. 1846 1 Rappen. Shield/wreath (C) **5.00**

Neuchatel. 1817 1 Kreuzer. Crowned arms/cross (Billon) **5.00**

St. Gall. 1790 6 Kreuzer. Bear l./wreath (Billon)........................ **17.50**

Schaffhausen. 1809 1/2 Batzen. Arms/ wreath (Billon) **22.00**

Schwyz. 1655 Schilling. Two-headed eagle/saint (Billon) **12.00**

Solothurn. 1830 2-1/2 Rappen. Shield/ cross, C at center (Billon) **6.00**

Thurgau. 1808 1 Kreuzer. Shield/wreath (Billon)........................**20.00**

Ticino. 1835 3 Soldi. Shield/wreath (Billon)......................... **7.00**

Unterwalden. 1812 1/2 Rappen. Shield/ wreath (Billon) **30.00**

	F

Uri. 1811 1/2 Rappen. Shield/wreath (Billon).......................**45.00**

Vaud. 1816 2-1/2 Rappen. Shield/wreath (Billon)........................ **10.00**

Zug. 1783 1 Schilling. Arms/Saint Wolfgang (Billon) **20.00**

Zurich. ca. 1628 3 Haller............ **4.00**

Zurich. 1842 2 Rappen. Arms/wreath (Billon)........................ **4.50**

1810 Ducat. Lion with shield (G) **600.00**

REPUBLIC

	F

1802 1 Rappen. Fasces/wreath (Billon) **7.50**

1801 10 Batzen. Figure with flag and sword/wreath (S)............. **75.00**

CONFEDERATION

	VF

1895 1 Rappen. Arms/wreath (C) **6.00**

1910 1 Rappen. Same (C)........... **8.00**

1899 2 Rappen. Similar (C)......... **6.00**

1942 5 Rappen. Head of Helvetia (CN)........................... **1.00**

1850 10 Rappen. Arms/wreath (Billon)....................... **15.00**

1907 20 Rappen. Head of Helvetia (N) **1.50**

1920 20 Rappen. Same (N) .... **.50**

1906 1/2 Franc. Helvetia stg./wreath (S) **2.00**

Switzerland 1950 5 Francs

Switzerland 1984 5 Francs

Switzerland 1956 1 Franc

Switzerland 1963 5 Francs

Switzerland 2003 20 Francs

	VF
1894 1 Franc. Similar (S)	**10.00**
1907 1 Franc. Similar (S)	**5.00**
1939 2 Francs. Similar (S)	**2.25**
1865 5 Francs. Woman and child/shield in cross (S)	**125.00**
1934 5 Francs. 18th century soldier/arms (S)	*Unc.* **60.00**
1950 5 Francs. William Tell/shield (S)	**6.50**
1883 20 Francs. Head of Helvetia/wreath (G)	**70.00**

	Unc.
1963 2 Rappen. Cross/wheat ear (C)	**.45**
1993 5 Rappen. Head of Helvetia/wreath (CN)	**.20**
1956 1 Franc. Helvetia stg./wreath (S	**4.50**
1967 1 Franc. Helvetia stg./wreath (S)	**3.50**
1963 5 Francs. Red Cross commemorative. Nurse and patients in form of cross (S)	**10.00**
1984 5 Francs. High altitude balloon and deep water submarine (CN)	**7.00**
1922 10 Francs. Bust of Helvetia/radiant cross (G)	**70.00**
2003 20 Francs. Skier (S)	**22.00**

AFRICAN COINS

Coinage largely did not come to sub-Saharan Africa until the colonial era, when Europeans introduced it extensively for their territories, which at first lay along the coast, and later stretched inland. There were, however, some earlier exceptions. The most important and distinctive coinage of early sub-Saharan Africa was that of the ancient kingdom of Axum, located in present-day Ethiopia.

Beginning ca.270 and continuing as late as ca.640, the coins of this African monarchy were always of small size, but were struck in all three classical metals: gold, silver, and bronze. Its most unusual and impressive feature was the use of a gold inlay on many of the bronze coins. Sometimes this was just a dot in the center, other times a large area surrounding the king's bust. When intact, these inlays always make for a dramatic appearance.

Another notable feature of Axumite coinage is the first use of Christian symbolism as the primary motif of the design. The cross became quite common on these pieces. Also of interest was the use of Ge'ez, the distinctive Axumite alphabet which today has the distinction of being the alphabet frequently used in Ethiopia for liturgical purposes.

Just because coins came late to Africa does not mean the region did without currency. Many distinctive forms of exchange existed, and they are today a collecting field unique to itself. Broadly speaking, three of the most common categories of this money were cowries, beads, and metal objects of various forms, Cowrie shells constitute a primitive form of currency common to most continents. They were traded in Asia, the Pacific, and the Americas as well. Later they were replaced or supplemented by manufactured beads.

Trade beads were used as early as the 1400s in Niger, where they were made of terra cotta. Later more elaborate designs evolved in glass, simpler ones occasionally in stone. Many were made locally, and as trade with Europe expanded, more were imported.

By far the most famous currency of Africa is that of bronze and iron. The "kissie" or "Ghizzi" penny was popular among the Kissi, Bandi, Gbandia, Gola, Kpelle, Loma, Mandingo, and Mendi tribes living in the areas of modern Guinea, Liberia, and Sierra Leone. Used from the 1880s to the

1930s, they consisted of twisted rods of iron about 9" to 15" in length. One end was formed into a "T" and the other a paddle. Its strange shape ultimately derives from a hoe.

Another famous African metal trade currency were the various crosses of central Africa. Small H-shaped ingots and medium to large X-shaped ingots of copper were traded in Zambia and Katanga during the 1700s and 1800s.

A third class of metal trade goods was the bracelet. Originally of African manufacture, the Europeans quickly learned the utility of arriving with acceptable local currency and today most of the smaller, late forms of these "manillas" are actually believed to have been cast in Birmingham.

The first sub-Saharan countries to strike their own modern coins were, logically, the only two to avoid European colonization: Ethiopia and Liberia. Ethiopia's first modern coins were struck by King Menelik II who unified the country in the 1880s. Though there had long been a royal dynasty in Ethiopia, traditionally descended from the biblical King Solomon, before Menelik's reign actual power had been divided between local feudal princes.

The other country to strike early independent coinage, Liberia, was founded in 1822 as a refuge for freed American slaves. While the first Liberian cents of 1833 were distinctive in their design, later issues depicting a Liberty head looked more like United States patterns than African coins. It was, in fact, not until 1960 that Liberty took on African instead of European facial features.

A third independent African country, although not native in culture, also began issuing coins in 1874. This was the Dutch Zuid Afrikaansche Republiek (the Transvaal). Its coinage was short-lived, however, as the country was conquered by the British during the Boer War and incorporated into their empire in 1902.

Beginning in 1957, and finally completed in 1975, African countries began to gain their independence from the colonial powers. Most wasted little time in emphasizing their independence by exercising the sovereign prerogative of striking coins. Those new states not finding it useful to strike coins in quantity to circulate in commerce, at the very least struck them in limited numbers for presentation and commemorative purposes.

It is not unusual for central and west African countries not to strike their own coins for circulation. Many of these states have found benefit in belonging to one of two currency unions. A common currency throughout every country in such a union is used to facilitate both trade and economic stability.

The most common obverse design to be used on new African coinages was the portrait of a founding statesman. The coat of arms was also a common obverse, and when it was not used for that, often found its way onto the reverse. One of the most common motifs, however, is the wonderful proliferation of exotic animals that have graced African coins since the 1960s. Such devices have made even the circulation strikes of Africa popular with collectors worldwide.

Most of the precious metal coins of post-colonial Africa are struck solely for sale to collectors, and many are struck only in proof quality. Recently, countries such as Liberia and Somaliland, both caught in protracted civil wars, have started striking small denominations for export to collectors as well.

Specialized Books: Gill, Dennis. *The Coinage of Ethiopia, Eritrea and Italian Somalia*.

Krause, Chester and Mishler, Clifford. *Standard Catalog of World Coins*. 19th and 20th century volumes updated frequently.

Munro-Hay, Stuart and Juel-Jensen, Bent. *Aksumite Coinage*. Up-to-date scholarship on this frequently redated series.

Known counterfeits: The most commonly counterfeited African coins are the gold coins of Axum, and to an extent those in other metals. The most commonly counterfeited modern African coin is the gold Krugerrand of South Africa. Fraudulent pieces have been common since the 1970s, often cast, some with real gold shells around a tungsten core. Every example should be not only weighed, but also examined with a glass and given a "ring" test. Cast pieces will sound dull and have less resonance.

Angola 1999 50 Centimas

ANGOLA

	Unc.
1978 1 Kwanza, arms (CN)	**1.50**
(1977) 100 Kwanzas, arms (C)	**3.50**
1999 50 Centimas, arms (C clad St)	**1.00**

AXUM

	VF
Endybis, c.270-290. Bust between grain ears/similar (G, 16mm)	**950.00**
Ouazebas, c.400. Bust between grain ears/bust within circular gold inlay (C, 16mm)	F **85.00**
Kaleb, c.500-525. Bust in crown/bust in head cloth (S, 16mm)	**250.00**
Wazena, c.520. Bust holding barley/8-armed cross, gold inlay at center. (C, 16mm)	F **85.00**
Joel, c.550. Bust in crown/cross (C, 15mm)	F **75.00**

BENIN (DAHOMEY)

	Unc.
1971 1,000 Francs, Somba woman/arms (S)	PF **150.00**
1994 200 Francs, Tyrannosaurus Rex/arms (C)	**15.00**

BOTSWANA

	Unc.
1966 50 Cents, Seretse Khama/arms (S)	**5.00**
1991 1 Thebe, arms/head of Turako bird (AL)	**.30**

Central African States 2006 100 Francs

BURUNDI

	Unc.
1965 1 Franc, arms (B)	**3.00**
1993 1 Franc, arms (AL)	**1.25**
1965 10 Francs, King Mwanbutsa/arms (G)	**50.00**
1968 10 Francs, grain and bananas (CN)	**3.00**

CENTRAL AFRICAN STATES

	Unc.
1978 1 Franc, three giant eland (AL)	**2.00**
1961 50 Francs, similar (CN)	**10.00**
1968 100 Francs, similar (N)	**12.00**
2006 100 Francs, foliage (S)	**5.00**

CHAD

	Unc.
1970 100 Francs, Africa/Robert F. Kennedy (S)	PF **75.00**
1985 100 Francs, three giant eland (N)	**30.00**
1999 1,000 Francs. Galileo (S) PF only	**30.00**

Peoples Republic of Congo
1996 500 Francs

Equatorial Guinea 1970 75 Pesetas

DJibouti 1977 1 Franc

CONGO, Peoples Republic

	Unc.
1990 100 Francs, three giant eland (N)	**6.00**
1993 100 Francs, woman inscribing tablet/sailing ship (CN)	**10.00**
1996 500 Francs Same/Lionhead (S) .... *Proof Only*	**40.00**

CONGO, Democratic Republic (ZAIRE)

	Unc.
1965 10 Francs, lion face (AL)	**7.00**
1987 1 Zaire, President Mobutu (B) ..	**2.00**
1971 100 Zaires, same/Hotel Intercontinental (G) .... *PF*	**675.00**

DJIBOUTI

	Unc.
1977 1 Franc, arms/antelope bust (AL)	**2.50**
1991 100 Francs, arms/camels (CN) .	**5.50**

EQUATORIAL AFRICAN STATES

	Unc.
1990 1 Franc, three giant eland (AL)	**1.75**
1982 25 Francs, similar (ALB)	**2.25**
1977 500 Francs, woman r./stylized eland (CN)	**16.50**

EQUATORIAL GUINEA

	Unc.
1969 1 Peseta, tusks/arms (ALB)	**2.00**
1970 75 Pesetas Lenin (S) *Proof*	**21.50**
1970 100 Pesetas, arms and tusks/naked Maja (S) .... *PF*	**35.00**
1985 5 Francos, three eland (ALB) ...	**8.00**

ERITREA

	Unc.
1997 1 Cent, Soldiers with flag/antelope (N clad Steel)	**.25**

Ethiopia 1998 20 Birr

Gambia 1996 1 Dalasi

	Unc.
1997 25 Cents, same/zebra (N clad Steel)	1.00
1994 1 Dollar, arms/cheetah (CN)	8.00

ETHIOPIA

	VF
1892-93 1 Mahaleki, crown/inscription (S)	150.00
1897 1 Matonya, Menelik II/inscription (C)	8.00
1897 Birr, Menelik II/lion (C)	250.00
1903 1 Gersh, similar (S)	3.50
1897 1/4 Birr, similar (S)	10.00
1903 1 Birr, similar (S)	30.00
1925 1 Werk, Empress Zauditu/lion (G)	500.00
1931 50 Matonas, Haile Selassie crowned/lion (N)	2.50

	Unc.
1944 (1944-75) 1 Cent, Haile Selassie/lion (C)	.50
1944 (1952-53) 25 Cents, similar (C, scalloped and reeded)	3.00
1972 5 Dollars, similar (S)	PF 15.00
1966 100 Dollars, similar (G)	PF 550.00
1977 10 Cents, lion head/antelope (B)	1.50

	Unc.
1982 2 Birr, lion head/two soccer players (CN)	8.00
1998 20 Birr Children (S) *Proof Only*	50.00

GABON

	Unc.
1960 10 Francs, Leon Mba/arms (G)	PF 95.00
1984 100 Francs, three giant eland (N)	9.00

GAMBIA

	Unc.
1971 1 Butut, bust/peanuts (C)	.20
1971 1 Dalasi, bust/crocodile (CN)	7.50
1987 1 Dalasi, similar (CN, heptagonal)	5.50
1996 1 Dalasi. Arms/3 kings (CN)	16.50
1977 40 Dalasi, bust/aardvark (S)	24.00

GHANA

	Unc.
1958 3 Pence, Kwame Nkrumah/star (CN, scalloped)	1.00
1958 5 Shillings, same (S)	PF 12.50

Ghana 2003 10 Cedis

Kenya 2003 40 Shillings

	Unc.
1967 5 Pesewas, cocoa beans/arms (CN)	.75
1991 20 Cedis, cowrie/arms (N clad Steel)	1.00
1986 100 Cedis, drums/commonwealth games (S)	17.50
2003 10 Cedis. Arms/Gorillas (CN)	.75

GUINEA

	Unc.
1959 10 Francs, Ahmed Sekou Toure (ALB)	80.00
1962 1 Franc, similar (CN)	7.00
1971 1 Syli, bust l. (AL)	8.00
1985 5 Francs, arms/palm branch (B clad Steel)	1.00
1988 100 Francs, arms/basketball players (S)	65.00

GUINEA-BISSAU

	Unc.
1977 50 Centavos, arms/palm tree (AL)	9.00
(1995) 2000 Pesos, arms/agricultural scenes (N plated Steel)	17.50

IVORY COAST

	PF
1966 10 Francs, President Boigny/elephant (S)	PF 50.00
1966 similar (G)	525.00

KATANGA

	Circ.
1700s-1800s. Katanga cross or Baluba cross. Large X-shaped cast, copper cross, usually 9" across and 3" thick. Authentic ones usually have a raised central ridge. Used in Zambia and Angola also.	120.00
1961 1 Franc, Bananas/Katanga cross (C)	3.50

KENYA

	Unc.
1966 5 Cents, Jomo Kenyatta/arms (B)	1.00
1969 10 Cents, similar but legend around bust (B)	.65
1975 50 Cents, similar (CN)	.75
1980 1 Shilling, Daniel Arap Moi/arms (CN)	1.00
1994 10 Shillings, similar (B around CN)	4.50
	Unc.
1991 1,000 Shillings, similar (S). PF	275.00
2003 40 Shillings. Pres. Kibaki (B around CN)	6.00

LESOTHO

	Unc.
1979 1 Sente, King Moshoeshoe II/hut (B)	.40
1992 2 Lisente, arms/bull (B)	.75
1966 50 Licente, King Moshoeshoe I/arms (S)	10.00
1988 10 Maloti, Pope/arms (S) PF	45.00

Lesotho 1966 50 Licente

Liberia 1996 1 Dollar

LIBERIA

	VF
1833 1 Cent, Settler grasping tree, ship in distance (C)	**20.00**
1847 2 Cents, Liberty head in cap/palm tree (C)	**12.00**
1896 10 Cents, Liberty head/wreath (S)	**10.00**
193/ 1/2 Cent, elephant/palm tree (B)	**.25**

	Unc.
1968 1 Cent, elephant/palm tree and ship (C)	**.35**

	VF
2000 5 Cents, arms/dragon (AL)	**1.50**
1960 10 Cents, African Liberty/wreath (S)	**3.00**
1968 50 Cents, same (CN)	**1.50**
1995 1 Dollar, Captains James T. Kirk and Jean-Luc Picard/arms (CN)	**8.00**
1996 1 Dollar. Arms/fish (CN)	**27.50**
1964 20 Dollars, William V.S. Tubman/arms (G)	**275.00**

MALAWI

	Unc.
1964 1 Shilling, President Banda/corn (CNZ)	**1.50**
1971 1 Tambala, same/rooster (C)	**.75**
1995 5 Kwacha, President Muluzi/child reading (CN)	**8.50**

MALI

	Unc.
1961 5 Francs, hippopotamus head (AL)	**2.00**
1967 50 Francs, President Keita (G)	**PF 275.00**

MOZAMBIQUE

	Unc.
1975 5 Centimos, head r./plant (CZ)	**115.00**
1986 20 Meticais, arms/armored tank (AL)	**3.00**
1994 10 Meticais, arms/cotton plant (B clad Steel)	**1.25**

NAMIBIA

	Unc.

1993 10 Cents, arms/tree
(N plated Steel). **1.00**
1996 10 Dollars, arms/runner
and cheetah (S). . . . . *PF* **45.00**

NIGER

	PF

1300s-1400s Djenné beads. Narrow,
tubular terra cotta beads with tight
ridges, strand . . . . *Circ.* **20.00**
1960 500 Francs, President
Hamani/arms (S). **35.00**
1968 50 Francs, lion/arms (G) **450.00**

NIGERIA

	Unc.

1973 1/2 Kobo, arms (C) **3.50**
1991 1 Kobo, arms/oil wells
(C plated Steel). **25**
1993 1 Naira, arms/Herbert
Macaulay (N plated Steel) **1.75**

RWANDA

	Unc.

1965 1 Franc, head/arms (CN) **1.75**
1970 2 Francs, person pouring
grain/arms (AL, scalloped) **50**
1987 5 Francs, plant/arms (C) **1.85**
1990 2,000 Francs, Nelson
Mandela/arms (G). . . . . *PF* **200.00**

SIERRA LEONE

	Unc.

1964 1/2 Cent, Milton
Margai/two fish (C). **25**
1980 1/2 Cent, Siaka Stevens/arms (Unc.)
. . . . **1.00**
1978 10 Cents, Siaka
Stevens/arms (CN) **1.00**
1987 1 Leone, Joseph
Momoh/arms (B, octagonal) **1.50**
1998 10 Leones, arms/Princess
Diana (S). . . . . *PF* **42.50**

Somalia 1976 10 Senti

SOMALIA

	Unc.

1967 5 Centesimi, arms (B). **60**
1976 10 Senti, arms/lamb
(AL, polygonal) **35**
2000 10 Shillings, arms/snake (Steel)
. . . . **1.50**
1984 25 Shillings, arms/turtle (CN)
. . . .**20.00**

SOUTH AFRICA, Z.A.R.

	VF

1898 1 Penny, Paul Kruger/arms (C)
. . . . **3.00**
1897 6 Pence, Paul Kruger/wreath (S)
. . . . **3.00**
1874 1 Pond, Thomas
Burgers/arms (G) **3,000.00**
1900 1 Pond, Paul
Kruger/arms (G) **135.00**

SOUTH AFRICA, Republic

	Unc.

1963 Cent, Jan Van Riebeeck/two
sparrows confronted (B) **1.00**

Republic of South Africa 1990 1 Rand

Tanzania 1998 2,500 Shilingi

	Unc.
1961 1 Cent, Jan Van Riebeeck/wagon (B)	**1.50**
1969 1 Cent, similar/two sparrows (C)	**.50**
1971 2 Cents, arms/gnu (C)	**.35**
1978 5 Cents, arms/crane (N)	**.50**
1984 10 Cents, arms/aloe (N)	**.35**
1988 20 Cents, arms/protea (N)	**.60**
1992 50 Cents, arms/plant (B plated Steel)	**1.00**
1971 1 Rand, arms/Springbok (S)	**6.00**
1990 1 Rand arms/Springbok (S) *Proof*	**25.00**
1994 1 Rand, arms/building (S) *PF*	**22.50**
1994 5 Rand, similar (N plated C)	**5.50**

Above two for inauguration of Nelson Mandela.

1978 Krugerrand, Paul Kruger/Springbok (G, 1 ounce net)	**bullion + 3%**

SWAZILAND

	Unc.
1974 1 Cent, King Sobhuza II/pineapple (C)	**.20**
1996 20 Cents, King Msawati III/elephant (CN, scalloped)	**2.00**
1996 50 Cents, King Msawati III/arms (CN)	**3.75**

TANZANIA

	Unc.
1966 10 Senti, Julius Nyerere/ostrich (B)	**1.50**
1972 1 Shilingi, same/armswith torch (CN)	**1.50**
1992 20 Shilingi, Ali Hassan Mwinyi/ mother and baby elephants (N clad Steel)	**3.25**
1974 1500 Shilingi, Julius Nyerere/cheetah (G)	**420.00**
1998 2500 Shilingi, Arms/lions (S) *PF*	**100.00**

UGANDA

	Unc.
1966 10 Cents, tusks (C)	**.35**
1966 2 Shillings, arms/crowned crane (CN)	**5.00**
1987 10 Shillings, arms (Steel, heptagonal)	**3.50**
1993 10,000 Shillings,arms/Pope (S) *PF*	**37.50**

WEST AFRICA

	Circ.
1700s-early 1900s Aggry beads. Millefiore-type multicolored glass beads composed of cross-sections of component parts pressed against a central tube. Many are of Venetian manufacture	**each 3.00**

Zambia 1998 100 Kwacha

Zimbabwe 2001 5 Dollars

	Circ.
1700s-early 1900s Aggry beads. Similar but wholly extruded, not composite	**strand 15.00**
1500s-1948 Popo manilla. Cast bronze bracelet of varying size. They have an opening about 1/2" to 1-1/2" separating two enlarged flat ends. Mostly manufactured in Birmingham. At the time British colonial authorities forced their withdrawal they circulated at about 3 pence. 2" to 3-1/2"	**12.00**
Similar but 12" across	**150.00**
1880s-1930s Kissie penny. Twisted rod of iron 9" to 15" long. One end was formed into a "T" and the other a paddle.	**8.00**

WEST AFRICAN STATES

	Unc.
1961 1 Franc, Ibex/root (AL).	**.60**
1980 25 Francs, chemist/root (ALB). .	**1.75**
1972 5,000 Francs, root/seven shields (S)	**40.00**

ZAMBIA

	Unc.
1964 6 Pence, shield/morning glory (CNZ)	**1.20**
1968 1 Ngwee, Kenneth Kaunda/aardvark (C)	**.80**
1972 50 Ngwee, same/arms (CN, polygonal).	**4.00**
1992 5 Kwacha, arms/oryx (B)	**1.50**
1998 100 Kwacha, Arms/ antelopes (S)	**55.00**

ZIMBABWE

	Unc.
1600s-1700s, H-shaped cast, copper ingot of variable size, ranging from 1" to 12"	*Circ.* **125.00**
1980 1 Cent, ancient bird sculpture (C)	**.40**
1980 50 Cents, same/sunrise (CN) . . .	**2.25**
1996 10 Dollars, Victoria Falls Bridge/lions (S)	*PF* **40.00**
2001 5 Dollars, Ancient bird sculpture/ rhinoceros (Steel in brass)	**8.50**

ASIAN, NORTH AFRICAN & PACIFIC COINS

Most early Asian coins fit neatly into the category of either Islamic or Oriental. Some pieces, particularly those of Southern India and South East Asia, had a distinctive appearance reflecting neither of these influences. However, over the course of the 1800s, nearly all coinage based on these traditions, be they Islamic, Oriental, or local were replaced by machine-made European-style coinage. The images on these new, modern coins varied from an attempt to preserve traditional designs with modern forms, to overt imitation of European motifs.

Trends in Islamic coinage changed following the fall of the Ottoman Empire after World War I. Today, very few countries follow the strict Muslim prohibition from depicting persons or animals on coins. The traditional toughra symbol rarely appears these days and Turkey even abandoned the Arabic alphabet for the Roman one. Also, a great number of Islamic countries produce bilingual coins. Often, English or French appear on the coins in a secondary position to Arabic. This is almost always the case with commemorative coins, which are to a large extent produced for the international collector market.

It is ironic that the militant Taliban government of Afghanistan struck collector market commemoratives depicting ancient pagan deities while it was making plans to destroy the ancient statues of deities. Also Western A.D. calendar dates often supplement the Islamic A.H. date as the former is used in some Islamic countries for business purposes.

In the center of the Middle East is its one non-Moslem country, Israel. It was founded in 1948 as a safe haven for Jews persecuted throughout the world, and who sought to return to their biblical homeland. It is the only nation whose coins are inscribed in Hebrew, although Arabic and English are found on many issues as well. Israeli minor coins frequently have motifs from ancient Judaean coinage. The extensive series of commemoratives features an extremely diverse array of motifs, often rendered in modern styles of art. During the 1960s and 1970s, Israeli commemorative coins were so widely purchased by the collecting public that now the number of coins and mint sets available from that point in time greatly exceeds demand, resulting in very low prices. This was further complicated by the use of government issued holders composed of a plastic corrosive to the coins' surfaces. Lower mintages and distribution, especially during the 1990s have resulted in collector issues of somewhat more stable value.

Those looking for coinage struck by India before the colonial era will find listings for a sampling of numerous small states with unfamiliar names. This is because until 1947 India was not one unified country, but a group of hundreds of princely states. Even during the period of British rule, only about half the country was directly controlled by the crown. Princely states, from the size of a city to those larger than most modern countries, often struck their own coins.

The first ancient Indian coins were not struck with a pair of dies, like Western coins, nor cast in molds like Chinese coins. Instead they were impressed by several different punches on each side, each being some indication of sequence or authority. After the invasion of Alexander the Great, Western methods gradually took over. For a few hundred years after, most Indian coins were stylistic descendants of either Greek or Sassanian (Persian) coins. After the advent of Islam in the eighth century most of central and northern India, regardless of the religion of the population, used the Islamic-style coins discussed above. The largest states during this period were the Sultanate of Delhi, and later the Moghul Empire. While all this occurred, southern India followed a different course. Most of the coins of this region freely bore images, generally of Hindu deities or their symbols. Gold, silver, and copper were common in both the north and the south during most periods. Interestingly, however, Indian gold included very tiny pieces called *fanams*. Struck in great quantities by both princes and merchants, they were common from the 1600s to the 1800s, but some are much earlier.

By the 1700s, most Indian coins were very thick and were struck with dies larger than their blanks, thus only part of the design was impressed. The nickname for this style coin is "dump" coinage. Sometimes broad, ceremonial versions were struck of the very same coins. These are *nazarana* coins and are scarce for all but a few states. As time progressed, thinner European-style coins began to replace dump coinage. Also from the 1700s to the present century, designs consisting solely of inscriptions gradually gave way to images. In the case of one of the largest of the Muslim-ruled states, Hyderabad, the prohibition of living things resulted in beautiful architectual depictions, or a toughra similar to that of the Ottoman Empire.

It is interesting to note that Indian states coins are presently so poorly published and sparsely collected that completely uncataloged dates and varieties of many coins will occasionally sell for only a few dollars over the price a common one would fetch. Many of the silver and gold coins from this period bear small digs, called shroff marks, applied by bankers. If moderate, they only moderately reduce the value of coins in average condition.

After independence from Britain was achieved, the Indian subcontinent was divided into Bangladesh, the Republic of India, and Pakistan, with Ceylon, now Sri Lanka off the coast. India's coinage is among the most common in the world with massive mintages. Its designs almost always feature the Asoka Pillar, a third century B.C. sculpture featuring lions facing in four directions. Recent Pakistani coins have omitted English legends, but are characterized by the star and crescent motif. Both Bangladesh and India have used their coins extensively to promote increased agricultural production.

Until recently, Himalayan countries rarely placed portraits on their coins, but like non-Islamic India, they used religious symbols. Tibetan coins show some temporary Chinese influence in the 1800s. Other Central Asian countries during the medieval through early modern ages are properly discussed under Islamic coins. They then fell under Russian domination, first Czarist then Communist. Only Mongolia and Tuva maintained modern coinage during this period, that of the latter being quite scarce. After the fall of the Soviet Union, many of these areas resumed coinage, combining European style coinage with traditional artistic motifs.

Late in the 1800s, domestically made silver coins became common in China. These pieces struck with European-style machinery by the Imperial Government generally depicted a dragon, a motif picked up by Japan and Korea as well. As the Western-style silver became common, so Western-style copper coins, generally without a central hole, began to replace the old cast cash coins. All three monarchies frequently dated their coins by the regnal year of their emperors. China also used the traditional Oriental cyclical calendar. When the Republic replaced the Empire, portraits of politicians replaced the imperial dragon on silver, and flags replaced it on copper. Architecture also became common beginning in the 1940s, both in China and Japan. Today portraiture is not overwhelmingly favored in the Far East, but plants and animals have become popular, especially when they are symbolically significant.

In addition to China, discussed above, many other areas of Asia progressed through a stage of primitive implement money. What is unusual about some of this, is that it occasionally followed the initial introduction of coinage proper and continued in use concurrently with it. This is particularly true of South East Asia. Most of the coinage of Vietnam over the last several hundred years has been cast copper, although silver was slightly more common than in China. As European-style coinage was adopted in Southeast Asia, portraiture became common. Those depicted were usually kings in the case of Thailand and Cambodia, politicians in the case of Vietnam. This trend continued in the postwar era in many countries, although buildings, flora and fauna became common too, particularly with the independence of Indonesia, Malaysia, and Singapore. None of these countries have issued precious metal coinage for circulation since 1942.

Independent Pacific coinage is a relatively recent phenomenon. Many nations did not even begin coinage until the 1970s. All the circulating coins are base metal, and a large percentage of the coins in both base and precious metals are struck for international collector distribution, rather than circulation. Some countries, such as the Marshall Islands, have bolstered sales by making virtually false claims of legal tender status. As a result, many are traded today at a fraction of their nominal face values or issue prices.

Specialized Books: Bruce, Colin R., et al. *The Standard Guide to South Asian Coins and Paper Money.*

Haffner, Sylvia. *The History of Modern Israel's Money.*

Japanese Numismatic Dealers Association. *The Catalog of Japanese Coins and Banknotes* (Contains annually updated prices, in Japanese, but usable.)

Krause, Chester and Mishler, Clifford. *Standard Catalog of World Coins* (17th, 18th, 19th, and 20th century editions, frequently updated.)

Mitchiner, Michael. *Oriental Coins and their Values: The Ancient and Classical World.*

Mitchiner, Michael. *Oriental Coins and their Values: Non-Islamic and Colonial Series.*

Opitz, Charles. *Odd & Curious Money—Descriptions and Valuations.*

Known Counterfeits: Most portrait silver dollars of China have been extensively counterfeited. The ones depicting Sun Yat Sen are often less deceptive than the others. Dragon dollars and Yuan Shih Kai dollars (called by many Chinese "Fat Man" dollars) have been counterfeited by the thousands. Many have a grey cast or are of incorrect weight. Counterfeits of dragon coppers made originally to circulate are often worth more than the real thing. In addition there are now many fantasy "silver dollars" made of base metal, apparently originating in the same factories. Some feature completely new designs in the 1875 to 1930s style. Others are combinations of accurately engraved obverses and reverses, which were never originally combined. Be careful not to take these to be real rarities. If it is not in any of the books, there is a far better chance that it is fake than that no one has discovered it in the last century of study.

The Japanese 1000 Yen for the 1964 Olympics has been counterfeited. The details of the mountain differ. A number of experts have challenged the Japanese government's claims that counterfeits exist of the gold 100,000 Yen. Counterfeits exist of both the Japanese silver Yen of the Meiji reign and of the Korean silver Whan of the late 1800s.

There have been a number of circulating counterfeits made of Thailand's coins, particularly in the mid-1800s and 1970s. More dangerous counterfeits of rarer coins may also have been made to fool collectors.

A large percentage of 19th Century Annamese (Vietnamese) silver should be considered with doubt.

AFGHANISTAN, Kingdom

	VF
1289 AH 1 Rupee,	**10.00**
1306 SH 2-1/2 Afghani, Toughra/mosque (S)	**20.00**
	Unc.
1316 SH 2 Pul, Mosque (C)	**1.00**
	VF
1330 SH 50 Pul, Mosque (C)	**1.00**
1340 SH 5 Afghani, Bust of shah (N clad Steel)	**1.50**

Republic, 1973-78

	BU
1352 SH 25 Pul, State seal (B clad Steel)	**2.00**
1352 SH 50 Pul, State seal (C clad Steel)	**3.50**

Democratic Republic, 1978-92

	BU
1978 AD 500 Afghani, State seal/Siberian crane (S)	**25.00**
1357 SH 50 Pul, Inscribed wreath (ALB)	**2.50**

Afghanistan 1999 500 Afghanis

Algeria 2002 100 Dinars

Islamic State, 1992-2001

	BU
1999 50 Afghanis, State seal/Athena & Equestrian (CN)	**7.50**
1999 500 Afghanis, Arms/globe (S) PF.	**30.00**

Note: The Taliban Islamic State struck no coins for circulation, just for the collector market.

AJMAN

MEMBER OF UAE

	Unc.
1969 1 Riyal, Flags and bird (S)	**9.00**
1970 7 1/2 Riyals, Emir/falcon (S)	**55.00**

ALGERIA

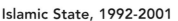

	Unc.
1354AH 5 Aspers, Inscriptions (base S or C)	VF **45.00**
1964 1 Centime, arms (AL)	**.25**
1964 50 Centimes, arms (ALB)	**1.00**
1974 5 Centimes, 1974-1977 inside gear (AL)	**.50**
1992 2 Dinars, camel head (Steel)	**5.00**
1979 10 Dinars, elaborate inscription (B)	**8.50**
1993 100 Dinars, horse head (Steel around ALB)	**22.50**
2002 100 Dinars, "40" (Steel around ALB)	**27.50**

Bahrain 1998 5 Dinars

BAHRAIN

	Unc.
1965 1 Fils, palm tree (C)	**.30**
1992 50 Fils, sailboats (CN)	**1.50**
1992 100 Fils, arms (B around CN)	**3.50**
1968 500 Fils, bust of Amir/arms (S)	**12.50**
2000 500 Fils, monument, STATE OF BAHRAIN (CN around Brass)	**6.00**
2002, same but KINGDOM OF BAHRAIN	**6.50**
1998 5 Dinars Amir/children (S) PF.	**40.00**

Bangladesh 2001 50 Poisha

Cambodia 1700s-1800s 2 Pe

Bhutan 1997 50 Ngultrum

BANGLADESH

	Unc.
1973 5 Poisha, state seal/hoe (AL, square)	.20
2001 50 Poisha. Same/foods (Steel)	1.50
1975 Taka, state seal/family (CN)	1.00
1992 Taka, state seal/runners (S) PF	32.50

BHUTAN

	VF
1835-1910 Deb Rupee, crude inscriptions in three registers (C)	3.50
(1928) 1/2 Rupee, king/symbols in nine compartments (S)	15.00
(1928-68) same but (N)	1.00

	Unc.
1975 5 Chetrums, king/wheel (AL, square)	.20
1974 20 Chetrums, farmer/four-fold ornament (ALB)	.50
1997 50 Ngultrum, dragons, mansion (S)	Proof 20.00
1995 300 Ngultrum, dragons/Dag Hammarskjold (S)	Proof 37.50

BURMA

PRESENTLY MYANMAR

	VF
1781 ¼ Pe, two fish (C)	145.00
1852 Rupee, peacock (S)	12.50

	Unc.
1952 1 Pya, lion (C)	.35
1966 25 Pya, Gen. Aung San (AL)	1.00
1953 1 Kyat, lion (CN)	3.00
1975 1 Kyat, rice plant (B)	2.00

CAMBODIA

	VF
802-1450AD Unit, dot and crescent pattern (Lead, hole)	5.00
1700s-1800s 2 Pe, bird (Billon)	10.00
1860 5 Cent, Norodom I/arms (C)	12.00

	Unc.
1959 10 Sen, bird (AL)	.65
1970 1 Riel, Angkor Wat (CN)	16.50
1974 10,000 Riels, bust of Lon Nol (S)	115.00
1979 5 Sen, arms (AL)	3.00
1993 4 Riels, flag/dinosaur (CN)	25.00
1994 100 Riels, Angkor Wat (Steel)	.50

CHINA, Empire

	VF
Anhwei 1902-1906 10 Cash, Dragon (C)	6.00
1 struck cash, four characters/two characters (Brass, round hole)	2.00
Peking 1851-1861 100 Cash (B)	50.00
Fukien 1896-1903 20 Cents, dragon (S)	6.00

China, Empire-Peking 1851-1861 100 Cash

China, Empire-Province Issue
Anhwei 1902-1906 10 Cash

	VF
Kiangsi 1890s 10 Cash, dragon (C)	**2.00**
Kwangtung 1890-1908 10 Cent, dragon (S)	**4.00**
Pei Yang (Chihli) 1908 Dollar, dragon, 34th year (S)	**15.00**
Taiwan, (1894) 10 Cents, dragon (S)	**175.00**
Szechuan 1906 10 Cash, Dragon (C)	**3.00**
Szechuan (1901-08) Dollar, dragon (S)	**25.00**

CHINA, Republic (General Issues)

	VF
1916 1/2 Cent, diamond with border of buds (C, holed)	**10.00**
1936 1/2 Cent, sun/ancient spade money (C)	**1.50**
Ca. 1920 10 Cash	**1.50**
(1912-27) 10 Cash, crossed flags (C)	**1.00**
1936 1 Cent, sun/Ancient spade money (C)	**.75**
1940 1 Cent, ancient spade money (AL)	**.25**
(1912-27) 20 Cash, crossed flags (C)	**2.50**
1933 2 Cents, diamond with border of buds (C, holed)	**60.00**
1936 5 Cents, Sun Yat-sen/ancient spade money (N)	**1.00**
1940 5 Cents, ancient spade money (AL)	**.60**

	VF
1914 1 Chiao, bust of Gen. Yuan Shi-kai (S)	**10.00**
1941 10 Cents, Sun Yat-sen/ancient spade money (CN)	**1.50**
1926 20 Cents, phoenix and dragon (S)	**15.00**
1927 20 Cents, Sun Yat-sen facing/crossed flags (S)	**25.00**
1914 1/2 Dollar, Yuan Shi-kai/wreath (S)	**30.00**
1942 1/2 Dollar, Sun Yat-sen/ancient spade money (CN)	**3.00**
1914 Dollar, Yuan Shi-kai/wreath (S)	**12.50**
1917 Dollar, Yuan Shi-kai in high hat/dragon (S)	**250.00**
(1912-27) Dollar, Sun Yat-sen/MEMENTO over wreath (S)	**10.00**
1932 Dollar, Sun Yat-sen/junk sailing into sunrise, birds over head (S)	**200.00**
1934 Dollar, similar but no birds or sun (S)	**12.50**
1916 10 Dollars, Yuan Shi-kai/dragon (G)	**2,000.00**

CHINA, Republic (Province Issues)

	VF
Chekiang 1924 10 Cents, crossed flags (S)	**7.00**
Fengtien 1929 1 Cent, sun over wreath (C)	**3.00**

China, Empire-Province Issue
Szechuan 1906 10 Cash

China, Republic-General Issue
ca. 1920 10 Cash

China, Republic-Province Issue
Kwangtung 1 Cent

China, Republic of Taiwan 1981 5 Dollars

	VF
Fukien 1923 20 Cents, three flags (S)	**7.00**
Honan (1912-27) 10 Cash, crossed flags (C)	**1.50**
Hunan (1912-27) 10 Cash, star (C)	**4.00**
Kansu 1928 Dollar, Sun Yat-sen/star (S)	**300.00**
Kiangsi 1912 10 Cash, star (C)	**5.00**
Kwangsi 1926 20 Cents, "20" (S)	**6.50**
Kwangtung 1919 20 Cents, "20" (S)	**1.25**
Kwangtung 1 Cent, value (C)	**5.00**
Kweichow 1928 Dollar, automobile (S)	**550.00**
Shensi (1928) 2 Cents, crossed flags and IMTYPEF (C)	**35.00**
Singkiang 1949 Dollar, value (S)	**30.00**
Szechuan 1912 Dollar, seal script (S)	**20.00**

CHINA, Republic of Taiwan

	Unc.
1949 1 Chiao, Sun Yat-sen/map of Taiwan (C)	**4.00**
1954 5 Chiao, similar (B)	**1.00**
1960 1 Dollar, flowers (CNZ)	**.50**
1970 5 Dollars, Chaing Kai-shek left (CN)	**.80**
1981 5 Dollars, Same (CN)	**.50**
1989 10 Dollars, Chaing Kai-shek facing (CN)	**.65**
2000 10 Dollars, Dragon/stylized dragon (CN)	**3.00**
1965 100 Dollars, Sun Yat-sen/deer (S)	**25.00**

CHINA, Peoples Republic

	Unc.
1976 1 Fen, arms (AL)	**.50**
1956 2 Fen, arms (AL)	**1.50**

China, Peoples Republic
1986 5 Yuan

Egypt 1938 1 Millieme

	Unc.
1986 5 Fen, arms (AL)	.45
1992 1 Jiao, arms/flower (AL)	.50
1980 1 Yuan, great wall (CN)	2.00
1986 5 Yuan Great wall/ship (BU)	35.00
1995 5 Yuan, monkey (C)	10.00
1995 10 Yuan, building/two pigs (S, scalloped)	PF 100.00
1996 20 Yuan, city gate/Yangtze river (S, rectangular)	PF 60.00
1989 100 Yuan, arms/snake (Platinum)	PF 900.00
1991 10,000 Yuan, Temple of Heaven/ panda encircled by coins (G), Proof only	120,000.00

DARFUR

PRESENTLY PART OF SUDAN

	F
1327AH, Piastre, Toughra in border (base S)	40.00

These coins are thin and crude.

EGYPT, British Occupation Issues

	VF
1917 1/2 Millieme, inscription (C)	3.50
1916 5 Milliemes, inscription (CN, hole	5.00

	VF
1917 2 Piastres, inscription (S)	2.50
1916 100 Piastres, inscription (G)	120.00

Fuad I, 1917-36

	VF
1935 1 Millieme, King Fuad (C)	.50
1935 5 Milliemes, King Fuad (CN)	1.00
1923 10 Piastres, King Fuad (S)	12.50
1930 50 Piastres, King Fuad (G)	70.00

Farouk I, 1936-52

1938 1 Millieme	2.50

	VF
1938 5 Milliemes, King Farouk (C, scalloped)	1.00
1938 10 Milliemes, King Farouk (C, Scalloped edge)	1.00
1941 10 Milliemes, King Farouk (CN)	1.00
1944 2 Piastres, King Farouk (S, hexagonal)	1.00
1938 100 Piastres, King Farouk (G)	150.00

Republic 1952-58

	Unc.
1956 1 Millieme, Sphinx (ALB)	5.00
1955 10 Piastres, Sphinx (S)	18.00
1957 25 Piastres, ancient Egyptian (S)	22.00
1958 1/2 Pound, ancient chariot (G)	185.00

United Arab Republic 1958-71

	Unc.
1962 2 Milliemes, falcon (ALB)	.60
1958 20 Milliemes, gear (ALB)	5.00

Hejaz 1334 AH 20 Piastres

Egypt 1992 10 Piastres

	Unc.
1960 5 Piastres, falcon (S)	**5.00**
1964 5 Piastres, dam (S)	**4.00**
1967 10 Piastres, falcon (CN)	**2.00**
1970 25 Piastres, Nasser (S)	**6.50**
1970 1 Pound, mosque (S)	**10.00**
1960 5 Pounds, dam (G)	**600.00**

Arab Republic 1958-71

	Unc.
1975 5 Milliemes, Nefertiti (B)	**.30**
1984 1 Piastre, Toughra/pyramids (ALB)	**.20**
1972 5 Piastres, falcon (CN)	**2.00**
1977 10 Piastres, clasped hands (CN)	**2.25**
1980 10 Piastres, Sadat (CN)	**3.50**
1992 10 Piastres, mosque (CN)	**1.25**
1973 1 Pound, dam (S)	**9.00**
1980 1 Pound, fist (S)	**8.00**
1994 5 Pounds, ancient hippopotamus figure (S)	PF **42.50**
1983 100 Pounds, Nefertiti (G)	PF **575.00**

FUJAIRAH
MEMBER OF UAE

	Unc.
1969 2 Riyals, Richard Nixon (S)	PF **28.50**
1969 10 Riyals, Apollo XI astronauts (S)	Proof **55.00**
1970 25 Riyals, Richard Nixon (G)	PF **140.00**

HEJAZ
PRESENTLY PART OF SAUDI ARABIA

	VF
(c.1916-20) 40 para countermark on Ottoman 40 para (N)	**25.00**
1334AH, year 5, 1/4 Piastre, Circle in X, inscriptions in spaces (C)	**20.00**
1334AH, year 8, 20 Piastres, inscriptions (S)	**100.00**

INDIA, ANCIENT
PRESENTLY PARTS OF INDIA, PAKISTAN, AND BANGLADESH

	F
Magadha, 462-414 BC, Karshapana, various punchmarks (S)	**25.00**
Mauryan Empire, c.272-232 BC, Karshapana, various punchmarks (S)	**20.00**
Nagas of Narwar, Unit, c.340 AD, bull/inscription (C, 10mm)	**9.00**
Indo-Sassanian, 800-950 AD, Drachm, peanut-shaped head/fire-altar composed of dots (S)	**20.00**
Hindu Shahis, 750-850 AD, Jital, bull/horseman (S)	**20.00**

	F
Hindu Shahis, 850-1008 AD, Jital, similar but linear style (S)	**15.00**
Delhi Rajas, 1100s, Jital, similar but smaller (base S or C)	**6.00**
Cholas of Tanjore, 985-1014 AD, Unit, leaping figure/enthroned figure (C, 17mm)	**9.00**
Vijayanagar, 1509-29, Unit, bull (C, 15mm)	**8.00**

INDIAN STATES

PRESENTLY PARTS OF INDIA, PAKISTAN, AND BANGLADESH

	VF
Assam 1818 Rupee, four lines Sanskrit inscription each side (S, octagonal)	**50.00**
Baroda 1885 Paisa, horse hoof over sword (C)	**1.25**
Bijapur 1600s, leaf containing dot pattern both sides (C)	**5.00**
Bikanir 1937 Rupee, facing bust (S)	**16.50**
Dungarpur 1944 Paisa, arms (C, square)	**25.00**

	F
Gwalior 1942 1/4 Anna, bust left (C)	**.60**
Hyderabad 1364 AH, 2 Pai, inscriptions (C, holed)	**.25**
___. 1362 AH, Rupee, building with two towers (S)	**6.50**
Indore 1935 1/4 Anna, facing bust (c)	**2.00**
___. 1902 1/2 Anna, bull (C)	**4.00**
Jaipur 1944 1 Anna, bust/branch (B)	**.40**
Jaora 1893 Paisa, flag (C)	**6.50**
Kachar 1601-11 1/4 Rupee, three lines Sanskrit inscription each side (S)	**50.00**
Kutch 1928 5 Kori, Inscriptions (S)	**21.50**
Mewar 1928 Rupee, city walls (S)	**10.00**
Mysore 1700s Kasu, elephant/Grid pattern (C)	**5.00**
Mysore 1800s Fanam, stylized Narasimha (G)	**13.50**
Nawanagar 1570-1850 Dokdo, barbarized inscription (C)	**1.50**
Pudokkatai 1889-1906 1 Cash, Goddess Brihadamba (C)	**.50**

	F
Tonk 1932 Pice, arms/leaf (C)	**1.00**
Travancore (1790-1895) Fanam, design rendered in series of dots and lines (G)	**12.50**
Travancore (1938-49) 1 Cash, conch shell (C)	**.25**
Tripura 1934 Rupee, lion (S)	**37.50**

INDIA

	Unc.
1950 1 Pice, Asoka pillar/horse (C)	**1.50**
1954 1 Anna, similar/bull (CN, scalloped)	**1.25**
1950 1 Rupee, similar/two ears of grain (N)	**4.50**
1972 1 Paisa, Asoka pillar (AL, square)	**.50**
1961 2 Paise, similar (CN, scalloped)	**.80**
1970 3 Paise, similar (AL, hexagonal)	**.50**
1957 5 Paise, similar (CN, square)	**1.00**
1993 10 Paise, similar (Steel)	**.35**
1968 20 Paise, similar/Lotus (ALB)	**1.50**
1996 25 Paisa, Rhinoceros/Asoka pillar (Steel)	**.35**
1972 50 Paise, couple with flag/similar (CN)	**.85**
1964 1 Rupee, Nehru/similar (N)	**2.00**
1991 1 Rupee, Rajiv Gandhi/similar (CN)	**.60**
1997 1 Rupee, Asoka pillar/two ears of grain (Steel)	**.30**
1994 2 Rupees, water drop/Asoka pillar (CN)	**2.00**
1997 2 Rupees, map/similar (CN)	**.40**

	Unc.
(1985) "1984" 5 Rupees, Indira Gandhi/similar (CN)	**3.00**
1994 5 Rupees	**1.50**
(1969-70) 10 Rupees, Mahatma Gandhi/similar (S)	**6.00**
1974 10 Rupees, family in triangle/similar (CN)	**4.50**
1986 20 Rupees, fishermen/similar (S)	**10.00**
1975 50 Rupees, woman and ear of grain/similar (S)	**11.50**
1982 100 Rupees, games logo/similar (S)	**17.50**

INDONESIA

	Unc.
1952 1 Sen, rice (AL, hole)	1.00
1970 1 Rupiah, bird (AL)	.25
1971 10 Rupiah, wreath (CN)	.45
1991 100 Rupiah, eagle/cow racing (ALB)	.75
1993 1,000 Rupiah, eagle/tree (CN around B)	4.00
1974 100,000 Rupiah, eagle/Komodo dragon (G)	450.00

IRAN,

QAJAR DYNASTY, TO 1925

	VF
1295AH 50 Dinars, sunface (C)	20.00
1332AH 50 Dinars, wreath/lion and sun (CN)	2.00
1323AH 1,000 Dinars, Shah with large moustache/lion and sun (S)	30.00
1342AH 5000 Dinars, Shah with fat cheeks/lion and sun (S)	15.00
1228 AH 1 Toman (F)	90.00
1343AH 1 Toman, same/wreath (G)	50.00

Pahlavi dynasty, 1925-79

	XF
1304SH 1 Kran, inscription/lion and sun (S)	10.00
1306SH 2 Kran, Reza Shah/lion and sun (S)	8.00
1310SH 1 Dinar, lion and sun (C)	30.00
1320SH 10 Dinars, similar (ALB)	2.00
1311SH 1 Rial, similar (S)	5.00
1346SH 10 Rials, Shah/lion and sun in wreath (CN)	1.00
1338SH 10 Rials, similar but FAO under lion (CN)	1.00
1971AD 100 Rials, ruins of Persepolis (S)	PF 25.00
1352 1 Pahlavi, Shah/lion in wreath (G)	120.00

Islamic Republic

	Unc.
1358SH 50 Dinars, lion and sun without crown (B)	25.00

Iran 1383 500 Rials

	Unc.
1371 5 Rials, Tomb of Hafez (B)	2.75
1370 50 Rials, oil refinery/map (CN)	7.50
1372 100 Rials, Shrine (CN)	6.50
1383 500 Rials, Birds & flowers (CN around ALB)	8.50
1375 1 Azadi, Mosque/Khomeini (G)	125.00

IRAQ
Kingdom

	VF
1933 1 Fils, Faisal I (C)	3.00
1932 1 Riyal, Faisal I (S)	15.00
1938 4 Fils, Ghazi I (C)	1.00
1938 20 Fils, Ghazi I (S)	3.00
1953 100 Fils, Faisal II (S)	7.50

Republic

	Unc.
1959 1 Fils, grain in star (C, polygonal)	.75
1971 5 Fils, palm trees (Steel, scalloped)	.75
1970 100 Fils, similar (CN)	1.50
1973 1 Dinar, oil tanker (S)	20.00
1981 1 Dinar, Saddam Hussein and airplanes (N)	20.00
1971 5 Dinars, two soldiers (G)	225.00

ISRAEL

	Unc.
1949 25 Mils, grapes (AL)	25.00
1949 1 Prutah, anchor (AL)	2.00

Israel 1952 10 Prutah

Israel 1984 10 Sheqalim

Israel 1980 1 New Agorah

Israel 1995 10 New Sheqalim

	Unc.
1949 5 Prutah, lyre (C)	2.50
1952 10 Prutah, ancient jug (AL, scalloped)	2.50
1954 100 Prutah, date palm (N clad Steel)	3.00
1949 500 Prutah, three pomegranates (S)	25.00
1965 1 Agorah, three ears of grain (AL, scalloped)	.25
1979 1/2 Lirah, menorah (CN)	.50
1967 10 Lirot, sword and olive branch/ Western Wall (S)	8.00
1969 10 Lirot, helmet and inscription (S)	10.00
1974 25 Lirot, David Ben-Gurion/Menorah (S)	10.00
1980 1 New Agorah, date palm (AL)	.10
1982 1/2 Sheqel, lion (CN)	.50
1984 1 Sheqel, Theresianstadt lamp (S)	15.00
1984 10 Sheqalim, Ancient ship (CN)	1.50
1984 100 Sheqalim, ancient coin with menorah (CN)	2.00
1986 1 New Sheqel, lily (CN)	1.50
1988 1 New Sheqel, Maimonides (N)	1.75
1996 1 New Sheqel, Yitzak Rabin (S)	30.00
1998 1 New Sheqel, Noah (S)	25.00
1995 10 New Sheqalim, date palm (Bimetallic)	7.00
1991 10 New Sheqalim, Jumbo jet and immigrants (G)	PF 395.00

JAPAN
Meiji

治 明

(JAPANESE FOR MEIJI),
1867 = YEAR 1

	VF
1883 1 Rin, chrysanthemum (C)	6.00
1875 1 Sen, dragon (C)	2.00
1889 5 Sen, sunburst (CN)	5.00
1907 20 Sen, sunburst (S)	5.50
1905 50 Sen. dragon (S)	10.00
1903 1 Yen, dragon (S)	27.50
1873 5 Yen, dragon/sunburst, wreath and banners (G)	1,000.00
1876 Trade Dollar, dragon (S)	650.00

Taisho

正 大

(JAPANESE FOR TAISHO),
1912 = YEAR 1

	VF
1916 5 Rin, Paulowina crest (C)	1.00
1913 1 Sen, sunburst (C)	3.00
1917 10 Sen, sunburst (S)	2.00
1925 50 Sen, sunburst/two phoenixes (S)	1.50

Japan 1905 50 Sen

Japan 1977 100 Yen

Showa

和 昭

**(JAPANESE FOR SHOWA),
1926 = YEAR 1**

	Unc.
1941 1 Sen, Mt. Fuji (AL)	**.50**
1938 10 Sen, cherry blossom/Waves (ALB, hole)	**4.75**
1946 50 Sen, Phoenix (B)	**2.50**
1968 5 Yen, rice plant (B)	**.15**
1978 50 Yen, chrysanthemums (CN, hole)	**1.00**

	Unc.
1958 100 Yen, phoenix (S)	**6.00**
1977 100 Yen, bridge/chrysanth. (CN)	**6.00**
1964 1,000 Yen, Mt. Fuji (S)	**40.00**
1986 100,000 Yen, chrysanthemum/two phoenixes (G)	**1,250.00**

Heisei

平 成

**(JAPANESE FOR HEISEI),
1989 = YEAR 1**

	Unc.
1990 Yen, sapling (AL)	**.10**
1997 10 Yen, temple (C)	**.45**
1994 50 Yen, chrysanthemums (CN, hole)	**1.00**
1989 500 Yen, Paulowina (CN)	**10.00**
1993 5,000 Yen, chrysanthemum/two cranes (S)	**70.00**

Jordan 2000 5 Piastres

JORDAN

	Unc.
1949 1 Fils, crown (C)	**2.25**
same but Fils misspelled "Fil"	**3.50**
1975 50 Fils, King Hussein (CN)	**1.25**
1977 2-1/2 Dinars, King Hussein/gazelle (S)	**22.00**
1995 1 Dinar, similar/FAO logo (B)	**10.00**
1981 60 Dinars, similar/Palace of Culture (G)	*PF* **250.00**
2000 5 Piastres, King Abdullah (N clad Steel)	**2.00**

KAZAKHSTAN

	Unc.
1993 2 Tyin, arms (B)	**.45**

Kazakhstan 2000 50 Tenge

Noth Korea 1997 10 Won

Kiribati 1997 5 Dollars

	Unc.
1995 20 Tenge, arms/U.N. logo (CN)	3.50
1996 20 Tenge, arms/musician (CN)	3.50
2000 50 Tenge, arms/mosque (CN)	3.00
1995 100 Tenge, arms/old man and hut (S)	PF 35.00

KIRIBATI

	Unc.
1979 5 Cents, arms/Tokai lizard (CN)	1.50
1979 1 Dollar, arms/outrigger sailboat (CN)	4.00
1997 5 Dollars, arms/castle (S) PF	40.00

KOREA

	VF
1898 5 Fun, two dragons (C)	4.00
1910 10 Chon, dragon (S)	18.00
1893 1 Whan, two dragons (S)	5,900.00

KOREA, NORTH

	Unc.
2002 1/2 Chon, arms/snake (AL)	1.25
1959 1 Chon, arms (AL)	1.00
1987 1 Won, building/arms (AL)	3.50
1995 10 Won, arms/cartoon cat (CN)	15.00
1997 10 Won, flower/arms (S)	55.00

KOREA, SOUTH

	Unc.
1959 100 Hwan, Syngman Rhee/two phoenixes (CN)	6.00
1978 1 Won, rose of Sharon (AL)	.15
1973 50 Won, rice plant (CN)	3.50
1983 50 Won, similar	.45
1983 500 Won, Manchurian crane (CN)	2.50

South Korea 1998 10,000 Won

	Unc.
1984 10,000 Won, cross/saints (S)	**20.00**
1998 10,000 Won, logo (S)	**35.00**

KURDISTAN

	Unc.
2003 1 Dinar, mountains/Saladin on horse (C)	**5.00**

This fantasy was struck privately in the United States, with the endorsement of certain Iraqi Kurdish exiles.

KUWAIT

	BU
1976 1 Fils, ship (B)	**.50**
1962 50 Fils, ship (CN)	**1.25**
1976 2 Dinars, two busts/oil well and ship (S)	**42.50**

LAHEJ

	VF
(1860) 1/2 Baisa, inscriptions (C)	**35.00**

LAOS

	Unc.
1952 20 Cents, elephants (AL)	**1.50**
1971 2,500 Kip, king/arms (S)	**35.00**

Laos 1995 50 Kip

Lebanon 2002 25 Livre

	Unc.
1980 20 Att, arms/plower (AL)	**.85**
1995 50 Kip, Dinosaur (S) *PF*	**30.00**

LEBANON

	VF
1925 1 Piastre, wreath/lion heads (CN, hole)	**7.50**
1925 2 Piastres, cedar/phoenician ship (B)	**8.00**
1929 25 Piastres, cedar/two cornucopias (S)	**7.00**
	Unc.
1955 1 Piastre, wreath (ALB, hole)	**.25**
1975 10 Piastres, cedar (B)	**.20**
1952 50 Piastres, cedar (S)	**3.50**
	VF
1968 1 Livre, cedar/fruit (N)	**3.00**
2002 25 Livre, value (N clad Steel)	**1.50**
1980 400 Livre, monogram/Olympic logo (G)	*PF* **600.00**

Malaysia 2003 1 Sen

LIBYA

	Unc.
1952 1 Millieme, King Idris (C)	.50
1952 5 Milliemes, King Idris (C)	1.00
1965 10 Milliemes, crowned arms (CN)	.50
1975 10 Dirhams, eagle (CN clad Steel)	2.75
1979 100 Dirhams, horseman with rifle (CN)	15.00
1981 70 Dinars, hands embracing handicapped symbol/logo (G)	.450.00

MALAYSIA

	Unc.
Malacca 1247AH 1 Keping, rooster (C)	VF 5.00
1967 1 Sen, building (C)	.15
1989 5 Sen, top (CN)	.15
1993 1 Ringgit, dagger and scabbard (B)	2.00
1976 500 Ringgit, Malayan Tapir (G)	580.00
2003 1 Sen. Drum (C clad Steel)	.25

MARSHALL IS.

	Unc.
1986 1 Dollar, arms/Triton shell (S)	PF 25.00
1988 5 Dollars, arms/space shuttle Discovery (CN)	4.00
1989 5 Dollars, arms/man on moon (CN)	4.50
1993 10 Dollars, arms/Elvis Presley (B)	16.50
1995 50 Dollars, arms/Marilyn Monroe (S)	PF 56.00
1993 50 Dollars, arms/dolphins (S)	40.00

Marshall Islands 1993 50 Dollars

MECCA,

PRESENTLY PART OF SAUDI ARABIA

	VF
1344AH, year 2, 1/2 Ghirsh, Toughra (C)	25.00

MESOPOTAMIA,

PRESENTLY IRAQ

	F
1223AH, year 26, 5 Piastres, Toughra (Billon)	60.00
1231AH 5 para, name in interlocking squares (C)	60.00

MONGOLIA

	XF
1925 1 Tugrik, national emblem (S)	22.50
1937 20 Mongo, similar (CN)	10.00
1937 5 Mongo, similar (ALB)	6.00
1945 5 Mongo, arms (ALB)	5.00
1959 2 Mongo, wreath (AL, hole)	.85
1981 1 Mongo, arms (AL)	1.25
1992 250,000 Tugrik, Chengis Khan/ national emblem (G)	PF 25,000.00

Morocco 1320AH 5 Mazunas

Nepal 2003 500 Rupees

MOROCCO

	VF
1314AH 1 Dirham, six-pointed star each side (S)	**7.00**
1320AH 5 Mazunas, value (C)	**5.00**
1340AH 10 Mazunas, star/ornamental pattern (C)	**1.50**
1951 1 Franc, star (AL)	**.10**
1953 100 Francs, star within star (S)	**2.50**

	Unc.
1975 5 Santimat, arms/wheel and fish (R)	**.30**
1965 1 Dirham, Hasan II/arms (N)	**1.00**
1987 5 Dirham, similar (Steel around ALB)	**7.50**

	VF
1986 100 Dirhams, Pope and king/Arms (S)	**70.00**
2002 5 Dirhams, Mohammed VI/Arms (Steel around ALB)	**7.00**

MYANMAR

	Unc.
1999 5 Kyat, Lion (B)	**1.00**
1999 50 Kyat, Lion (CN)	**4.00**

NEJD,

PRESENTLY PART OF SAUDI ARABIA

	VF
ca.1917, "Nejd" countermarked in Arabic on Egypt 5 Piastres (S)	**100.00**

These have been counterfeited.

NEPAL

	VF
Patan 1654 ¼ Mohar, sword/lion (S)	**100.00**
Patan 1685 1 Mohar, Interlocking squares / 8-pointed star (S)	**35.00**
Kathmandu 1669 1 Mohar, triangle/circle (S)	**45.00**
1715 1 Mohar, lion within petals/six-pointed star with letter in each angle (S)	**37.50**
1891 1 Paisa, footprints above two knives (C)	**5.00**
1902 1 Paisa, inscription in square (C)	**4.00**
1953 5 Paisa, urn (CN)	**1.00**
1822 1 Rupee, trident/sword (S)	**9.00**
1934 1 Rupee, similar but neater (S)	**5.00**

Niue 1997 5 Dollars

Oman 1975 5 Baisa

	Unc.
1980 5 Paisa, mountain/cow (AL)	.40
1993 25 Paisa, crown (AL)	.50
1971 50 Paisa, Trident/sword (CN)	.90
1968 10 Rupees, King with plumed helmet (S)	6.50
1993 500 Rupees, bear (S)	PF 40.00
2003 500 Rupees, Mount Everest (S)	25.00

NIUE

	Unc.
1997 1 Dollar, arms/Princess Diana (CN)	7.50
1997 5 Dollars, arms/Queen mother (S) PF	20.00
1997 10 Dollars, arms/Princess Diana (S)PF	20.00
1992 5 Dollars, arms/HMS Bounty(S)	13.50

OMAN,

FORMERLY MUSCAT AND OMAN

	Unc.
1311AH 1/4 Anna, Castle/Arabic inscription (C)	F 20.00
1315AH 1/4 Anna, English and Arabic inscriptions (C)	F 5.00
1975 5 Baisa, dagger & swords (C)	.45
1980 1/4 Rial, same (B)	2.00
1994 1/2 Rial, Sultan/dagger & swords (S)	110.00

Pakistan 1976 50 Paisa

PALESTINE MANDATE

	VF
1927 1 Mil, branch, (C)	2.00
1927 20 Mils, wreath (CN, hole)	12.00
1942 50 Mils, branch (S)	6.00

PAKISTAN

	Unc.
1951 1 Pie, Toughra (C)	2.50
1948 2 Annas, Toughra/star and crescent (CN)	1.00
1974 1 Pice, Tower, star and crescent (AL)	.30
1962 5 Paisa, Toughra, star and crescent/ Ship (B)	.70

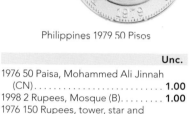

Philippines 1979 50 Pisos

Qatar 1973 50 Dirhems

	Unc.
1976 50 Paisa, Mohammed Ali Jinnah (CN)	**1.00**
1998 2 Rupees, Mosque (B).	**1.00**
1976 150 Rupees, tower, star and crescent/crocodile (S)	**40.00**

PHILIPPINES

	Unc.
1958 1 Centavo, arms/man seated with hammer (C)	**.25**
1964 25 Centavos, arms/woman with hammer (CNZ).	**.35**
1947 50 Centavos, MacArthur/arms (S).	**4.00**
1967 1 Peso, flaming sword/arms (S).	**7.50**
1974 1 Sentimo, bust of Lapulapu (AL)	**.10**
1983 50 Sentimos, bust of Pilar/eagle (CN).	**.50**
1970 1 Piso, Marcos/Pope (N).	**3.00**
1990 2 Pisos, Bonafacio/tree (CN).	**1.25**
1974 25 Pisos, arms/national bank (S)	**8.00**
1979 50 Pisos, child (S)	**10.00**
1992 10,000 Pisos, Corazon Aqino/map (G)	PF **900.00**

QATAR

	Unc.
1973 1 Dirhem, ship and trees (C)	**.50**

	Unc.
1973 50 Dirhems, similar (CN).	**2.00**
(1998) 500 Riyals, similar/bank building (G)	**600.00**

QATAR & DUBAI

	Unc.
1966 1 Dirhem, Gazelle (C)	**.75**

RAS AL KHAIMAH,

MEMBER OF UAE

	Unc.
1970 50 Dirhams, falcon (CN)	**20.00**
1970 2 1/2 Riyals, emir/falcon (S)	**25.00**
1970 10 Riyals, US President Eisenhower (S).	**15.00**

SAUDI ARABIA

	VF
1344AH 1/4 Ghirsh, inscription (CN)	**6.00**
1346AH 1/2 Ghirsh, same (CN).	**8.00**
1344AH 1 Ghirsh, same but countermarked "65" in Arabic (CN).	**80.00**
1376AH 1 Ghirsh, palm and swords (CN).	**.25**
1378AH 4 Ghirsh, same	**.50**
1354AH 1/4 Riyal, inscription (S).	**2.50**
1354AH 1 Riyal	**3.50**

Saudi Arabia 1383AH 1 Halala

Saudi Arabia 1978 100 Halala

Sri Lanka 2003 5 Rupees

	VF
1374AH 1 Riyal, similar (S)	**2.50**
1397AH 10 Halala, palm and swords (CN)	.25

	Unc.
1383AH 1 Halala	3.00
1978 100 Halala	3.50
1414AH 100 Halala, similar (CN)	**4.00**
1419AH 100 Halala, palm tree (B in CN, bimetallic)	**6.50**
1377AH 1 Guinea, inscription and palms (G)	160.00

SEIYUN and TARIM,
PRESENTLY PART OF YEMEN

	VF
1258AH 3 Khumsi, crescent/scales (C)	**55.00**
1315AH 6 Khumsi, wreath and inscriptions (S)	10.00

SOUTH EAST ASIA

	VF
Funan 190-627AD Unit, sun/temple with symbol inside (S)	**75.00**
Mekong River valley 1600s-1800s Long ingot with rounded ends and rough bumps on one side, called "Tiger tongue" money (Billon, 5")	**20.00**
__. 1700s to late 1800s, similar but no bumps, called "Canoe" money (Base Billon, 3")	10.00

SHARJAH

	Unc.
1964 5 Rupees, John F. Kennedy/crossed flags (S)	**15.00**

SINGAPORE

	Unc.
1986 1 Cent, arms (C)	.10
1971 5 Cents, fish (AL)	.35
1967 20 Cents, swordfish (CN)	.60
1974 50 Cents, zebra fish (CN)	1.10
1978 10 Dollars, satellite dish (S)	7.50
1981 5 Dollars, airport (CN)	**6.50**
1990 100 Dollars, arms/lion head (G)	485.00

Sudan 1975 10 Ghirsh

Syria 1971 5 Piastres

Syria 2003 25 Pounds

SOUTH ARABIA

	Unc.
1964 1 Fils, daggers (AL)	.25
1964 50 Fils, boat (CN)	1.25

SRI LANKA (CEYLON)

	Unc.
1963 1 Cent, arms (AL)	.10
19/5 25 Cents, arms (CN)	.25
1981 2 Rupees, dam (CN)	1.25
1995 5 Rupees, U.N. logo (ALB)	2.50

SUDAN

	F
1302AH 20 Piastres, Toughra (S)	325.00
1312AH 20 Piastres, Toughra (debased S)	12.00
	Unc.
1956 1 Millim, postman on camel (C)	.30
1970 10 Millim, similar (C, scalloped)	.90
1975 10 Ghirsh, arms (CN)	2.50
1989 25 Ghirsh, building (Steel)	2.25
1976 5 Pounds, hippopotami (S)	25.00

SYRIA

	VF
1919 Dinar, arms/wreath (G)	*rare*
1935 1 Piastre, lion heads (B, hole)	2.50
1926 5 Piastres, crossed grain (B)	2.00
1929 10 Piastres, ornamental design (S)	12.00
ND (World War II emergency issue) 1 Piastre, inscription (B)	5.00
	Unc.
1971 5 Piastres, arms/grain (ALB)	.35
1950 1 Lira, arms (S)	25.00
1978 1 Pound, President Assad/arms (N)	3.00
1995 25 Pounds, same (C around Steel)	7.00
2003 25 Pounds, Parliament (C around Steel)	4.50
1997 10 Pounds, arms/map & flag. Anniv. of Baath Party (CN)	2.50

TANNU TUVA,

PRESENTLY PART OF RUSSIA

	VF
1934 1 Kopejek, (ALB)	**45.00**
1934 20 Kopejek (CN)	**55.00**

TAJIKISTAN

	Unc.
2001 20 Drams, crown (B clad Steel)	**1.00**
2001 5 Somoni, bust of Rudaki (CNZ)	**5.00**

THAILAND

	VF
1782-1809 1 Baht "bullet money" with Conch countermark (S)	**25.00**
1760-1871 circulating gambling token (Porcelain)	**4.00**
(1862) 1/16th Fuang, three crowns/ elephant in border (Tin)	**6.00**
1890 1 Att, Rama V/Siam seated (C)	**12.00**
1908 1 Baht, Rama V l./elephants (S)	**2,50.00**
1918 1 Baht, Rama VI r./elephants (S)	**10.00**
1929 50 Satang, Rama VII l.,/elephant l. (S)	**7.00**
1946 25 Satang, Rama VIII as child/Garuda (Tin)	**2.50**

Rama IX

	Unc.
1957 5 Satang, bust/arms (B)	**.25**
1961 1 Baht, king and queen/arms (CN)	**2.00**
1972 5 Baht, bust/Garuda (CN, polygonal)	**1.20**
1980 10 Baht, bust/wheel (N)	**2.50**
1996 20 Baht, king with camera/king and people (CN)	**3.50**
2002 20 Baht, two kings/arms (CN)	**3.50**
1971 50 Baht, bust/wheel (S)	**14.00**

Thailand 2002 20 Baht

TIBET

	VF
1795 1 Sho, Chinese inscription around square/Tibetan inscription around square (S)	**60.00**
1875-1930 Ga-den Tanka, lotus/symbols (S)	**8.00**
1919 1 Sho, lion (C)	**4.00**
1937 3 Srang, lion before mountains (S)	**9.00**
1952 10 Srang, similar (S)	**10.00**
1918 20 Srang, lion (G)	**400.00**
1902-42 Rupee, Chinese bust/floral wreath (S) *Struck by Chinese*	**14.00**

TIMOR, EAST

	Unc.
2003 10 Centavos, rooster (N clad Steel)	**4.00**
2004 50 Centavos, coffee plant (CNZ)	**8.00**

TONGA

	Unc.
1967 1 Seniti, Queen Salote (C)	**1.00**
1981 20 Seneti, King Taufa'ahau/roots (CN)	**1.50**

Tonga 1996 1 Pa'anga

Turkey 1979 1 Kurus

	Unc.
1985 1 Pa'anga, king/dove (CN, heptagonal)	**4.00**
1981 5 Hau, king/Charles and Diana (G)	**250.00**
1996 1 Pa'anga, arms/Eliz. II (S) *PF*	**35.00**

TUNISIA

	VF
1249AH 1 Kharub, inscriptions (Billon)	**22.00**
1289AH 2 Kharub, inscriptions (C)	**6.00**
1891 1 Franc, branches/ornamental border (S)	**20.00**

	Unc.
1954 5 Francs, monogram/crescent (CN)	**4.00**

	VF
1960 2 Millim, tree (AL)	**.25**
1976 1/2 Dinar, Bourguiba/hands (CN)	**9.00**
1969 1 Dinar, Bourguiba/Hannibal (S)	*PF* **10.00**
1982 75 Dinars, same/children (G)	*PF* **235.00**

TURKEY

	VF
1341 100 Para, wheat/oak branch (ALB) Arabic alphabet	**2.50**
1928 25 Kurus, similar. Arabic alphabet (N)	**3.00**
1936 1 Kurus, star in crescent (CN)	**1.00**
1948 1 Lira, star and crescent (S)	**3.00**

	Unc.
1979 1 Kurus, girl in veil/branch (C)	**3.00**
1959 5 Kurus, similar/oak branch (C)	**.30**
1967 1 Lira, Ataturk (Steel)	**.50**

	VF
1979 5 Lira, Ataturk on horse (Steel)	**1.00**
1960 10 Lira, Ataturk/symbols of revolution (S)	**8.00**
1988 50 Lira, Ataturk (ALB)	**.15**
1997 5,000 Lira, Ataturk (B)	**.75**
1992 500,000 Lira, ship (Turkish Jews) (G)	*PF* **320.00**
1998 500,000 Lira, wreath/Ataturk	*Unc.* **18.00**
2000 150,000,000 Lira, mint logo/U.S. President Clinton (G in S, bimetallic)	*PF* **350.00**

United Arab Emirates 1990 50 Dirhams

Vietnam 1992 100 Dong

TURKMENISTAN

	Unc.
1993 1 Tennesi, President Nyyazow (C plated Steel)	.25
1993 50 Tennesi, same/Rhyton (N plated steel)	2.00

UNITED ARAB EMIRATES

	Unc.
1973 1 Fils, palm trees (C)	.20
1973 50 Fils, oil wells (CN)	1.50
1995 1 Dirham, pitcher (CN)	1.85
1981 5 Dirhams, falcon (CN)	6.50
1990 50 Dirhams, bust of Sheikh/Dubai Intl. Trade Center (S)	70.00

UZBEKISTAN

	Unc.
1994 3 Tiyin, arms (B clad Steel)	.30
1997 10 Som, arms (N clad Steel)	1.50

VIETNAM

	VF
1832 7 Tien, sun/dragon (S)	300.00
1848-83 1 Tien, scepter and swastika (S)	120.00

	Unc.
1976 1 Hao,arms (AL)	2.50
1987 10 Dong, arms/orangutan (CN)	17.50
1989 20 Dong, Ho Chi Minh (B) . PF	14.50
1992 100 Dong, Soccer player (S) PF	25.00

VIETNAM, NORTH

	XF
1946 5 Hao, stove/star (AL)	18.00
1958 1 Xu, wreath (AL, hole)	2.00

VIETNAM, SOUTH

	Unc.
1953 10 Su, three women (AL)	1.00
1960 1 Dong, bust/rice (AL)	2.50
1966 5 Dong, rice (CN, scalloped)	1.00
1974 10 Dong, farmers (B clad Steel)	.60
1975 50 Dong, rice farmers (N clad Steel)	500.00

WESTERN SAMOA

	Unc.
1967 1 Sene, king (C)	.20
1974 50 Sene, king/bananas (CN)	1.75
1974 1 Tala, boxers/arms (CN)	4.50
1988 100 Tala, arms/Kon-Tiki (G)	PF 125.00

Yemen 1974 50 Fils

Yemen 1963 1 Buqsha

YEMEN

Kingdom

	VF
1343AH 1 Zalat, inscription (C)	**40.00**
1381AH 1/80th Riyal, crescent (C)	**.75**
1368AH 1/16th Riyal, crescent (S, pentagonal)	**5.00**
1974 50 Fils, arms (CN)	**1.25**

Arab Republic

	Unc.
1963 1 Buqsha, leaves (ALB)	**.50**
1963 1 Riyal, leaves (S)	**12.00**
1985 50 Fils, eagle (CN)	**2.50**
1975 100 Riyals, eagle/Arab Jerusalem (G)	**325.00**

Peoples Democratic Republic

	Unc.
1981 100 Fils, building (CN, octagonal)	**3.00**

Republic

	Unc.
1995 10 Riyals, stone bridge (Steel)	**2.75**

COINS OF THE AMERICAS

The images and symbolism that adorned the newly independent Latin American countries' coins in the early 1800s found their origins in the coinages of the early United States and the French Revolution. This was only natural. After all, most of these states had rejected monarchy in favor of a representative republican form of government, quite unusual on earth at the time. There were few examples of republican coinages on which to base theirs. The United States' was the closest, and its struggle showed that a colony *can* throw off its master's yoke. The French Republic had been the most important in terms of the development of political thought.

Hence, the first generations of Latin American coins were mostly dominated by female personifications of liberty, as well as symbols of liberty and prosperity, such as the liberty cap and the cornucopia. This was not to the exclusion of real human portraiture. Haïti, the hemisphere's second oldest independent nation, Mexico, and Brazil all established monarchies. These and many other countries depicted their heads of state, be it king or president, or the liberator Simon Bolivar. Almost all the new countries proudly displayed their new, distinctly American coats of arms.

If the primary inspiration for images was the United States and France, the primary source for the physical form and standard of the coinage was clearly Spain, the former colonizing power for most of the New World. Most countries retained a silver coin the size of the old Spanish milled dollar or eight-real piece. Some even kept its division into pieces of eight. Many gold pieces were also struck on the old escudo standard as well. Many of the big bullion exporting areas during colonial days continued to do so after independence, and the Mexican eight real peso was a favorite coin in the Orient until the early 1900s.

Latin American coinage proved to be far less stable than the old Spanish colonial coinage. Within a generation or two many of these new eight reales or pesos began to decline in weight or purity. Some were even replaced by copper emergency coins. By 1967 all Latin American and Caribbean countries had abandoned precious metal for all but bullion and commemorative coins.

Iconography remained fairly consistent throughout the 1800s. Some of the biggest changes in the imagery reflected the overthrow of the Haitian

(1806, 1821, 1858), Mexican (1823, 1867), and Brazilian (1889) monarchies. The extremely diverse and creative allegories of Bolivian proclamation coins often incorporated books, buildings, crowds, and dragons, as well as images of the presidents, who seemed to take power and be forced out with the vagaries of fate.

Another change was the replacement of the screw press with steam-powered machinery for the manufacture of coinage, generally within the first 50 years of independence. As a transition to modern minting technology, many Latin American countries towards the end of the century contracted to have their coins struck in Paris, Brussels, Birmingham (England), or Waterbury (Connecticut). Improvements in local die engraving were spotty, however, and images usually varied from quaint to cartoon-like. European mints provided not only high capacity machines capable of producing uniform coins, but expert die engraving as well.

New images began to appear toward the beginning of the 20th century, along with new metals. Commemoratives were introduced, first in Colombia in 1892 to honor the 400th anniversary of Columbus's discovery of America. During the period before the 1950s, Brazil and Mexico were the only other countries to release commemorative coins. Late in the twentieth century, most New World countries struck commemoratives, both for circulation and for sale to collectors at a premium. The flora and fauna depicted on many Caribbean and Central American coins have given them particular appeal to collectors.

Many New World collectors' issues have been distributed in Europe and North America by marketing firms. Overdistribution, particularly in the case of Caribbean collector issues caused a sharp drop in their market prices, and many can today be purchased well below their original issue prices. Unknowingly, some collectors have further reduced the value of their holdings by discarding the original mint holders in which collector coins must remain to maintain their maximum value.

One of the most fascinating aspects of Latin American numismatics is plantation or hacienda tokens. Some plantations were so large that they constituted company-run towns with exclusively company-run stores. This was also true of some mines. Often the workers were paid with tokens issued by the plantation or mines that were good at these stores. They were usually simple, devoid of all but inscriptions and numbers, but form a valuable record of local history.

Specialized Books:

Bruce, Colin R. *Standard Catalog of Mexican Coins, Paper Money, Stocks, Bonds and Medals.*

Burnett, Davis. *Bolivian Proclamation Coinage.*

Rulau, Russell. *Latin American Tokens.*

Known Counterfeits: Contemporary counterfeits of the early coppers of Brazil are quite common and actively collected. Cast counterfeits exist of Cuban 1915 10, 20 and 40 centavos and Peso, and 1932 Peso. A counterfeit of the 1928 Ecuador 1 Condor was struck with cast dies. Early Haitian silver coins were counterfeited at the time, but the counterfeits are collected along with the official issues. Contemporary counterfeits of Mexican cap-and-rays 8 reales abound. Most are struck either nickel-silver (an alloy of copper, nickel and zinc, but no silver), or of a baser silver alloy. A partial list includes 1835PiJS, 1836ZsOM, 1840GJ, 1843MoML, 1894MoAM and 1904ZsFM (peso). Counterfeits of two and four reales of this type also exist. There are collector counterfeits of several of the Mexican revolutionary issues, and very dangerous counterfeits of some of the Mexican 20th century bullion gold coins, the 1947 50 Peso in particular. Examine the latter carefully. A 1982 counterfeit Mexico silver onza is not dangerous due to its significant difference in style. It has been suggested that there are dangerous counterfeits of the 1889 Paraguay 1 Peso, but this is not certain. Another bullion piece, the Peru 1962 100 Soles has been the victim of a dangerous counterfeit of about 75 percent pure gold.

ARGENTINA

	VF
Buenos Aires 1823 1 Decimo, arms (C)	**12.00**
Buenos Aires 1844 2 Reales, wreath/ wreath (C)	**12.00**
Cordoba 1849 2 Reales, castle/sun (S)	**32.00**
1861 2 Reales, value (C)	**65.00**
Entre Rios 1867 ½ Real, arms (S)	**150.00**
La Plata 1826 2 Soles, Sun face/ Arms (S)	**25.00**
1815 8 Soles, similar (S)	**200.00**
1826 8 Escudos, Sun face / Arms over cannons (G)	**2,000.00**

Argentina 1861 2 Reales

Argentina 2000 50 Centavos

	VF
1829 8 Escudos, similar (G)	*Rare*
1854 1 Centavo, sun face (C).	**15.00**
1884 1 Centavo, arms/Liberty head (C)	**1.00**
1897 10 Centavos, head of Argentina/ wreath (S)	**1.50**
1903 5 Centavos, similar (CN).	**.50**
1915 10 Centavos, similar (CN)	**1.00**
1926 20 Centavos, similar (CN).	**.50**
1941 50 Centavos, similar (N)	**1.00**
1882 1 Peso, head of Argentina/arms (S).	**85.00**

	Unc.
1959 1 Peso, similar (N clad Steel) . . .	**1.50**
1963 5 Pesos, sailing ship (N clad Steel)	**2.00**
1963 10 Pesos, Gaucho (N clad Steel)	**2.00**
1973 1 Centavo, head of Argentina/olive branch (AL).	**.30**
1986 5 Centavos, wildcat (B)	**1.50**
2000 50 Centavos (ALB).	**2.50**
1991 1000 Australes, 14 coats of arms/ globes and pillars (S).	*PF* **45.00**
1997 1 Peso, Eva Peron (CN around B)	**3.75**
1994 50 Pesos, three coats of arms/book (G)	*PF* **255.00**

BAHAMAS

	Unc.
1974 1 Cent, arms/starfish (B)	**.40**
1975 25 Cents, arms/sloop (N)	**1.00**
1974 50 Cents, arms/swordfish (CN) .	**2.00**
1994 5 Dollars, arms/golf course (S).	*PF* **45.00**

Bahamas 2000 2 Dollars

Barbados 1996 5 Dollars

	Unc.
1974 10 Dollars, arms/Milo Butler (CN)	**12.00**
2000 2 Dollars Elizabeth. II/ Queen Mother (S)	*PF* **50.00**

BARBADOS

	Unc.
2001 5 Cents, Arms/Lighthouse (B). . . .	**.25**
1973 1 Dollar, Arms/Flying fish (CN) .	**1.50**
1970 4 Dollars, Arms/Plant (CN). . . .	**12.50**
1996 5 Dollars, Arms/Royal couple (S).	*PF* **40.00**

Unc.

1981 10 Dollars, Arms/Neptune (CN)
.... **12.50**
1994 50 Dollars, arms/SIDS conference
logo (G) .... *PF* **550.00**

BELIZE

Unc.

1977 1 Cent, arms/swallow-tailed kite (AL,
scalloped)........................ **.25**
1974 10 Cents, arms/hermit bird (CN) **2.00**
1977 25 Cents, arms/motmot bird
(CN)............................ **2.00**
1981 5 Dollars, arms/toucan (CN) ... **6.50**
1982 100 Dollars, arms/kinkajou (G)
.... **450.00**
Same but Proof **175.00**

BOLIVIA

VF

1828 2 Soles, Bolivar/tree between llamas
(S)............................ **20.00**
1831 8 Soles, similar (S)............ **45.00**
1844 8 Scudos, Bolivar/mountain (G)
.... **650.00**
1839 1 Sol, Phoenix rising from flames/
angel stg., lion at feet (S) typically
holed......................... **20.00**
1852 1 Sol, Victory or Fame blowing
trumpet/small temple (S) typically
holed......................... **18.00**
1868 1/8th Melgarejo, bust of Melgarejo/
dragon about to be beat by hand with
club (S) **25.00**
1873 1 Boliviano, arms/wreath (S) .. **25.00**
1883 5 Centavos, similar (CN, hole).. **8.00**
1897 20 Centavos, similar (S)........ **5.00**
1900 50 Centavos, similar (S)........ **9.50**
1909 5 Centavos, mountain scene/
Caduceus (CN) **1.00**
1935 10 Centavos, similar (CN)...... **1.00**
1942 20 Centavos, similar (Zinc) **2.50**

Unc.

1951 5 Bolivianos, arms (C) **3.50**
1951 10 Bolivianos, Bolivar/wreath
(C) **3.50**
1965 50 Centavos, Mountain scene (N
clad Steel)..................... **1.50**

Bolivia 1951 5 Bolivianos

Bolivia 1991 10 Centavos

Bolivia 1991 50 Centavos

VF

1979 200 Pesos Bolivianos, arms/children
(S). .... *PF* **16.50**
1991 10 Centavos, arms (Steel)....... **.50**
1987 20 Centavos, arms (Steel)....... **.75**
1991 50 Centavos, arms (Steel)....... **.75**
1998 1 Boliviano, arms/bank emblem
(S). .... *PF* **65.00**
(1876) 5 Centavos token of Daniel
Quiroga, Cochabamba. Eagle-topped
fountain (CN)
.... **8.50**

BRAZIL, Empire

VF

1868 10 Reis, similar (C) **2.00**
1826 20 Reis, wreath/arms (C)...... **15.00**
(1835) 40 Reis, 40 in circle
counterstamped on 80 reis like above
(C) **12.50**

Brazil 1901 100 Reis

Brazil 1957 1 Cruzeiro

Brazil 1980 5 Cruzeiros

Brazil 2002 1 Real

	VF
1831 80 Reis, similar (C)	**10.00**
1871 200 Reis, arms/value (CN)	**1.50**
1888 1,000 Reis, Pedro II/arms (S) . .	**12.50**
1847 1,200 Reis,wreath/arms (S) . . .	**175.00**
1887 2,000 Reis, Pedro II/arms (S) . .	**30.00**
1857 20,000 Reis, Pedro II/arms (G)	**260.00**

BRAZIL, Republic

	VF
1889 20 Reis, star (C).	**4.50**
1896 100 Reis, Constellation (CN) . . .	**3.00**
1901 100 Reis, Bust/star (CN)	**1.50**
1900 400 Reis, cross/wreath (S)	**25.00**
1900 4,000 Reis, Cabral with flag/Arms of Portugal and Brazil (S)	**300.00**

Above two commemorate the 400th anniversary of the discovery of Brazil.

1918 50 Reis, female bust r. (CN)	**.35**
1918 100 Reis, similar (CN).	**1.50**
1938 200 Reis, Maua/locomotive (CN)	**.75**
1937 300 Reis, Oswaldo Cruz/lamp (CN).	**1.50**
1925 400 Reis, similar (CN)	**1.75**
1936 1,000 Reis, Jose de Anchieta/open book (ALB).	**1.00**
1936 5,000 Reis, Dumont/wing (S). . .	**2.00**
1922 10,000 Reis, bust of Brazil/arms (G)	**400.00**

	VF
1947 20 Centavos, Getulio Vargas (ALB)	**.15**

	Unc.
1953 1 Cruzeiro, map of Brazil (ALB) .	**1.00**
1957 1 Cruzeiro, arms (AL)	**2.50**
1961 2 Cruzeiros, arms (AL)	**1.00**
1972 1 Cruzeiro, two portraits/Map of Brazil (N).	**1.65**
1972 300 Cruzeiros, similar (G)	**300.00**
1980 5 Cruzeiros, coffee (Steel)	**.75**
1988 100 Cruzados, child's portrait (Steel)	**3.00**
1992 500 Cruzeiros, sea turtle (Steel) .	**.75**
1993 5 Cruzeiros Reals, two parrots (Steel)	**.60**
1998 5 Centavos, bust of Tiradentes (C plated Steel)	**.45**
1999 1 Real, portrait (B around CN, *bimetallic*).	**2.65**
2002 1 Real, Kubitschek (B around CN, *bimetallic*)	**3.00**
(1995) 3 Reals, BC30/Jerusalem Cross (S). *PF*	**40.00**

Chile 1938 10 Centavos

Chile 2001 100 Pesos

CENTRAL AMERICAN REPUBLIC

	VF
1842 1/4 Real, mountains/tree, no legends (S)	**15.00**
1831 1 Real, similar with legends (S)	**50.00**
1825 8 Reals, similar (S)	**60.00**
1850 2 Escudos, similar (G)	**200.00**

CHILE

	VF
1817 1 Peso, volcano/column (S)	**650.00**
1817 1 Peso, similar with assayer's initials (S)	**150.00**
1834 1/2 Real, similar (S)	**40.00**
1848 2 Reales, condor/arms (S)	**8.00**
1851 1 Centavo, star/wreath (C)	**12.50**
1861 1/2 Decimo, condor flying/wreath (S)	**10.00**
1879 1 Decimo, condor with shield/wreath (S)	**2.00**
1883 1 Peso, condor with shield/Arms (S)	**12.00**
1892 10 Pesos, arms/Chile stg. (G)	**235.00**
1904 1 Centavo, bust/wreath (C)	**2.00**
1915 5 Centavos, condor/wreath (S)	**3.00**
1938 10 Centavos, same (CN)	**.50**
1922 20 Centavos, similar (CN)	**.75**
1933 1 Peso, similar (CN)	**.50**
(1903-05) 2 Pesos token, Compania de Salitres.../CSA monogram (Vulcanite, various colors)	**5.00**
(1900-10) 2 Pesos token. Oficina Brac / $2 (Vulcanite, green/brown)	**6.50**
1916 20 centavos token, bust of girl (CN)	**5.00**

Chile 1976 10 Pesos

	Unc.
1946 100 Pesos, Female bust l./arms (G)	**300.00**
2001 100 Pesos, Mapuche/arms (B around CN)	**3.00**
1969 10 Centavos, condor (ALB)	**5.00**
1975 1 Peso, O'Higgins (CN)	**.25**
1980 5 Pesos, liberty breaking chains (CN)	**2.00**
1995 100 Pesos, arms (ALB)	**2.50**

COLOMBIA

	VF
1820 1/4 Real, Liberty cap/pomegranate (S)	**60.00**
1831 1 Real, Fasces between two cornucopiae/wreath (S)	**17.50**
1842 2 Reales, "Nueva Granada" and bird over cornucopia/wreath (S)	**55.00**
1855 1 Decimo, pomegranate between two cornucopiae/wreath (S)	**8.00**
1864 1/2 Decimo, pomegranate/BOGOTA and stars (S)	**9.50**
1874 2 Decimos, Liberty head/arms (S)	**11.50**
1881 2-1/2 Centavos, Liberty cap (CN)	**.25**

Colombia 1933 2 Centavos

Costa Rica 1997 5 Colones

Colombia 2004 20 Pesos

COSTA RICA

	VF
1847 1 Real, tree/bust (S)	30.00
(1846) 4 Reales, dies of 1 Real stamped on American Half Dollar	8,000.00
1855 1/8th Peso, arms/Tree (S)	22.50
1875 25 Centavos, similar (S)	18.00
1899 20 Colones, arms/Columbus (G)	225.00
1903 2 Centimos (CN)	1.00
1936 5 Centimos, arms/wreath (B)	.75
1948 25 Centimos, similar (CN)	.20
1954 1 Colon, similar (Steel)	.35
	Unc.
1982 25 Centimos, similar (AL)	.25
1970 5 Colones, arms/Renaissance portrait (S)	PF 20.00
1997 5 Colones, arms/value (B)	.50
1970 20 Colones, Venus de Milo (S) Proof	40.00
1974 50 Colones, arms/sea turtle (S)	17.50
1997 50 Colones, arms (B)	3.00
2000 500 Colones, arms/bank (B)	2.50

COLOMBIA

	VF
1892 50 Centavos, Columbus/arms (S)	10.00
1897 10 Centavos, Liberty head/arms (S)	1.50
1918 1 Centavo, Liberty bust (CN)	12.00
1921 2 Centavos, similar (CN)	.75
1935 5 Centavos, similar (CN)	1.50
1942 10 Centavos, Bolivar/arms (S)	1.25
(1839-40) 1 Mitad token of Manuel Angulo, cannon/logo (C)	100.00
	Unc.
1971 20 Centavos, Santander (N clad Steel)	.20
1965 50 Centavos, Gaitan/arms (CN)	.60
1956 1 Peso, old mint doors/arms (S)	25.00
1919 5 Pesos, stone cutter/arms (G)	125.00
1981 10 Pesos, equestrian statue/Map (CNZ)	1.25
2004 20 Pesos, Head l.	.15
1993 500 Pesos, tree (CN around ALB)	4.00
Leprosarium. 1921 2 Centavos, cross inscribed LAZARETO (CN)	VF 8.00

The above coin was struck for use inside government run leper colonies. Brazil, Costa Rica, Panama and Venezuela also struck such pieces.

CUBA

	VF
1916 2 Centavos, arms/star (CN)	1.00
1943 5 Centavos, similar (B)	1.00
1915 10 Centavos, similar (S)	4.00
1920 20 Centavos, similar (S)	3.00
1916 40 Centavos, similar (S)	75.00
1952 40 Centavos, lighthouse and flag/ tree growing through wheel (S)	2.50
1953 50 Centavos, Jose Marti/scroll (S)	2.50
1932 1 Peso, arms/star (S)	9.50

Cuba 1993 5 Pesos

Dominican Republic 2002 5 Pesos

	VF
1916 2 Pesos, Jose Marti/arms (G)	**75.00**
1916 10 Pesos, similar (G)	**225.00**
	Unc.
1963 1 Centavo, arms/star (AL)	**.60**
1972 20 Centavos, similar (AL)	**2.50**
1982 1 Peso, Don Quixote and Sancho Panza/arms (CN)	**6.50**
1990 3 Pesos, Che Guevara/arms (CN)	**6.00**
1987 5 Pesos, Slave breaking chains/arms (S)	**32.50**
1993 5 Pesos, ship/arms (S)	PF **18.00**
1993 20 Pesos, Fidel Castro/arms (S)	PF **90.00**

DOMINICAN REPUBLIC

	VF
1844 1/4 Real, value (B)	**8.50**
1877 5 Centavos, book (CN)	**20.00**
1888 2-1/2 Centavos, arms (CN)	**2.00**
1897 20 Centavos, arms/Indian head (Billon)	**7.50**
1937 1 Centavo, arms/palm tree (C)	**1.50**
1942 10 Centavos, arms/Indian head (S)	**2.00**
1956 25 Centavos, similar (S)	**2.50**
	Unc.
1955 1 Peso, arms/Trujillo (S)	**25.00**
1984 1 Centavo, arms/Caonabo (C plated Zinc)	**.25**

Ecuador 1841 4 Reales

	Unc.
1991 25 Centavos, arms/horse cart (N clad Steel)	**.60**
1967 1/2 Peso, similar (CN)	**1.50**
1976 1 Peso, arms/Duarte (CN)	**2.00**
1983 1 Peso, arms/three portraits (CN, polygonal)	**2.50**
2002 5 Pesos. Sanches (B around Steel)	**2.50**
1979 100 Pesos, arms/pope (G)	**160.00**

ECUADOR

	VF
1834 1 Real, Fasces between two cornucopiae/Sun over two mountains (S)	**60.00**
1849 2 Reales, Liberty as on 1830s United States coin/arms (S)	**65.00**
1841 4 Reales, arms/mounts. (S)	**7,500.00**
1855 8 Escudos, Bolivar/arms (G)	**1,750.00**
1858 5 Francos, Liberty / Arms (S)	**350.00**

El Salvador 1868 1 Real (Countermark on 1786 Spanish Colonial Real)

Guatemala 1993 1 Centavo

	VF
1886 1/2 Decimo, arms (CN)	**16.50**
1893 1 Decimo, Sucre/arms (S)	**1.75**
1909 1 Centavo, arms/wreath (CN)	**7.50**
1912 1/2 Decimo, Sucre/arms (S)	**1.25**
1928 10 Centavos, arms/bust (N)	**1.00**
1937 20 Centavos, arms/wreath (N)	**.50**
1928 50 Centavos, Sucre/arms (S)	**2.00**

	Unc.
1928 1 Condor, Bust/arms (G)	**350.00**
1943 5 Sucres, Sucre/arms (S)	**10.00**
1946 5 Centavos, arms/wreath (CN)	**1.00**
1964 10 Centavos, similar (N clad Steel)	**.50**
1979 50 Centavos, similar (N clad Steel)	**.50**
1964 1 Sucre, arms/bust of Sucre (N clad Steel)	**.75**
1988 same but smaller	**.40**
1991 10 Sucres, arms/ancient sculpture (N clad Steel)	**1.00**
2000 25 Centavos (of a Dollar), Jose de Olmedo (Steel)	**1.25**

EL SALVADOR

	VF
1828 2 Reales, Pillar/mountain (S)	**165.00**
1835 1 Real, similar (S)	**275.00**
1868 1 Real (Countermark on 1786 Spanish Colonial Real) (S)	**75.00**
1889 1 Centavo, Morazán (CN)	**3.00**
1892 50 Centavos, arms/flags with hands (S)	**50.00**
1892 1 Centavo, Hat (C)	**45.00**
1904 1 Peso, arms/Columbus (S)	**15.00**
1914 5 Centavos, arms/wreath (S)	**3.00**
1942 1 Centavo, Morazán (C)	**.50**
1951 10 Centavos, similar (CN)	**1.50**
1953 20 Centavos, priest l./wreath (S)	**1.00**
1890s 4 Reales token of Finca (Plantation) San Luis (N plated Z)	**9.50**

	VF
c.1890-1920, Josefa de Diaz/serial number (CN) illus.	**9.00**

	Unc.
1976 1 Centavo, Morazán (B)	**.20**
1970 50 Centavos, similar (N)	**.60**
1988 1 Colon, Columbus (Steel)	**2.25**
1992 2,500 Colones, four interlocking hands (G)	**350.00**

GUATEMALA

	VF
1829 1 Real, sun over five mountains/tree (S)	**225.00**
1859 1/2 Real, Carrera/arms (S)	**30.00**
1861 4 Reales, Carrera/wreath (G)	**30.00**
1874 1 Real, shield/wreath (S)	**16.50**
1880 1/2 Real, Guatemala std./scroll, wreath and rifles (S)	**4.50**
1895 2 Reales, similar (S)	**4.50**
(1890-1910) Token, Las Mercedes / ViJ (AL)	**5.00**
(1893-97) 1 Dia token of Las Camelias (AL, triangular)	**17.50**
1900 1/4 Real, mountains/wreath (CN)	**.35**
1915 12-1/2 Centavos (C)	**1.25**
1923 5 Pesos, Barrios (B)	**2.75**
1932 1 Centavo, arms (B)	**1.00**
1993 1 Centavo, Las Casas (B)	**.25**
1949 5 Centavos, arms/tree (S)	**1.50**
1958 10 Centavos, arms/Monolith (S)	**1.25**

	Unc.
1963 25 Centavos, arms/female portrait (S)	**5.50**
1978 25 Centavos, similar (CN)	**.85**
1992 1 Quetzal, arms/Carlos Merida (S)	PF **50.00**

Haïti 1995 50 Centimes

Honduras 1991 50 Lempiras

HAÏTI

	VF
1807 15 Sols, Liberty/arms (S)	**125.00**
1814 (year 11) 12 Centimes, snake grasping tail/arms (S)	**30.00**
1827 (year 24) 25 Centimes, President Boyer/arms (S)	**16.00**
1831 (year 28) 50 Centimes, similar (S)	**20.00**
1846 1 Centime, wreath/fasces (C)	**3.00**
1850 6-1/4 Centimes, Emperor Faustin/ arms (C)	**9.50**
1863 10 Centimes, President Geffrard/ arms (C)	**4.50**
1881 1 Centime, head of Haïti/arms (C)	**3.50**
1894 20 Centimes, similar (S)	**4.50**
1904 5 Centimes, Pedro Nord-Alexis/arms (CN)	**4.00**
1906 10 Centimes, similar (CN)	**1.50**
1949 10 Centimes, Dumarsais Estime/ arms (CN)	**.25**

	Unc.
1953 10 Centimes, Paul Magliore/arms (CNZ)	**1.25**
1970 20 Centimes, Francois Duvalier/arms (CN)	**.80**
1981 50 Centimes, Jean-Claude Duvalier/ plant (CN)	**1.50**
1986 50 Centimes, Peralte/arms (CN)	**1.00**
1995 50 Centimes Similar (N clad Steel)	**1.25**
1995 1 Gourde, fortress/arms (ALB)	**1.75**
1970 40 Gourdes, Emperor Dessalines/ arms (G)	*PF* **220.00**

HONDURAS

	F
1832 1 Real, sun over five mountains/Tree (33% silver)	**22.50**
1845 2 Reales, similar (20% silver)	**15.00**
1852 4 Reales, similar (6-1/4% silver)	**13.50**
1854 4 Reales, similar (4% silver)	**10.00**
The above four are all extremely crude.	
1862 1 Peso, pyramid/tree (C)	**7.50**
1871 25 Centavos, arms/tree (S)	**5.50**
ca.1880 Municipalidad de la Ceiba, 1 Real, star (B)	**500.00**
1911 similar, no star (B)	**20.00**

	VF
1884 50 Centavos, Female stg. with book/ arms (S)	**15.00**
1892 1 Peso, similar (S)	**45.00**
1907 1 Centavo, pyramid (C)	**1.50**
1912 2 Centavos, pyramid (C)	**2.50**
1922 1 Peso, Liberty head/arms (G)	**250.00**
1939 1 Centavo, arms (C)	**.50**
1949 2 Centavos, arms (C)	**.25**
1934 1 Lempira, arms/Indian (S)	**3.50**

	Unc.
1956 5 Centavos, arms (CN)	**.60**
1967 50 Centavos, arms/Indian (CN)	**1.25**
1978 50 Centavos, arms/Indian (CN)	**1.00**
1992 100 Lempiras, arms/sailing ship (S)	*PF* **60.00**
1992 500 Lempiras, arms/Morazan (G)	*PF* **240.00**

Jamaica 1979 10 Dollars

JAMAICA

	Unc.
1969 1 Cent, arms/ackee fruit (C)	.25
1977 10 Cents, arms/butterfly on plant (CN)	.40
1982 25 Cents, arms/hummingbird (CN)	1.00
1976 50 Cents, Marcus Garvey/arms (CN, polygonal)	1.50
1972 10 Dollars, Bustamante and Manley/arms (S)	15.00
1979 10 Dollars, arms/child (CS)	PF 17.00
1995 25 Dollars, parrots/arms (S)	PF 45.00
1995 50 Dollars, Bob Marley/arms (S)	PF 40.00

MEXICO, Pre-Columbian

	Circ.
1500s Mushroom-shaped or T-shaped, thin copper sheet with upturned edge. Usually 4-5" high by 6" wide	85.00
1500s Chisel-shaped, thin copper sheet with unfinished edge. Usually 7" high by 2" wide	25.00

MEXICO, Local Copper

	F
Chiapas 1911 Token of Guatimoc Plantation, Coffee plant (B)	7.00
Chihuahua 1835 1/4 Real, Indian/wreath (C)	12.00
Colima 1830 1 Octavo, inscription (C, 23mm)	40.00

Examples 33mm wide are counterfeit, as are many other similar pieces.

Durango 1852 1/8th Real, eagle/large 8o (C)	8.00
Guanajuato 1856 1 Quartilla, eagle/hands about to strike coin (C)	11.00
Jalisco 1860 1/2 Octavo, Flag, bow and quiver/Liberty std. (C)	10.00
San Luiz Potosi 1828 1/4 Real, book/std. figure (C)	6.75
Sinaloa 1866 1/4 Real, Liberty head in wreath/wreath (C)	4.00
Sonora 1835 Cuartillo, two quivers/cap and rays (C)	11.00
Tacambaro ND 1/8th Real, Caduceus (C)	25.00
Zacatecas 1853 1 Quartilla, monument/cherub (B)	8.00

MEXICO, Empire of Iturbide

	VF
1822 1/2 Real, Emperor Augustin I/eagle (S)	**25.00**
1823 2 Reales, similar (S)	**45.00**

Mexico 1903C 1 Centavo

MEXICO

REPUBLIC, REALES

	VF
1824 2 Reales, hook neck eagle/cap and rays (S)	**50.00**
1830 1/8th Real, eagle/wreath (C)	**5.00**
1842 1/8th Real, Liberty std./wreath (C)	**10.00**
1847 1/4 Real, Liberty head (S)	**4.00**
1852 1/2 Real, eagle/cap and rays (S)	**5.00**
1858 1 Real, similar (S)	**6.00**
1862 2 Reales, similar (S)	**10.00**
1869 4 Reales, similar (S)	**30.00**
1893 8 Reales, similar (S)	**12.00**
1840 1/2 Escudo, eagle/hand holding liberty cap and pointing to book (G)	**60.00**
1856 1 Escudo, similar (G)	**100.00**
1868 2 Escudos, similar (G)	**200.00**
1829 4 Escudos, similar (G)	**450.00**
1839 8 Escudos, similar (G)	**500.00**

EMPIRE OF MAXIMILIAN

	VF
1864 1 Centavo, eagle/wreath (C)	**60.00**
1864 5 Centavos, similar (S)	**20.00**
1864 10 Centavos, similar (S)	**25.00**
1866 50 Centavos, head r./arms (S)	**95.00**
1866 1 Peso, head r./arms with supporters (S)	**45.00**
1866 20 Pesos, similar (G)	**800.00**

REPUBLIC, DECIMAL

	VF
1863 1 Centavo, Liberty std./wreath (C)	**18.00**
1886 1 Centavo, eagle/wreath (C)	**3.00**
1883 1 Centavo, bow and quiver/wreath (CN)	**.75**
1900 1 Centavo, eagle/1 over 4 (C)	**4.00**

	VF
1903C 1 Centavo, Eagle (C)	**12.50**
1903M 1 Centavo, Same (C)	**2.00**
1883 2 Centavos, bow and quiver/wreath (CN)	**.75**
1867 5 Centavos, eagle/cap and rays (S)	**40.00**
1888 5 Centavos, eagle/wreath (S)	**2.50**
1882 5 Centavos, bow and quiver/wreath (CN)	**1.00**
1868 10 Centavos, eagle/cap and rays (S)	**40.00**
1891 10 Centavos, eagle/wreath (S)	**3.00**
1898 20 Centavos, similar (S)	**8.00**
1884 25 Centavos, eagle/scroll, cap and balance scale (S)	**20.00**
1878 50 Centavos, similar (S)	**25.00**
1872 1 Peso, similar (S)	**20.00**
1898 1 Peso, eagle/cap and rays (S)	**10.00**
1870 1 Peso, eagle/wreath (G)	**60.00**
1889 2-1/2 Pesos, similar (G)	**300.00**
1900 5 Pesos, eagle/scroll, cap and balance scale (G)	**300.00**
1889 10 Pesos, similar (G)	**500.00**
1891 20 Pesos, similar (G)	**600.00**

ESTADOS UNIDOS

	XF
1916 1 Centavo, eagle (C)	**165.00**
1961 1 Centavo, eagle/wheat (B)	**.15**
1906 2 Centavos, eagle/2 over 4 (C)	**20.00**

The small 1915 coppers were struck by Zapata, the famous revolutionary.

1915 2 Centavos, similar but smaller (C)	**13.50**
1941 2 Centavos, as 1906 2c	**1.25**
1906 5 Centavos, eagle (N)	**3.25**
1927 5 Centavos, eagle/5 over 4 (C)	**27.50**
1937 5 Centavos, eagle/value in Aztec border (CN)	**1.00**
1944 5 Centavos, eagle/Josefa left (C)	**.35**

Mexico 1919 50 Centavos

Mexico 1977 100 Pesos

XF

1950 5 Centavos, eagle/Josefa rt. (CN)**1.50**
1974 5 Centavos, eagle/Josefa (B)......**.15**
1928 10 Centavos, eagle/cap and rays
(S)................................. **2.75**
1935 10 Centavos, eagle/10 over 4 (C)
..............................**25.00**
1936 10 Centavos, eagle/value in Aztec
border (CN)................... **2.00**
1967 10 Centavos, eagle/Juarez (C).....**.15**
1976 10 Centavos, eagle/corn (CN).... **.20**
1935 20 Centavos, eagle/20 over 4 (C)**8.50**
1942 20 Centavos, eagle/cap and rays
(S)............................. **2.00**
1944 20 Centavos, eagle/pyramid (C). **.65**
1979 20 Centavos, eagle/Madero (CN) **.15**
1983 20 Centavos, eagle/Olmec sculpture
(B)................................ **.25**
1951 25 Centavos, eagle/Balance scale
(Billon).......................... **.75**
1964 25 Centavos, eagle/Madero (CN) **.15**
1943 50 Centavos, eagle/cap and rays
(S)............................. **3.75**
1919 50 Centavos, eagle/cap and rays
(S)........................ VF **8.00**
1950 50 Centavos, eagle/realistic portrait
of Cuauhtemoc (Billon) **1.80**
1956 50 Centavos, eagle/stylized portrait
of Cuauhtemoc (C)............. **1.00**

Unc.

1979 50 Centavos, similar (CN)........**.50**
1983 50 Centavos, eagle/Palenque face
(Steel) **1.50**

Unc.

1910 1 Peso, eagle/horsewoman (S)
..........................XF **45.00**
*Note: Many examples of the above have
been cleaned and if so are worth less.*
1945 1 Peso, eagle/cap and rays (S). **5.00**
1947 1 Peso, eagle/Morelos r. (S).... **4.00**
1950 1 Peso, eagle/Morelos 3/4 left
(Billon)........................ **6.00**
1957 1 Peso, eagle/Juarez (Billon) .. **12.50**
1962 1 Peso, eagle/Morelos r. (Billon) **1.75**
1978 1 Peso, eagle/Morelos l. (CN) ... **.65**
1985 1 Peso, eagle/Morelos 3/4 r. (Steel)
................................**.50**
1921 2 Pesos, eagle/Independence
winged (S) ....XF **60.00**
1945 2 Pesos, eagle (G) **30.00**
1945 2-1/2 Pesos, eagle/Hidalgo (G)**35.00**
1955 5 Pesos, similar (G)...........**60.00**
*Almost all 1945 2 and 2-1/2 Pesos, and
1955 5 Pesos are restrikes.*
1955 52-1/2 Pesos, eagle/Hidalgo (G)
..............................**35.00**
1948 5 Pesos, eagle/Stylized portrait of
Cuauhtemoc (S) **8.50**
1953 5 Pesos, eagle/Hidalgo (S)..... **7.00**
1955 5 Pesos, same, smaller (S)...... **5.00**
1957 5 Pesos, Juarez (S) **13.50**
1959 5 Pesos, Carranza (S).......... **6.50**
1971 5 Pesos, eagle/Vicente Guerrero
(CN).......................... **2.50**
1980 5 Pesos, eagle/Quetzalcoatl (CN)
.... **1.75**
1988 5 Pesos, Eagle (B).............. **.35**

Mexico 2002 1 Peso

Mexico 2001 10 Pesos

Mexico 2002 5 Pesos

	Unc.
1959 (1959-72) 10 Pesos, eagle/Hidalgo (G, .24 oz. net) . . . . **bullion + 7%**	
1956 10 Pesos, eagle/Hidalgo (S). . . . **8.00**	
1957 10 Pesos, eagle/Juarez (S) **42.50**	
1960 10 Pesos, eagle/Hidalgo and Madero (S) **9.00**	
1975 10 Pesos, eagle/Hidalgo (CN, heptagonal) **6.50**	
1988 10 Pesos, eagle/Hidalgo (Steel) . . **.25**	
1959 (1960-96) 20 Pesos, eagle/ Aztec calendar (G, .48 oz. net) . . . . **bullion + 7%**	
1980 20 Pesos, eagle/Mayan figure (CN) **2.50**	
1988 20 Pesos, eagle/G. Victoria (B) . . . **.50**	
1968 25 Pesos, eagle/Aztec playing ball (S) **5.00**	
1972 25 Pesos, eagle/Juarez (S) **5.50**	
1921 (1947-72) 50 Pesos, eagle/winged Independence (G, 1.2 oz. net) . . . . **bullion + 3%**	
1988 50 Pesos, eagle/Juarez (Steel). . . **.75**	
1977 100 Pesos, eagle/Morelos (S) . . **6.00**	
1984 100 Pesos, eagle/Carranza (ALB) **2.50**	
1985 200 Pesos, eagle/four revolutionaries (CN) **3.25**	
1985 250 Pesos, eagle/soccer ball (G) **100.00**	
1987 500 Pesos, eagle/Madero (CN). **2.00**	

	Unc.
1988 1,000 Pesos, eagle/Juana de Asbaje (ALB) **3.45**	
1986 2,000 Pesos, eagle/soccer (G) **900.00**	
1988 5,000 Pesos, eagle/monument (CN) **7.75**	

NEW PESOS

	Unc.
1992 5 Centavos, eagle (Steel) . . . . **.25**	
1993 10 Centavos, eagle (Steel) . . . . . . **.25**	
1994 20 Centavos, eagle/wreath (ALB) **.35**	
1995 50 Centavos, eagle (ALB) . . . . **.75**	
1992 1 New Peso, eagle/N$1 (Steel around ALB) **1.00**	
1993 1 New Peso, eagle/warrior with Eagle helmet (S) **10.00**	
1996 1 Peso, eagle/$1 (Steel around ALB) **1.00**	
2002 1 Peso, Same **1.25**	
1993 2 New Pesos, eagle/N$2 (Steel around ALB) **2.00**	
1997 2 Pesos, eagle/$2 (Steel around ALB) **2.00**	

Mexico 1985 1 Oz. Bullion Issue

	Unc.
1992 5 New Pesos, eagle/N$5 (Steel around ALB)	**3.50**
1998 5 Pesos, eagle/$5 (Steel around ALB)	**4.50**
2002 5 Pesos (Unc.)	**4.00**
1992 10 New Pesos, eagle/Aztec image, N$10 (ALB around S)	**6.75**
1996 10 Pesos, similar but $10 (ALB around S)	**6.75**
1998 10 Pesos, similar (B around CNZ)	**7.00**
2000 10 Pesos, similar but AÑO 2000 (B around CN)	**6.75**
2001 10 Pesos	**5.00**
1994 20 New Pesos, eagle/Hidalgo, N$20 (ALB around S)	**11.00**
1996 20 Pesos, similar but $20 (ALB around S)	**13.50**
2000 20 Pesos, eagle/Xiutecuhtli (B around CN)	**16.50**
2000 20 Pesos, eagle/Octavio Paz (B around CN)	**16.50**
1995 50 New Pesos, eagle/Niños Heroes, N$50 (ALB around S)	**25.00**
1996 50 Pesos, similar but $50 (ALB around S)	**22.00**

BULLION ISSUES

	Unc.
1991- 1/20 oz., eagle/winged Independence (S)	**3.00**
1991- 1/10 oz., similar (S)	**3.50**
1991- 1/4 oz., similar (S)	**5.00**
1991- 1/2 oz., similar (S)	**7.00**
1949 1 oz., coining press/balance scale (S)	**17.50**
1978-80 1 oz., similar (S)	**12.00**
1982- 1 oz., eagle/winged Independence (S)	**12.50**
2000 1 oz., eagle surrounded by 10 eagles/winged Independence (S)	**11.50**
1996- 2 oz., similar (S)	**24.00**
1996- 5 oz., similar (S)	**48.00**
1987- 1/20 oz., eagle/winged Independence (G)	**bullion + 30%**
1987 1/15 oz., similar (G)	**bullion + 25%**
1991-93 1/10 oz., similar (G)	**bullion + 20%**
1981-93 1/4 oz., similar (G)	**bullion + 11%**
1981-93 1/2 oz., similar (G)	**bullion + 8%**
1981-93 1 oz., similar (G)	**bullion + 3%**
1943 1.2057 oz., similar (G)	**550.00**
1989 1/4 oz., similar (Platinum)	PF **350.00**

REVOLUTIONARY ISSUES

	VF
Aguascalientes 1915 5 Centavos, eagle/cap and rays (C)	**25.00**
__. 1915 20 Centavos, similar (C)	**9.00**
Atlixtac 1915 10 Centavos, eagle/wreath (C)	**6.50**
Chihuahua 1915 5 Centavos, cap and rays/5 over ¢ (C)	**3.50**
Durango 1914 1 Centavo, date/wreath (C)	**35.00**
Jalisco 1915 2 Centavos, cap and rays/2 over 4 (C)	**17.50**
Oaxaca 1915 1 Centavo, inscription (C, rectangular)	**125.00**
Oaxaca 1915 5 Centavos, Juarez (C)	**4.50**
Puebla 1915 10 Centavos, eagle/X over C (C)	**17.50**
Sinaloa 1915 20 Centavos, eagle/value (S, cast)	*rare*

Coins of
the Americas

<table>
<tr><td>Nicaragua 2002 25 Centavos</td><td>Panama 2001 1/2 Balboa</td></tr>
</table>

NICARAGUA

	VF
1800s Token, Hacienda Elvira, tree (CN)	**45.00**
ca.1900 5 Centavos token, Lopez i Mallaño (B)	**50.00**
1912 1/2 Centavo, arms in triangle/wreath (C)	**2.50**
1878 1 Centavo, arms/wreath (CN)	**6.00**
1928 1 Centavo, arms in triangle/wreath (C)	**4.00**
1899 5 Centavos, similar (CN)	**1.50**
1936 5 Centavos, similar (CN)	**1.00**
1887 10 Centavos, arms in triangle/wreath (S)	**2.50**
1936 10 Centavos, Francisco Hernandez de Cordoba/Sun over five mountains (S)	**2.00**
1946 25 Centavos, similar (CN)	**.50**
1912 1 Cordoba, similar (S)	**75.00**

	Unc.
1954 50 Centavos, similar (CN)	**5.00**
1972 1 Cordoba, similar (CN)	**4.00**
1967 50 Cordobas, triangular arms/Ruben Dario (G)	**550.00**
1975 50 Cordobas, similar/USA's Liberty bell (S)	**21.50**
1974 5 Centavos, triangular arms (AL)	**.50**
2002 25 Centavos, Same (B clad Steel)	**.60**

	VF
1981 50 Centavos, Sandino (CN)	**1.75**
1987 5 Cordobas, Sandino's hat (ALB)	**4.00**
1994 10 Centavos, triangular arms/dove flying over Nicaragua (Steel)	**.75**
1997 1 Cordoba, triangular arms (N clad Steel)	**2.50**

PANAMA

	VF
1907 1/2 Centesimo, Balboa (CN)	**1.50**
1937 1 Centesimo, Uracca (C)	**3.50**
1904 2-1/2 Centesimos, Balboa/Arms (S) *Popularly called the "Panama Pill"*	**12.00**
1929 2-1/2 Centesimos, Balboa (CN)	**3.50**
1904 5 Centavos, Balboa/Arms (S)	**5.00**
1930 1/10th Balboa, arms/Balboa (S)	**4.00**
1947 1/4 Balboa, similar (S)	**2.00**
1904 50 Centesimos, Balboa/Arms (S)	**30.00**

	Unc.
1953 1 Centesimo, Uracca (C)	**2.00**
1966 1/10th Balboa, arms/Balboa (CN clad C)	**1.50**

Paraguay 2002 1 Guaranie

	Unc.
1971 1/2 Balboa, similar (S clad Billon).	PF **3.00**
1983 1/2 Balboa, similar (CN clad C)	**1.50**
2001 1/2 Balboa, similar (CN clad C).	**1.50**
1947 1 Balboa, allegory of Panama stg. with arms/Balboa (S)	**16.00**
1970 5 Balboas, discus thrower/arms (S)	**8.00**
1982 20 Balboas, Balboa up to knees in water/arms (S).	PF **115.00**
1999 100 Balboas, President Moscoso/Panama Canal (G).	PF **300.00**
1983 500 Balboas, butterfly/arms (G, scalloped).	PF **750.00**

PARAGUAY

	VF
1845 1/12 Real, lion with radiant cap on pole (C).	**20.00**
1870 1 Centesimo, star in wreath (C).	**5.00**
1903 5 Centavos, lion (CN)	**2.00**
1925 50 Centavos, star (CN)	**1.50**
1889 1 Peso, star in wreath/lion with cap on Pole (S)	**125.00**
1938 2 Pesos, star (AL)	**1.50**
	Unc.
1947 5 Centimos, passion flower (ALB)	**1.00**

	Unc.
1953 50 Centimos, lion/wreath (ALB, scalloped).	**.75**
2002 1 Guaranie ship/bank (S)	PF **55.00**
1975 5 Guaranies, woman with jar (Steel)	**.50**
1988 50 Guaranies, Estigarribia/dam (Steel)	**1.00**
1974 150 Guaranies, Einstein/arms (S).	PF **85.00**
1968 300 Guaranies, Stroessner/lion (S).	**9.00**
1997 500 Guaranies, Caballero/bank building (B)	**2.50**

PERU

	VF
1826 1/4 Real, Llama (S)	**14.00**
1833 1/2 Real, arms/Liberty stg. (S).	**6.00**
(ca.1860s) 1/2 Real token of Hotel of Commerce, Trujillo. Chicken on plate/wreath (C).	**scarce**
1849 2 Reales, similar (S)	**15.00**
1853 8 Reales, similar (S)	**200.00**
1854 4 Reales, similar (S)	**25.00**
1863 1 Centavo, sun/two cornucopiae (CN)	**2.50**
1876 2 Centavos, similar (C).	**3.00**
1888 1/5th Sol, arms/Peru std. (S)	**3.50**
1891 1 Sol, similar (S).	**7.00**
1901 1 Centavo, sun/two cornucopiae (C)	**2.50**
1919 2 Centavos, similar (C).	**.75**
1921 10 Centavos, head of Peru/fern branch (CN)	**.75**
1945 10 Centavos, similar (B).	**.50**
1935 1/2 Sol, arms/Peru std. (S)	**2.50**
1951 1 Sol, arms (B)	**.50**
	Unc.
1966 1 Sol, arms/Llama (B).	**1.00**
1972 10 Soles, arms/Tupac Amaru (CN)	**1.25**
1962 100 Soles, arms/Peru std. (G)	**650.00**
1973 100 Soles, arms/flower (S)	**12.50**
1984 100 Soles, Adm. Grau (B)	**1.00**
1987 1 Inti, arms/Adm. Grau (CN)	**.75**
1986 100 Intis, Marshall Caceres/arms	**17.50**

Uruguay 1942 1 Peso

Uruguay 1953 5 Centesimos

Peru 1997 1 Nuevo Sol

URUGUAY

	VF
1991 5 Centavos, arms (B)	.45
1996 1 Nuevo Sol, miner and oil derrick/ arms (S)	4.00
1997 1 Nuevo Sol, arms/Barrenechen (S)	PF 55.00
1994 5 Nuevos Soles, arms/bird (Steel around B)	6.50
1926 1 Libra, arms/Indian (G)	160.00

SURINAME

	Unc.
1962 1 Cent, arms (C)	.75
1987 100 Cents, arms (CN)	2.00
1985 25 Gulden, dove/fist on star (S)	55.00

TRINIDAD & TOBAGO

	Unc.
1966 1 Cent, arms (C)	.15
1971 10 Cents, arms (CN)	.30
1979 50 Cents, steel drums (CN)	1.50
1973 1 Dollar, cerico bird (CN)	3.00
1976 5 Dollars, arms/Ibis (S)	10.00
1982 10 Dollars, arms/flag (CN)	20.00
1994 10 Dollars, arms/bird (S)	PF 47.50
1984 200 Dollars, arms/bank building (G)	PF 110.00

	VF
1844 1 Peso, arms (S)	350.00
1857 5 Centesimos, sun face/wreath (C)	12.00
1869 1 Centesimo, similar (C)	2.00
1877 10 Centesimos, arms/wreath (S)	6.00
1895 1 Peso, similar (S)	25.00
1901 1 Centesimo, sun (CN)	.75
1924 2 Centesimos, sun (CN)	1.00
1936 5 Centavos, sun (CN)	1.00
1930 10 Centesimos, head of Uruguay/ cougar (ALB)	2.50
1917 50 Centesimos, arms/Artigas (S)	7.00
1942 1 Peso, Artigas/cougar (S)	2.25
early 1900s 10 Centesimos token of Villegas Bros. Vinyard, Carmelo (B)	10.00

	XF
1948 2 Centesimos, sun (C)	1.00
1953 5 Centesimos, Artigas (CN)	.50
1960 5 Centesimos, Artigas (B)	.25

	Unc.
1977 1 Centesimo, sun with face (AL)	.25
1977 5 Centesimos, bull (AL)	.45
1976 10 Centesimos, horse (ALB)	.80

Uruguay 1981 2 Nuevos Pesos

Venezuela 1858 1 Centavo

Uruguay 2000 10 Pesos

Venezuela 1945 2 Bolivares

Unc.

1965 1 Peso, Artigas/arms (ALB) . . . . . . **.60**
1961 10 Pesos, Gaucho/wreath (S) . . . **7.00**
1981 2 Nuevos Pesos, five ears of grain
  (CNZ). **1.00**
1989 10 Nuevos Pesos, sun (Steel). . . . . **.50**
1989 100 Nuevos Pesos, Gaucho (Steel) **.75**
1981 5,000 Nuevos Pesos, dam/
  Uruguayan and Argentine arms (S)
  Proof **15.00**
1994 2 Pesos Urugayos, Artigas (B) . . **1.50**
2000 10 Pesos, Artigas
  (Steel around B) **3.50**
2000 250 Pesos Urugayos, couple on
  horse (S) . . . . *PF* **47.50**

VENEZUELA

F

Guaiana 1814 1/2 Real, castle/lion (C)
  . . . . **25.00**
1822 1/4 Real, star around "19" (S)
  . . . . **275.00**

VF

1830 1/4 Real, cornucopia/wreath (S)
  . . . . **38.50**
1843 1/4 Centavo, Liberty head/wreath
  (C) **7.50**
1858 1 Centavo, similar (C) **6.00**
1863 10 Reales, Esclarecido/wreath (S)
  . . . . *rare*
1876 1 Centavo, arms/wreath (CN) . . **6.00**
1886 1/2 Bolivar, Bolivar/arms (S) . . . **20.00**
1893 1 Bolivar, similar (S) **12.00**

VF

1858 1 Real token of J.B. Hellyer, alligator
  (C) **45.00**
1887 1 Real token of F.B. Leon (CN)
  . . . . **70.00**
1921 5 Centimos, arms (CN) **2.00**
1938 12-1/2 Centimos, arms (CN). . . . . . **.30**
1944 12-1/2 Centimos, arms (B) **4.50**
1929 1/4 Bolivar, Bolivar/arms (S) . . . . . **.75**
1935 1/2 Bolivar, similar (S). . . . . **.75**
1911 1 Bolivar, similar (S). **5.00**
1954 1 Bolivar, similar (S) **1.25**

Venezuela 1977 1 Bolivar

Venezuela 1999 500 Bolivares

Venezuela 1983 100 Bolivares

	Unc.
1977 5 Bolivares, similar (N)	**1.50**
1973 10 Bolivares, Bolivar in rounded rectangle/arms in rounded rectangle (S)	PF **10.00**
2000 20 Bolivares, Bolivar/arms (N clad Steel)	**.25**
1975 50 Bolivares, arms/Armadillo (S)	**25.00**
1980 75 Bolivares, Sucre/donkey running (S)	**10.00**
1983 100 Bolivares, Bolivar standing/ building (S)	PF **17.50**
1975 500 Bolivares, Bolivar in rounded rectangle/oil wells in rounded rectangle (G)	**12,000.00**
1990 500 Bolivares, Jose Paez/arms (S)	PF **25.00**
1998 500 Bolivares, Bolivar/arms (Steel)	**.75**
1999 500 Bolivares, similar	**1.50**
Leprosarium. 1913 1/8 Bolivar, Maracaibo/ Bs 1/8 (B)	VF **12.00**

The above coin was struck for use inside government-run leper colonies. Brazil, Colombia, Costa Rica, and Panama also struck such pieces.

	VF
1945 2 Bolivares, similar (S)	**2.75**
1902 5 Bolivares, similar (S)	**16.00**
1936 5 Bolivares, similar (S)	**11.50**
1912 20 Bolivares, similar (G)	**70.00**

	Unc.
1983 5 Centimos, arms (N clad Steel)	**.10**
1971 10 Centimos arms (CN)	**.25**
1977 25 Centimos, Bolivararms (N)	**.20**
1960 50 Centimos, similar (S)	**2.00**
1977 1 Bolivar, similar (N)	**.65**
1960 2 Bolivares, similar (S)	**3.50**

WORLD PAPER MONEY

Paper money was created to make several things possible. The original reason for the invention of paper money in China in the 1200s was to permit the government to spend an increased amount of money without having to occur the expense of actually making coins of that value. Such deficit financing has, over the last few centuries, been the cause for hundreds of countries printing literally billions of pieces of paper money. Most governments have had the ability to force their citizens to accept their paper money through coercion, but they have not always had to. Historically, most governments' notes have been backed up by full or partial reserves of precious metal, and such notes have been able to be redeemed for that bullion under specified conditions. This has been less and less the case over the last thirty or so years. There are also advantages to the general public in the use of paper money. It permits the convenient transportation of a fixed amount of value. Because it is physically small, it is also easier to hide, therefore making such transportation and storage not only more convenient, but also more secure. Unfortunately, when a government that has issued paper money is overthrown, its paper, unlike its precious metal coins, often becomes worthless. Many countries even declare their own paper money obsolete every ten or twenty years as a matter of course.

There are no surviving examples of the first paper, issued in China 700 years ago, but specimens are known of notes printed on mulberry bark paper in the 1300s during the Ming dynasty. The first European notes were printed in France in the 1600s when the king of France wished to raise funds without having to part with gold or silver bullion. It was at that time a failure, and it was over a century later that paper money became accepted in any serious way by any European population. This was during the French Revolution, when the government printed *assignats* backed up by confiscated Church property.

Over the last decade, the market in collectible paper money has been very strong. Many prices have increased and over-the-counter sales at shows are far more brisk than they were a decade ago. Like coins, the value of a piece of paper money varies based on its state of preservation.

GRADING PAPER MONEY

State of preservation is as important for paper money as it is for coins. Paper money is primarily graded to describe the amount of wear. Other factors can influence value though. Many of the terms used to describe the grades of paper money are the same as for coins. Of course the physical nature of paper requires a whole different set of definitions. They are briefly described here.

Crisp Uncirculated (CU)—This note is as pristine as when issued. It is literally crisp, with sharply pointed corners. It must have absolutely no folds, tears, or edge rounding. It can have no stains or staple holes either.

Extremely Fine (XF)—This is a particularly nice note with only the slightest sign of wear. It will still be crisp to the touch. Slight rounding of the corner points is possible, but no significant folds or creases. No tears, stains or staple holes at all.

A convenient method of detecting creases in a note is to hold the note pointed at a narrow light source and look at it from an acute angle, though not directly in the direction of the light.

Very Fine (VF)—This is a nice clean note with obvious, but moderate, signs of wear. Creases which break the ink will be visible, but generally only one in each direction, and neither crease too deep. Its corner points will be dull. While not limp, it will have only some of the crispness of better grade notes. No significant stains are visible.

Fine (F)—This is a worn, but not worn-out note. It has no crispness left. It will have heavy creases, but none that threaten the structural integrity of the note. Its edges may not be perfectly smooth, but are not irregularly worn. Trivial ink marks and smudges are acceptable.

Very Good (VG)—This note is worn and limp. It has serious deep creases. The edges are worn and not even. Some ink marks or smudges are visible. Tiny tears may be present, but no parts missing. Small staple or pin holes are acceptable.

Good (G)—This condition is not considered collectible for most purposes. Only the rarest of notes in this grade could find a home with most collectors. It is usually limp, heavily creased, stained, ripped, and pinned or stapled. Some of the creases will permit spots of light to shine through the note at their intersections.

Many collectors consider grades below strictly Uncirculated unacceptable for common notes. Grades below this may be worth a fraction of the prices indicated for Uncirculated. It is important to realize that most examples of world paper money in low grades such as G to VG may have virtually no wholesale value.

Also, collectors should be aware that certain practices are designed to take an authentic note and make it appear to be in a better grade of preservation than it is. These include ironing a note to make it look less worn, and expertly gluing tears. Hold your note up to a light. Light will pass through the glue differently than through normal currency.

HANDLING AND TREATMENT OF PAPER CURRENCY

The most important thing to know about handling currency is to **never fold paper money**. This instantaneously reduces its value. When in doubt as to whether a note has value or not, place it flat in a book until you can consult a numismatist or coin dealer. Do not carry an interesting note around in your wallet. When handling a note, remember that its most fragile parts are its corners. Never touch them. Also never repair a tear in a note with tape. The tape usually is a greater detriment to the note's value than the tear. Attempts to clean a note are also likely to cause damage.

COUNTERFEITS

Because of the potential for counterfeiting, most paper money is made with a number of deterrents incorporated, all of which are intended to make reproduction difficult. Several countries have even considered replacing paper (actually combinations of paper and cloth) with plastic notes. Australia has circulated these plastic notes for years with great success. Multicolored inks and intricately engraved designs may have been intended to thwart counterfeiters, but they have had the secondary result of encouraging collecting.

When choosing a rare currency dealer, make sure the person has the skills to know a note is real, and the ethics to accept it back if it is not. There are specialized organizations that enforce codes of ethics. Two of the largest are the International Banknote Society (IBNS) and the Professional Currency Dealers Association (PCDA). These insignia in advertising ndicate that the dealer is a member.

DATES

The dates of the notes listed following are the series or law dates appearing on the notes themselves. However, dates appearing on paper money are not necessarily the actual dates of printing, which often can be told only by an analysis of the signatures printed on the notes. Dates in parentheses are actual issue dates, which do not appear in the notes.

A book such as this can do no more than simply introduce the collector to this aesthetically pleasurable hobby. Thus, it is particularly important for anyone interested in collecting world paper money to acquire one or more of the excellent specialized books listed following.

Specialized Books: Cuhaj, George and Shafer, Neil, eds. *Standard Catalog of World Paper Money, Specialized Issues. 9th edition.*

Cuhaj, George S., ed. *Standard Catalog of World Paper Money, Modern Issues. 10th edition.*

Monetary Research Institute. *MRI Bankers' Guide to Foreign Currency.*

Shafer, Neil and George Cuhaj, eds. *Standard Catalog of World Paper Money, General Issues. 10th edition.*

Known Counterfeits: Good counterfeits of British notes were made during World War II by the Germans, and allied counterfeits of Ottoman notes were made during World War I. Many counterfeits are not made by the same process as the real notes they imitate. Often the counterfeits will lack the precise detail of the originals. Notes of significant value should be authenticated by an expert.

AFGHANISTAN

	VF
1299SH (1920) 1 Rupee, coins/blank	**7.00**
	Unc.
1340 SH (1961) 10 Afghanis, king/mosque	**1.00**
1352 SH (1973) 10 Afghanis, president/arch	**2.25**
1357 SH (1978) 50 Afghanis, national seal (Inscription in wreath)/Building	**20.00**
1370 SH (1991) 500 Afghanis, horsemen racing/fortress	**1.50**
1372 SH (1993) 5,000 Afghanis, mosque with minaret/hexagonal mosque	**2.00**

Note: The 1996-2001 Taliban regime issued no paper money.

1381 SH (2002) 1 (New) Afghani, bank seal/mosque with two domes	**.50**

ALBANIA

	F
1926 5 Franka Ari, boy in fez	**20.00**
1939 20 Franga, Roma std.	**7.00**
	Unc.
1957 10 Leke, Arms	**2.00**
1964 1 Lek, peasant couple/mountain fortress	**1.50**
1976 5 Leke, bridge/freighter ship	**1.25**

Afghanistan 1372SH (1993) 5,000 Afghanis

Albania 2001 1,000 Leke

Argentina 1991 100,000 Australes

Australia 1938-1952 1 Pound

Unc.

1992 1,000 Leke, Skanderbeg/arms and tower......................**22.50**
2001 1,000 Leke, D. Bogadani/church **14.50**

ANGOLA

VF

1861 1,000 Reis, Portuguese arms . . . *rare*
1921 1 Escudo, Francisco de Oliveira Chamico and steamship/woman looking out at ships............**50.00**
1956 20 Escudos, Porto r./gazelle running **4.00**

Unc.

1962 20 Escudos, dock/gazelles running **25.00**
1976 100 Kwanzas, Antonio Neto/ agricultural workers............**5.00**
1995 1,000 Kwanzas Reajustados, Jose Dos Santos and Antonia Neto/ antelope......................**3.00**

ARGENTINA

F

1884 5 Centavos, Avellanda **15.00**
1900 1 Peso, Argentina std. (grey-blue-pink)........................**110.00**

Unc.

1935 1 Peso, Similar (blue on pink paper) **3.50**
1960 5 Pesos, Young Jose de San Martin/ people in plaza.................**5.50**
1983-84 1 Peso Argentino, Old Jose de San Martin/mountainlake..........**.75**
1991 100,000 Australes, M. Quintana/ progress std. with torch **45.00**

AUSTRALIA

VF

1923 1 Pound, George V **700.00**
1938-52 1 Pound, George VI/shepards and sheep **10.00**

Unc.

1961-65 10 Shillings, M. Flinders/ parliament building...........**125.00**

Unc.

1974-83 1 Dollar, Elizabeth II/aboriginal art **1.25**
1994-01 20 Dollars, Biplane and Rev. J. Flynn/sailing ship and M. Reiby. .**27.50**

AUSTRIA

F

1759 10 Gulden, inscriptions .... *rare*
1847 100 Gulden, Austria, Atlas and Minerva.....................**600.00**
1858 100 Gulden, Austria I., Danube r. **450.00**
1880 100 Gulden, boys with sheaf and book **800.00**
1919 2 Kronen, female heads **1.00**

VF

1919 1,000 Kronen, imperial eagle, female bust r...........................**.75**
1927 10 Schilling, Mercury/harvest .**20.00**
1936 100 Schilling, woman with Edelweiss **600.00**
1945 10 Schilling, woman/mountain .**2.00**

Unc.

1956 20 Schilling, A. von Welsbach/ mountain village **15.00**
1967 20 Schilling, C. Ritter von Ghega/ railway bridge over Semmering Pass **4.50**
1986 20 Schilling, M. Daffinger/Albertina Museum, Vienna...............**3.25**
1985 50 Schilling, Sigmund Freud/ Josephinum Medical School **7.00**
1988 5,000 Schilling, Wolfgang A. Mozart/ opera house, Vienna **575.00**

BAHAMAS

VF

1870s Bank of Nassau 5 Shillings, Victoria I.................**scarce**
1919 1 Pound, George V and ship .**525.00**
1936 4 Shillings, George VI and ship**40.00**
1953 4 Shillings, Elizabeth II and ship **7.50**

Unc.

1965 1/2 Dollar, Elizabeth II/underwater scene of fish....................**7.50**

Austria 1919 2 Kronen

Bahamas 2001 1/2 Dollar

	Unc.
2001 1/2 Dollar, Elizabeth II/smiling woman at market	**2.75**
1996 100 Dollars, Elizabeth II/swordfish	**185.00**

BAHRAIN

	Unc.
1964 100 Fils, boats/palm trees	**5.00**
1973 (1986-98) 1/2 Dinar, weaver/ "Aluminum Bahrain" facility	**3.50**
2001 20 Dinars, Emir/Ahmed al-Fateh Islamic Center	**100.00**

BELARUS

	Unc.
1992 50 Kapeek, knight/squirrel	**.30**
1995 50,000 Rublei, Medieval gateway/ modern star-shaped gateway	**8.00**

BELGIUM

	VF
1851-52 100 Francs, two cherubs	*rare*
1910-20 20 Francs, Minerva and lion	**12.00**
1919 1,000 Francs, allegorical figures	**300.00**
1927-32 100 Francs, Albert and Elizabeth	**2.50**
1952-59 100 Francs, Leopold I	**5.50**
	Unc.
1964 20 Francs, King Baudouin/molecule	**2.00**
1978-81 100 Francs, H. Beyaert/geometric design	**25.00**
1995-, 100 Francs, J. Ensor and theatrical masks/beach scene	**7.50**
1992-97 10,000 Francs, King Baudouin and Queen Fabiola/greenhouses at Laeken	**600.00**
1997 10,000 Francs, King Albert II and Queen Paola/same as above	**350.00**

BERMUDA

	F
1914 1 Pound, arms	**1,750.00**

	F
1920-35 5 Shillings, George V/ship	**800.00**
	VF
1937 5 Shillings, George VI and Hamilton harbor	**40.00**
1952-57 5 Shillings, Elizabeth II and Hamilton harbor	**7.50**
	Unc.
1966 5 Pounds, Elizabeth/arms	**850.00**
1970 1 Dollar, Elizabeth II/two sailboats	**22.50**
1988 5 Dollars, Elizabeth II/lighthouse and harbor scene	**8.50**
1996 100 Dollars, Elizabeth II/House of Assembly	**175.00**

Note: Many Bermuda notes after 1978 marked SPECIMEN trade below their nominal values.

BOLIVIA

	VF
1902 1 Boliviano, arms and vegetation	**5.00**
1928 1 Boliviano, Bolivar and mountain	**1.00**
1942 500 Bolivianos, miner	**85.00**
1945 500 Bolivianos, Busch/miners	**1.50**
	Unc.
1962 5 Pesos Bolivianos, G. Villarroel/oil refinery	**12.00**
1981 500 Pesos Bolivianos, Avaroa/Puerto de Antofagasta in 1879	**2.00**
1986 50 Bolivianos, M. Perez de Holguin/ early church	**17.50**

BOSNIA-HERZEGOVINA

	Unc.
1992 100 Dinara, Dove of Peace	**12.00**
1992 100 Dinara, shield containing arm with sword	**1.75**
1994 500 Dinara, shield containing six fleurs-de-lis	**6.00**

Bahrain 1973 1/2 Dinar

Bermuda 1966 5 Pounds

Bolivia 1986 50 Bolivianos

Bosnia-Herzegovina 1992 100 Dinara

Brazil 1991-1993 10,000 Cruzeiros

Bulgaria 1997 10,000 Leva

BRAZIL

F

1833 1 Mil Reis, arms l., Commerce std. center/blank **45.00**

1860-68 5 Mil Reis, arms between Justice and Commerce. **50.00**

1870 1 Mil Reis, Pedro II and arms . .**15.00**

1885 2 Mil Reis, Pedro II and church/Rio de Janeiro Post Office. **30.00**

Estampa 3A (1893) 500 Reis, woman with sheep **12.00**

Estampa 11A (1907) 5 Mil Reis, woman std. with flowers and fruit **30.00**

Estampa 17A (1925) 10 Mil Reis, Pres. Manuel Ferraz de Campos Salles . **6.00**

Estampa 17A (1936) 100 Mil Reis, A. Santos Dumont. **20.00**

VF

1943 10 Cruzeiros, Getullio Vargas/ allegory of Industry **5.00**

Estampa 1A (1955-59) 50 Cruzeiros, Princess Isabel/allegory of Law . . . **4.00**

Estampa 2A (1954-61) Similar **1.25**

Unc.

(1961-62) 5 Cruzeiros, bust of male Indian/ flower floating. **1.25**

Unc.

(1972-80) 1 Cruzeiro, Liberty head in circle/bank building in circle . . . . **.50**

(1988) 5,000 Cruzados, bust of C. Portinari/C. Portinari painting **4.00**

(1991-93) 10,000 Cruzeiros, Vital Brazil and snake being milked for venom/one snake swallowing another. **1.00**

BULGARIA

F

1885 20 Leva, arms **575.00**

1904 5 Leva, value/arms. **25.00**

1922 5 Leva, arms/beehives **4.50**

1942 500 Leva, Tsar Boris III/allegorical woman **7.00**

1943 200 Leva, Tsar Simeon II and arms/ view of Tirnovo **5.00**

Unc.

1947 20 Leva, Bank building **10.00**

1951 100 Leva, G. Dimitrov and arms/ woman with grapes . . . . **.25**

1962 1 Lev, arms/war monument . . . **1.75**

1974 2 Leva, arms/woman picking grapes **1.75**

1991 20 Leva, portrait of medieval duchess/Boyana church . . . . **.25**

1997 10,000 Leva, Dr. P. Beron/Telescope **17.50**

CAMBODIA

VF

(1955) 10 Riels, Temple of Banteay Srei/ Phnom-Penh central market **10.00**

Unc.

(1963-72) 100 Riels, Preah Vihear Temple/ Areal view of Preah Vihear Temple **1.00**

Unc.

(1973) 1,000 Riels, Children at desks/ ancient stone face **1.00**

1998 5,000 Riels, King Sihanouk/Phnom-Penh central market. **6.50**

CANADA

A much fuller treatment of Canadian paper money is provided here than for any other country. This is due to the wide popularity of collecting in North America.

As in the United States, many of Canada's earlier notes were actually issued by banks and not by the government. They were gradually eliminated by the 1940s. Fractional notes, with face values under one dollar, were common well into the 20th century. They are frequently found in very worn condition.

Note that the prices here are for the most common date appearing on the note and most common variety for each design described. There are sometimes many varieties, and a specialized reference should be consulted.

Additional Specialized Reference: Charlton, J.E. *Standard Catalogue of Canadian Charter Bank Notes.*

Charlton, J.E. *Standard Catalogue of Canadian Government Paper Money.*

Known Counterfeits: The series of 1954 is known to have been counterfeited in the 20, 50, 100, and 1,000 dollar denominations. Counterfeits are also known of some of the earlier private bank notes.

Many Canadian notes have small colored discs called plachets embedded in the paper. This is a counterfeit deterrent. Those which are simply printed (without plachets) are counterfeit.

Canada 1967 1 Dollar

Twenty Five Cents

	VF
1870 Bust of Britannia	50.50
1900 Britannia std.	12.50
1923 Bust of Britannia	12.50

One Dollar

	F
1866 Champlain and Cartier	1,000.00
1870 Cartier and woman with child and globe	500.00
1878 Countess of Dufferin	135.00

	VF
1897 Countess and Earl of Aberdeen, lumberjacks between/Parliament building	125.00
1911 Earl and Countess of Grey/ parliament building	125.00
1917 Princess of Connaught	75.00
1923 George IV	50.00
1935 George V	45.00
1937 George VI	8.00

	Unc.
1954 Elizabeth II with "Devil's face" in hair/Prairie scene	37.50
1954 similar, no "Devil's face"	12.50
1967 Elizabeth II/Parliament	3.50
1973 Elizabeth II/floating logs in river near Parliament	5.00

Two Dollars

	F
1866 Indian woman, Britannia scene, sailor	2,200.00
1870 Gen. Montcalm, Indian chief, Gen. Wolfe	2,500.00
1878 Earl of Dufferin	1,850.00
1887 Marchioness and Marquis of Lansdowne	450.00

	VF
1897 Prince of Wales and fishermen in boat/wheat threshing scene	250.00
1914 Duke and Duchess of Connaught/ arms	200.00
1923 Prince of Wales	120.00

	VF
1935 Queen Mary	75.00
1937 George VI	15.00

	Unc.
1954 Elizabeth II with "Devil's face" in hair/Quebec scene	55.00
1954 similar, no "Devil's face"	15.00
1974 Elizabeth II/Inuit scene	9.50
1986 Elizabeth II/two robins	3.00

Four Dollars

	F
1882 Duke of Argyll	750.00

	VF
1900 Countess and Earl of Minto, ship in lock between/Parliament building	1,000.00
1902 similar but ship on Canadian side of lock	1,200.00

Five Dollars

	F
1866 Victoria, arms, sailing ship	4,500.00

	VF
1912 Locomotive	350.00
1924 Queen Mary	2,000.00
1935 Prince of Wales	150.00
1937 George VI	15.00

	Unc.
1954 Elizabeth II with "Devil's face" in hair/Otter Falls	80.00
1954 similar, no "Devil's face"	30.00
1972-79 Sir Wilfred Laurier/fishing boat	25.00
1986 Sir Wilfred Laurier/kingfisher	6.50

Ten Dollars

	F
1866 Sailors, lion and beaver	9,000.00

	VF
1935 Princess Mary	100.00
1937 George VI	20.00

	Unc.
1954 Elizabeth II with "Devil's face" in hair/Mt. Burgess	85.00

Canada 1973 1 Dollar

Canada 1974 2 Dollars

Canada 1986 2 Dollars

Canada 1986 5 Dollars

	Unc.
1954 similar, no "Devil's face"	**45.00**
1971 Sir John MacDonald/oil refinery	**40.00**
1989 Sir John MacDonald/osprey	**12.00**
2001 same/memorial	**7.00**

Twenty Dollars

	F
1866 Princess of Wales, Beaver, Prince Albert	*rare*

	VF
1935 Princess Elizabeth	**350.00**
1937 George VI	**30.00**

	Unc.
1954 Elizabeth II with "Devil's face" in hair/Laurentian Hills	**140.00**
1954 similar, no "Devil's face"	**65.00**
1969-79 Elizabeth II/Lake Moraine and Rocky Mountains	**55.00**
1991 Elizabeth II/loon	**22.50**

Twenty Five Dollars

	VF
1935 George V and Queen Mary	**1,200.00**

Fifty Dollars

	VF
1935 Duke of York	**600.00**
1937 George VI	**65.00**

	Unc.
1954 Elizabeth II with "Devil's face" in hair/Nova Scotia coastline	**200.00**
1954 similar, no "Devil's face"	**150.00**
1975 W.L. MacKenzie King/mounted police in formation	**150.00**
1988 W.L. MacKenzie King/snowy owl	**50.00**

One Hundred Dollars

	VF
1935 Duke of Gloucester	**450.00**
1937 Sir John MacDonald	**140.00**

	Unc.
1954 Elizabeth II with "Devil's face" in hair/Okanagan Lake	**250.00**
1954 similar, no "Devil's face"	**200.00**
1975 Sir Robert Borden/Nova Scotia harbor scene	**190.00**
1988 Sir Robert Borden/Canada goose	**95.00**

Five Hundred Dollars

	VF
1896 Genius, Marquis of Lorne and Parliament building *Cancelled*	**6,500.00**
1911 Queen Mary	**8,000.00**
1925 George V	**3,850.00**
1935 Sir John MacDonald	**3,500.00**

One Thousand Dollars

	VF
1896 Queen Victoria. *Cancelled*	**6,500.00**
1901 Lord Roberts... *Cancelled*	**6,500.00**
1911 George V *VG*	**3,500.00**
1924 Lord Roberts... *Cancelled*	**5,000.00**
1925 Queen Mary	**6,500.00**
1935 Sir Wilfred Laurier	**990.00**
1937 similar	**1,150.00**

	Unc.
1954 Elizabeth II with "Devil's face" in hair/landscape	**2,250.00**
1954 similar, no "Devil's face"	**1,300.00**
1988 Elizabeth II/two pine grosbeaks	**900.00**

Five Thousand Dollars

	VF
1896 J.A. MacDonald *Cancelled*	**6,500.00**
1901 Queen Victoria. *Cancelled*	**3,500.00**
1918-24 similar *Cancelled*	**5,000.00**

Fifty Thousand Dollars

	VF
1918-24 George V and Queen Mary *Cancelled*	**6,000.00**

Chile 1970-1976 10 Escudos

CHILE

	F
1881 5 Pesos, Village and Gen. Freire	**60.00**
1918-22 5 Pesos, Chile std. with shield	**10.00**
1929 1,000 Pesos, Condor	**200.00**

	VF
1939-47 20 Pesos, Capt. Valdivia/park scene	**3.50**
1958-59 5 Pesos, O'Higgins	**.25**

	Unc.
1962-70 1/2 Escudo, Bernardo O'Higgins/ early explorer	**3.00**
1970-76 10 Escudos, J.M. Balmaceda/ battle scene	**2.00**
1975-81 50 Pesos, Capt. A. Prat/sailing ship	**2.00**

	Unc.
1989-95 10,000 Pesos, Capt. A. Prat/ Hacienda	**45.00**

CHINA, EMPIRE

	F
1368-99 300 Cash, three strings of coins	**rare**
1856-59 5,000 Cash, inscription with dragons	**60.00**

	VF
1904 5 Dollars, "Imperial Bank of China," Confucius stg./same in Chinese, Confucius stg.	**125.00**
1910 10 Dollars, Prince Chun l., dragon above Great Wall	**900.00**

China (People's Republic) 1990 2 Yuan

China (People's Republic) 1999 10 Yuan

China (Taiwan) 1999 50 Yuan

Colombia 1997-2001 5,000 Pesos

CHINA, REPUBLIC

	VF
1931 5 Yuan, Temple of Heaven	**5.00**
1937 5 Yuan, Sun Yat-sen/skyscraper	**.25**
1940 10 Cents, Temple of Heaven	**.75**
1947 1,000 Customs Gold Units, Sun Yat-sen/building	**2.00**

Republic of Taiwan

	Unc.
1946 1 Yuan, Bank building and Sun Yat-sen/naval battle	**6.00**
1954 1 Yuan, Sun Yat-sen/bank building	**5.00**
1961 1 Yuan, Sun Yat-sen/presidential office building	**3.00**
1972 50 Yuan, Sun Yat-sen/Chungshan building	**6.00**
1987 100 Yuan, similar	**7.00**
1999 50 Yuan, Bank building, polymer plastic	**4.00**

CHINA, PEOPLES REPUBLIC

	Unc.
1948 5 Yuan, sheep	*XF* **18.00**
1953 2 Fen, airplane	**.25**
1953 5 Fen, freighter	**.30**
1962 1 Jiao, farm workers	**.50**
1972 5 Jiao, textile workers	**.75**
1980 1 Jiao, two Taiwanese	**.50**
1990 2 Yuan, 2 portraits, seascape	**.75**
1990 50 Yuan, three portraits/waterfalls	**12.50**
1979 10 Fen Foreign Exchange Certificate, waterfall	**.50**
1999 10 Yuan, Mao Tse Tung/3 gorges	**2.50**

COLOMBIA

	F
1819 2 Reales/25 Centavos donkey with pack	**100.00**
1860s 1 Peso = 10 Reales, steamship	**150.00**

	F
1888 1 Peso, Arms and Bolivar	**18.00**

	VF
1929-54 1 Peso, Santander and Bolivar/liberty	**.75**
1953-63 10 Pesos, Gen. Nariño/bank	**7.50**

	Unc.
1959-77 1 Peso Oro, Bolivar and Santander/Condor	**3.00**
1974-78 200 Pesos Oro, Bolivar/coffee picker	**20.00**
1997-2001 5,000 Pesos, J. Asuncion Silva/woman amid trees	**8.00**

COSTA RICA

	F
1871 2 Pesos, arms l., woman r.	**400.00**
1910-14 1 Colon, Columbus and arms	**70.00**
1914-32 10 Colones, coffee pickers	**65.00**

	VF
1942-48 10 Colones, Carazo/sailing ship	**15.00**
1951-62 10 Colones, Echeverria/oxcart	**20.00**

	Unc.
1963-67 5 Colones, B. Carrillo/coffee worker	**45.00**
1977-88 100 Colones, R. Jimenez/Supreme Court building	**15.00**
1996 5000 Colones, Ancient sculpture/ancient stone sphere and animals	**45.00**

CROATIA

	Unc.
1941 10 Kuna	**10.00**
1991 1 Dinar, R. Boskovic and geometry/Zagreb Cathedral	**.10**
1995 10 Kuna, J. Dobrila/Pula Arena	**4.00**

CUBA

	F
1857-59 100 Pesos, allegorical scene	*rare*
1872-83 5 Centavos, arms/allegory	**7.50**

Cuba 1949-1960 1 Peso

Czechoslovakia 1961 3 Korun

	F
1905 10 Pesos, T. Palma	*rare*
1934-48 10 Pesos, Cespedes	**80.00**

	VF
1949-60 10 Pesos, Cespedes	**4.50**

	Unc.
1949-60 1 Peso, Jose Marti	**22.50**

1961-65 1 Peso, Jose Marti/Castro entering Havana **7.50**
1971-90 20 Pesos, C. Cienfuegos/soldiers on beach **10.00**
1995 3 Pesos, Ernesto Che Guevara/ Guevara cutting sugar cane **1.50**
1985-, 1 Peso Foreign Exchange Certificate, San Salvador de la Punta castle **3.50**

CZECHOSLOVAKIA

	VF
1919 1 Koruna, Arms	**1.50**

1920 100 Korun, Bohemian lion and Pagan priestess/female portraits at each side **60.00**
1932 1,000 Korun, Figure scanning globe **40.00**
1945 1,000 Korun, King George Podebrad/castle **3.00**
1953 25 Korun, equestrian statue/view of Tabor **7.50**

	Unc.
1961 3 Korun, arms	**2.00**

1973 500 Korun, soldiers in rain gear/ medieval fortress **30.00**
1986 10 Korun, P. Orszagh Hviezdoslav/ Orava mountains **2.00**

DENMARK

	F
1713 5 Rigsdaler, Crowned F4 monogram	
. . . .	*rare*

1819 1 Rigsbankdaler, inscriptions and ornaments **75.00**
1819 100 Rigsbankdaler, inscriptions **1,000.00**
1875-90 10 Kroner, arms **450.00**
1916-21 1 Krone, value/arms **3.00**

	VF
1910-42 50 Kroner, fishermen pulling net into boat/arms within vine	**30.00**

	Unc.

1950-60 5 Kroner, B. Thorvaldsen and three graces/Kalundborg city view **25.00**
1972-78 10 Kroner, S. Kirchhoff/eider bird (duck) **4.00**
1997-2003 500 Kroner, N. Bohr/medieval relief of knight fighting dragon **105.00**

DOMINICAN REPUBLIC

	VF
1810 4 Escalins, arms	**rare**

1848 2 Pesos = 80 Centa with 40 Pesos overprint, Boy l., arms center . . . **225.00**
1867 10 Pesos, arms **175.00**
1947-59 100 Pesos, woman with coffee pot . . . . *VF* **90.00**

	Unc.

1961 10 Centavos Oro, Reserve Bank building **15.00**
1978-88 5 Pesos Oro, Sanchez/ hydroelectric dam **5.50**
1992 1000 Pesos Oro, National Palace/ Columbus' fortress **110.00**

ECUADOR

	VF
1928-38 5 Sucres, woman std. with fruit and sickle	**45.00**

1939-49 100 Sucres, woman scanning globe **60.00**

	Unc.

1957-74 10 Sucres, Conquistador . . . **15.00**
1957-80 100 Sucres, Bolivar/arms, American Banknote Co. **12.50**
1961-65 100 Sucres, same but T.DeLaRue **50.00**
1976-82 1000 Sucres, Ruminahui/arms **25.00**
1986 10 Sucres, Benalcazar at center/ arms **3.50**
1995 50,000 Sucres, E. Alfaro/arms . **10.00**

EGYPT

	VF
1899 50 Piastres, Sphinx	**1,750.00**
1917-51 25 Pistres, Nile scene	**8.50**
1940 5 Piastres, King Farouk	**3.00**
1952-58 5 Piastres, Queen Nefertiti	**1.75**

	Unc.
1961-66 25 Piastres, arms	**6.00**
1967-78 50 Piastres, Al Azhar Mosque/ Ramses II	**3.50**

	Unc.
1976-78 25 Piastres, statue and Sphynx/ arms	**3.50**
1995-, 50 Piastres, Al Azhar Mosque/ Ramses II	**.75**
1978-99 1 Pound, Sultan Quayet Bey Mosque/four statues from Abu Simbel	**1.50**
1989- 5 Pounds, Ibn Toulon Mosque/ Ancient Egyptian relief	**5.00**

1994-97 100 Pounds, mosque/Sphinx	**60.00**
1940 (1998-99) 5 Piastres, Queen Nefertiti, signed M. Elghareeb	**1.25**

EL SALVADOR

	VF
1934 5 Colones, woman reclining with branch/Columbus	**40.00**
1955-58 2 Colones, coffee bush/ Columbus	**10.00**

	Unc.
1963-66 1 Colon, Central Bank Building/ Columbus	**30.00**
1974-76 25 Colones, port/Columbus	**45.00**

	Unc.
1983 100 Colones, monument/Columbus	**37.50**
1997 200 Colones, monument/Columbus	**9.00**

Ecuador 1986 10 Sucre

Egypt 1994-1997 100 Pounds

El Salvador 1983 100 Colones

ETHIOPIA

	F
1915-29 10 Thalers, "Bank of Abyssinia," leopard . . . . *rare*	
1932-33 5 Thalers, head of gazelle.	**100.00**
1932-33 100 Thalers, elephant	**175.00**
1945 1 Dollar, Haile Selassie and farmer plowing.	**15.00**
1945 100 Dollars, Haile Selassie and palace.	**225.00**
1961 1 Dollar, Haile Selassie and coffee bushes	**8.00**

	Unc.
1966 100 Dollars, Haile Selassie and church cut from rock	**125.00**
1969EE (1976) 50 Birr, science students/ castle at Gondar.	**50.00**
1969EE (1991) 100 Birr, Menelik II/man with microscope	**45.00**
1989EE (1997) 1 Birr, portrait of boy/Tisisat Waterfalls on Blue Nile	**.75**

EUROPEAN UNION

In 2002, this currency replaced the issues of those European Union countries that chose to become part of the "Euro Zone." Intitially twelve, other countries may be admitted afterwards. The designs are uniform across borders, but the prefix of the serial number indicates the country where a particular note was issued as follows:

L	**Finland**		T	**Ireland**
M	**Portugal**		U	**France**
N	**Austria**		V	**Spain**
P	**Netherlands**		X	**Germany**
R	**Luxembourg**		Y	**Greece**
S	**Italy**		Z	**Belgium**

All notes have arches on the obverse, and a bridge on the reverse. These motifs are interpreted with a different style of architecture on each denomination. They are archetypal images, and no specific building or bridge is intended.

These values are for crisp notes. Circulated ones are worth only their face value. Values in all grades may fluctuate with the currency markets.

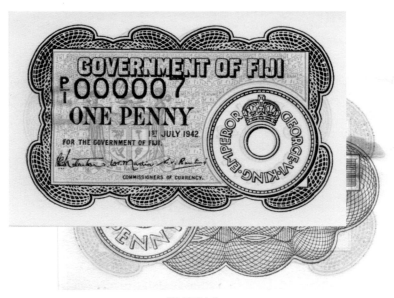

Fiji 1942 1 Penny

Finland 1918 1 Markkaa

Germany 1991-1993 1,000 Deutsche Mark

Great Britain 1929-1934

Greece 1997 5,000 Drachmes

Haiti 1973 5 Gourdes

	Unc.
2002 5 Euro, Classical	**8.50**
2002 10 Euro, Romanesque	**17.50**
2002 20 Euro, Gothic	**30.00**
2002 50 Euro, Renaissance	**75.00**
2002 100 Euro, Baroque	**150.00**
2002 200 Euro, late 19th century	**300.00**
2002 500 Euro, 20th century	**750.00**

FIJI

	VF
1873 50 Cents, C R	**150.00**
1942 1 Penny, coin/coin	**2.00**
	Unc.
1980-93 1 Dollar, Elizabeth II/crowds at fruit market	**2.50**

FINLAND

	F
1790 8 Skilling Specie, arms	**1,200.00**
1862 20 Mark, arms with supporters	**300.00**
1897 5 Markkaa, allegorical bust/arms	**20.00**
	VF
1918 25 Penniä, group of four flowers	**1.50**
1918 1 Markka, flowers/flower design	**1.50**
1939 50 Markkaa, allegorical group of six people, ship in background	**10.00**
1945 1,000 Markkaa, allegorical group of 13 people with heavy rope	**25.00**
	Unc.
1963 1 Markka, wheat/lion rampant with sword	**1.50**
1975 500 Markkaa, President Kekkonen/ arms	**150.00**
1986 100 Markkaa, Jean Sibelius/swans	**55.00**
1986 (1991) same but optical variable device added	**22.50**
1993 (1993-97) 20 Markkaa, V. Linna/ Tampere Street	**7.50**

FRANCE

	F
1701-07, 200 Livres, crowned monogram	**3,500.00**
1789-90, 1000 Livres, Louis XVI	**2,200.00**
	VF
1792 10 Sous, Value in triangle between allegorical figures	**4.00**
1792 50 Livres, Republic std	**16.00**
1864-66 50 Francs, two cherubs	*rare*
1889-1927 50 Francs, two cherubs, two portraits and ornate oval border	**60.00**
1939 20 Francs, Science and Labor/ scientist	**15.00**
1941-49 10 Francs, miner/farm woman	**.75**
1944 5 Francs, flag	**.40**
1946-51 50 Francs, Leverrier/Neptune	**3.50**
	Unc.
1966-70 5 Francs, Louis Pasteur/Louis Pasteur	**100.00**
1980-97 20 Francs, Claude Debussy/ Claude Debussy	**10.00**
1981-94 200 Francs, Baron de Montesquieu /Baron de Montesquieu	**70.00**
The backs of the above three notes are mirror images of their fronts.	
1996 200 Francs, A.G. Eiffel/base of Eiffel Tower	**40.00**

GERMANY

	F
1874 20 Mark, herald wearing tabbard	**8,000.00**
	VF
1908 100 Mark, eagle/medallic woman's head supported by two women kneeling	**.75**
1910 1000 Mark, inscription/arms with supporters	**1.00**
1923 1,000,000 Mark, inscription	**1.50**
1939 20 Reichsmark, woman with edelweiss	**6.00**
1944 1 Mark, Large M	**.75**
1948 5 Deutsche Mark, Europa on bull	**9.00**

Unc.

1960 5 Deutsche Mark, Young Venetian Woman by Albecht Dürer/oak leaves
.... **14.00**
1970-80 10 Deutsche Mark, Young Man by Albecht Dürer/sailing ship **12.00**
1989-1999 10 Mark, Gauss on right/ Sextant........................ **10.00**
1991-93 1,000 Deutsche Mark, Brothers Grimm/open book............**650.00**

GERMAN NOTGELD

Unc.

Frankfurt: G.M. Holz, 1921 25 pfennig, Golem...................... **5.00**
Schneidemuhl, c.1919 75 pfennig, Biplane **1.00**
These very common emergency notes were issued mostly by cities. Austria, Hungary, and other countries saw the same phenomenon during or after World War I.

GHANA

Unc.

1965 1 Cedi, Kwame Nkrumah/bank building **7.50**
1979-82 5 Cedis, old man with hat/men cutting tree **3.00**
1994-96 5000 Cedis, arms/freighter in harbor....................... **25.00**

GREAT BRITAIN

F

1694 5 Pounds, inscription (handwritten) .... *rare*
1751 10 Pounds, inscription (handwritten details)................... *rare*
1797 1 Pound, inscription and small arms .... *rare*
1855 5 Pounds, similar but "payable to the bearer".................... *rare*
1902 10 Pounds, similar **500.00**
1917 1 Pound, St. George and George V/ Parliament **100.00**

F

1929-34 1 Pound, Britannia at left, building .... *VF* **25.00**
1944-47 5 Pounds, inscription and small arms..........................**60.00**
(1957-67) 5 Pounds, head of Britannia and St. George/lion. .... *VF* **45.00**

Unc.

1960-70 10 Shillings, Elizabeth II/Britannia std.................... **10.00**
(1978-84) 1 Pound, Elizabeth II/Sir Isaac Newton........................ **8.00**
1990 (1990-2002) 5 Pounds, Elizabeth II/G. Stephenson **20.00**

GREECE

F

1822 100 Grossi, inscription and seals **350.00**
1822 1,000 Grossi, similar......... **600.00**
1852 10 Drachmai, arms ....**rare**
1897 5 Drachmai, arms and Stavros/ Athena **175.00**
1922 100 Drachmai, Stavros, reclining women, arms/Acropolis seen between columns **65.00**

VF

1946 10,000 Drachmai, Aristotle. ... **50.00**
1955 50 Drachmai, Pericles/Pericles speaking....................... **5.00**

Unc.

1964 50 Drachmai, Arethusa/shipyard **2.00**
1978 50 Drachmai, Poseidon/sailing ship **1.00**
1983 500 Drachmes, Capodistrias/fortress at Corfu **4.50**
1997 5,000 Drachmes, Kolokotronis/ church at Calamata **30.00**
1996 200 Drachmes, R. Velestinlis Ferios/ secret school of Greek priests.... **3.25**

GUATEMALA

F

1882 5 Pesos, locomotive......... **125.00**
1934-45 5 Quetzales, freighter between two quetzales **30.00**

1948-54 1/2 Quetzal, Building l., Quetzal flying at center/two figures **6.00**

Unc.

1966-70 100 Quetzales, Indio de Nahuala/ mountain **400.00**

1971-83 10 Quetzales, Gen. Granados/ National Assembly of 1872 ..... **22.50**

1994-95 100 Quetzales, F. Marroquin/Univ. of San Carlos de Borromeo **35.00**

HAITI

F

1790s 4 Escalins, arms .... *rare*

1851 2 Gourdes, arms **60.00**

1875 1 Piastre, Pres. Domingue l., Agriculture r. **25.00**

1914 2 Gourdes, J.J. Dessalines and arms/ mining scene **50.00**

Unc.

1919 (1964-67) Castle/arms **7.50**

Unc.

1973 1 Gourde, Francois Duvalier/arms **2.00**

1973 5 Gourdes, Francois Duvalier/arms **2.50**

1979 5 Gourdes, Jean-Claude Duvalier/ arms **4.00**

1989 1 Gourde, Toussaint L'Ouverture **.60**

1992 5 Gourdes, Statue of several figures/ arms **1.50**

HAWAII

VF

1880 10 Dollars, Sailing ship, cowboy, locomotive **10,000.00**

1895 5 Dollars, Woman, building, bull's head **15,000.00**

HONG KONG

VF

1931-56 10 Dollars, Chartered Bank of India, Australia and China .... F **75.00**

1935 1 Dollar, George V **325.00**

1949-52 1 Dollar, George VI **22.00**

1952-59 1 Dollar, Elizabeth II **2.00**

Unc.

1961-95 1 Cent, Elizabeth II .... **.25**

1962-70 (ND) 1 Dollar, Chartered Bank **50.00**

1973-76 500 Dollars, Hong Kong and Shanghai Banking Corp **200.00**

1985-91 10 Dollars, Standard Chartered Bank **6.00**

1994-00 20 Dollars, Bank of China issue **6.00**

HUNGARY

VF

1920 20 Korona, Matyas Church ...... **.50**

1929 10 Pengo, Deak/parliament ... **10.00**

1939 5 Pengo, girl/man playing balalaika **4.00**

Unc.

1965-89 50 Forint, Rakoczi/battle scene **3.00**

1990 500 Forint, Endre Ady/aerial view of Budapest **6.00**

1992-95 100 Forint, Kossuth at right/ horsedrawn wagon **3.50**

1997-2003 10,000 Forint, St. Stephen/view of Esztergom **75.00**

ICELAND

VF

1792-1801 1 Rigsdaler, inscription, triangle above .... *rare*

1928 10 Kronur, Sigurdsson **11.00**

1957 5 Kronur, Viking/farm **1.50**

Unc.

1961 10 Kronur, J. Eiriksson/ships at port **6.00**

1961 (1984-91) 1000 Kronur, Bishop Sveinsson/church **27.50**

1986 2,000 Kronur, J.S. Kajarval/Leda and the swan **40.00**

INDIA

VF

1861-65 10 Rupees, Queen Victoria .. *rare*

1910-20 10 Rupees, inscription .. F **40.00**

1917 1 Rupee, George V **3.50**

Hong Kong 1962-1970 10 Dollars

Hungary 1992-1995 100 Forint

Iceland 1986 2000 Kronur

India 1997 5 Rupees

Indonesia 1993 50,000 Rupiah

Iran 1974-1979 50 Rials

	VF
1937-43 5 Rupees, George VI	**1.50**

	Unc.
1957 1 Rupee, Coin	**5.00**
1966 1 Rupee, Coin	**3.00**
1962-67 5 Rupees, Asoka pillar	**10.00**

	Unc.
1996 10 Rupees, Mahatma Gandhi/tiger	**2.00**
1997 5 Rupees, Ghandi/tractor	**3.50**

INDONESIA

	Unc.
1945 1 Rupiah, President Sukarno/ smoking volcano	**6.00**
1964 2-1/2 Rupiah, President Sukarno	**7.50**
1964 50 Sen, Soldier	**.25**
1980 5000 Rupiah, diamond cutter/three Torajan houses	**20.00**
1993 50,000 Rupiah, President Soeharto/ airport	**35.00**

IRAN, Empire

	F
1890 1 Toman, lion and Nasr-ed-Din Shah	**200.00**
1924-32 50 Tomans, Nasr-ed-Din/lion	**1,250.00**

	VF
1315AH (1936) Reza Shah/mountains	**15.00**
1948 50 Rials, Shah Mohammad Reza/five ancient figures	**12.50**

	Unc.
1340SH (1961) 10 Rials, Shah Mohammad Reza/Amir Kabir Dam	**4.00**
1965-69 same/painting of hunters	**4.00**
1974-79 50 Rials, same/Tomb of Cyrus the Great	**3.00**
1979 same with Shah's portrait over-printed by the Islamic Republic	**7.00**
1971-72 5000 Rials, Shah Mohammad Reza/trees before Golestan Palace	**300.00**

IRAN, Islamic Republic

	Unc.
1981 200 Rials, Imam Reza Shrine/Tomb of Ibn-E-Sina	**6.00**
1992 1000 Rials, Ayatollah Khomeini/ Dome of the Rock in Jerusalem	**3.00**
1986-, 2,000 Rials, Revolutionaries before mosque/Kaaba in Mecca	**3.00**
1993-, 5,000 Rials, similar/flowers and birds	**7.50**

IRAQ

	VF
1931 1 Dinar, King Faisal I	**250.00**
1931 (1933) 1/4 Dinar, King Ghazi	**125.00**
1931 (1941) 1/4 Dinar, King Faisal II as child	**75.00**
1947 1 Dinar, King Faisal II as adult/ horseman	**50.00**
1959 1/4 Dinar, State seal/palm trees	**5.00**
1959 5 Dinars, same/Hamurabi receiving laws	**12.50**

	Unc.
1971 1/4 Dinar, ship at port/palm trees	**9.00**
1971 1 Dinar, oil refinery/doorway	**17.50**
1978-80 25 Dinars, horses/ courtyard	**22.50**
1986 25 Dinars, Saddam Hussein/ monument	**5.50**
1994 100 Dinars, Saddam Hussein/ building with tower	**5.50**
2003 50 Dinars, grain silo/date palms)	**.50**
2003 250 Dinars, Astrolabe/spiral minaret	**1.00**
2003 1,000 Dinars, Medieval coin/ university	**2.50**

IRELAND

	F
1808 1 Pound, Hibernia seated	*rare*
1890-1917 10 Pounds, Hibernia standing. l. and r.	**275.00**

Iraq 1994 100 Dinars

Japan 1984-1993 1,000 Yen

VF

1929-39 5 pounds, man plowing with horses **120.00**

Unc.

1962-68 10 Shillings, Lady Hazel Lavery/ face of river god **30.00**

1977-89 1 Pound, Queen Medb/Medieval writing **7.00**

1993-99 10 Pounds, James Joyce/ river allegory **25.00**

1995-01 50 Pounds, D. Hyde/statue of Parnell **110.00**

1995-01 100 Pounds, Hibernia seated/ statue **275.00**

ISRAEL

VF

(1948-51) 500 Mils, Anglo-Palestine Bank **80.00**

(1952) 1 Pound, Bank Leumi Le-Israel **16.00**

Unc.

1958 1/2 Lira, woman with oranges . . **8.00**

1968 5 Lirot, Albert Einstein/atomic reactor **10.00**

1975 500 Lirot, David Ben-Gurion/ Golden Gate **45.00**

1978 1 Sheqel, Moses Montefiore/ Jaffa Gate. **2.00**

Unc.

1983 1,000 Sheqelim, Maimonides/view of Tiberias. **10.00**

1986 1 New Sheqel, same **2.00**

1985-92 10 New Sheqelim, Golda Meir/ Jews in Moscow **15.00**

1991-94 200 New Sheqelim, Zalman Shazar/school girl writing **120.00**

ITALY

VF

1874 2 Lire, bust of Italia . . . . *F* **8.00**

1888-1925 10 Lire, Umberto I **12.00**

1926-36 50 Lire, Woman with three children/woman standing. **55.00**

1935-44 10 Lire, Victor Emmanuel III/Italia **2.00**

Unc.

1966-75 500 Lire, eagle and Arethusa **10.00**

1982 1,000 Lire, Marco Polo/Doge's Palace **3.00**

1990 1,000 Lire, Montessori/teacher and student **3.00**

1971-77 5,000 Lire, Columbus and Hippocamp **45.00**

1962-73 10,000 Lire, Michaelangelo/Piazza del Campidoglio **30.00**

1975 20,000 Lire, Titian/Painting **280.00**

1984-90 10,000 Lire, Volta/Mausoleum **12.50**

1984-90 50,000 Lire, Bernini/Equestrian statue **55.00**

1997 500,000 Lire, Raphael/Painting "School of Athens" **380.00**

JAMAICA

F

1904-18 2 Shillings 6 Pence, George V/ Woman with hat **1,250.00**

1939-48 10 Shillings, George VI/Value **40.00**

Unc.

1960 5 Shillings, Elizabeth II/River rapids **100.00**

1976 1 Dollar, Bustamante at left/harbor **5.00**

1978-81 10 Dollars, G.W. Gordon/Bauxite mining. **7.50**

1991-93 100 Dollars, D. Sangster/Dunn's River Falls **10.00**

JAPAN

VF

(1872) 1 Yen, two phoenixes and two dragons . . . . *F* **125.00**

(1930) 100 Yen, pavilion and Shotoku-taishi/Temple complex **55.00**

(1938) 50 Sen, Mt. Fuji. **1.25**

(1947) 10 Sen, dove/Diet building . . . . **.50**

(1950) 1,000 Yen, Shotoku-Yaishi/ Yumedono Pavilion **17.00**

Jordan 1992 5 Dinars

Kenya 1978 10 Shillings

	Unc.
(1969) 500 Yen, Iwakura Tomomi/Mt. Fuji	10.00
(1963) 1000 Yen, Hirobumi Ito/Bank of Japan	16.00
(1984-93) 1,000 Yen, Soseki Natsume/two cranes	15.00
(1993-) 5,000 Yen, Inazo Nitobe/Mt. Fuji	65.00

JORDAN

	Unc.
1959 1/2 Dinar, young King Hussein/Collonade	75.00
(1975-92) 1/2 Dinar, King Hussein/Jerash	3.25
(1975-92) 5 Dinars, King Hussein/Petra	22.50
1977-88 20 Dinars, King Hussein/electric power plant	70.00
1992 20 Dinars, King Hussein/dome of the Rock in Jerusalem	95.00
2002 5 Dinar, King Abdullah I/palace	10.00
2002 50 Dinars, King Abdullah II/palace	110.00

KENYA

	Unc.
1966-68 5 Shillings, Jomo Kenyatta/woman picking coffee	85.00
1978 10 Shillings, Jomo Kenyatta/cows	8.00
1980-88 50 Shillings, Daniel Arap Moi/airplane over airport	16.00
1995 20 Shillings, Daniel Arap Moi/runner and stadium	2.50

KOREA, SOUTH

	Unc.
1962 100 Hwan, mother and child	325.00
1962 10 Jeon, Value	.40
(1975) 1,000 Won, Yi Hwang/Do-San Academy	5.00

KUWAIT

	Unc.
1960 (1961) 1/4 Dinar, Amir Shaikh Abdullah/Port	45.00
1968 1 Dinar, Amir Shaikh Sabah/oil refinery	30.00
1968 (1980-91) 1 Dinar, arms/old fortress, red-violet and purple	5.50
1968 (1992) 1 Dinar, arms/old fortress, green and deep blue	9.00

Because many notes were stolen by invading Iraqi forces, the Kuwaiti government declared the paper money worthless and reissued it with similar designs but different colors after liberation. The above pair of notes is an example.

	Unc.
1968 (1994) 1/2 Dinar, Boys playing game	5.00

LATVIA

	VF
(1919) 5 Rubli, Head l./flame	10.00
1937-40 10 Latu, Fishermen/man sowing	5.00

	Unc.
1992 1 Rublis	.30
1992 5 Lati, Tree	15.00
1992 50 Latu, Sailing ship/crossed keys	125.00

LEBANON

	VF
1925 25 Piastres, Water mill	250.00
1939 5 Livres, Cedar tree r./city view	95.00
1942 25 Piastres, Umayyad mosque	8.00
1948 5 Piastres, Value	2.50
1952-64 1 Livre, Crusader castle/columns at Baalbek	8.00
1952-63 100 Livres, Beirut harbor/cedar	35.00

	Unc.
1964-80 10 Livres, Ancient arch/rocks in water	1.00
1964-88 50 Livres, Temple of Bacchus/building	1.25

Kuwait 1968 (1980-1991) I Dinar

Latvia 1919 5 Rubli

Lebanon 1952- 1964 1 Livre

Macedonia 1996 50 Denari

	Unc.
1988-93 500 Livres, Beirut city view/ ancient ruins	**3.00**
1994 5,000 Livres, Geometric pattern	**10.00**

LITHUANIA

	Unc.
1991 0.10 Talonas, Arms	**.25**
1993 500 Talonu, Wolves	**2.50**
1992 2 Litai, Bishop/castle	**3.00**
1993 10 Litu, Two pilots/early monoplane	**7.50**

LUXEMBOURG

	VF
1856 10 Thaler, Seated woman and three cherubs	*rare*

	VF
1944 5 France, Grand Duchess Charlotte	**5.00**

	Unc.
1961 50 Francs, Grand Duchess Charlotte/ landscape	**10.00**
1967 10 Francs, Grand Duke Jean/bridge	**5.00**
1972 50 Francs, Same/steel workers	**7.00**
1980 100 Francs, Same/city view	**7.50**
(1986) 100 Francs, Same	**4.50**

MACEDONIA

	Unc.
1992 10 Denari, Women harvesting	**.75**
1993 20 Denari, Tower/Turkish bath	**2.50**
1996 50 Denari, Archangel Gabriel/ Byzantine coin	**3.00**

MEXICO

A much fuller treatment of Mexican paper money is provided here than for any other country but Canada.

As in the United States, many of Mexico's earlier notes were actually issued by banks and not by the government. They were eliminated by the issues of the Bank of Mexico about 1920. This introductory reference only deals with federally issued notes.

Note that the prices here are for the most common date appearing on the note and most common variety for each design described. There are sometimes a wide number of varieties, and a specialized reference should be consulted.

Additional Specialized Reference: Bruce, Colin. *Standard Catalog of Mexican Coins, Paper Money Stocks, Bonds and Medals.*

Empire of Augustin Iturbide

	F
1823 1 Peso, arms	**25.00**
1823 2 Pesos, arms	**40.00**
1823 10 Pesos, arms	**25.00**

Fifty Centavos

	F
1920 Minerva	**15.00**

One Peso

	F
1920 Plenty with cherubs	**25.00**
(1936)-43 Aztec calendar/statue of Victory	**3.00**

	Unc.
1943-48	**6.00**
1948-50 similar	**12.00**
1954 similar	**12.00**
1957-70	**1.00**

Mexico 1925-1934 5 Pesos

Mexico 1978-1985 1,000 Pesos

Mexico 2001 20 Pesos

Morocco 1996 20 Dirhams

Five Pesos

	F
1925-34 G. Faure/Victory statue	**8.00**
1936	**50.00**

	Unc.
1937-50 similar	**5.00**
1953-54 similar	**4.00**
1957-70 similar	**2.50**
1969-72 Josefa/aquaduct	**1.50**

Ten Pesos

	F
1925-34 two winged Victories/statue of Victory	**8.00**
1936 similar	**15.00**

	Unc.
1937-42 woman with large headdress/ road to Guanajuato	**17.00**
1943-45 similar	**11.00**
1946-50 similar	**8.00**
1951-53 similar	**7.00**
1954-67 similar	**3.00**
1969-77 Hidalgo/Dolores Cathedral	**.75**

Twenty Pesos

	F
1925-34 freighter at dock by locomotive	**25.00**
1937 Josefa/Federal Palace courtyard	VF **26.00**

	Unc.
1940-45, similar	**16.00**
1948 similar	**11.00**
1950-70 similar	**7.50**
1972-77 Morelos/pyramid	**1.50**
2001 20 Pesos, Juarez/monument	**4.50**

Fifty Pesos

	F
1925-34 Navigation std./statue of Victory	**60.00**
1937-40, Zaragoza/city view	**125.00**

	Unc.
1941-45 de Allende/statue of Victory	**15.00**

	Unc.
1948-72 similar	**3.00**
1973-81, Juarez/Aztec deity	**1.00**

One Hundred Pesos

	F
1925-34 Maritime Commerce and Youth/ statue of Victory	**100.00**
1936 Madero/bank building	**225.00**

	VF
1940-42	**20.00**
1945 Hidalgo/coin	**20.00**

	Unc.
1950-61 similar	**25.00**
1974-82, Carranza/stone altar	**1.00**

Five Hundred Pesos

	F
1931-34 Electricity std./statue of Victory	**400.00**
1936 Morelos/miners' palace	**400.00**
1940-43 Morelos	VF **42.00**

	Unc.
1948-78 similar	**8.50**
1979-84, Madero/Aztec calendar	**2.50**

One Thousand Pesos

	F
1931-34 Wisdom with globe/statue of Victory	**1,350.00**
1936 Cuauhtemoc/pyramid	**450.00**
1941-45 Cuauhtemoc/pyramid	VF **42.00**

	Unc.
1948-77 similar	**5.00**
1978-85, de Asbaje/Santo Domingo plaza	**3.00**

Two Thousand Pesos

1983-89, J. Sierra/1800s courtyard. . . **2.25**

Five Thousand Pesos

	Unc.
1980-89 Cadets/Chapultepec castle	**3.00**

Ten Thousand Pesos

1943-53 Romero/government palace
.............................VF **300.00**
1978 Romero/national palace......**75.00**
1981-91 Cardenas/Coyolxauhqui....**6.00**

Twenty Thousand Pesos

1985-89 A. Quintana Roo/Pre-Columbian
art **12.50**

Fifty Thousand Pesos

1986-90 Cuauhtemoc/Spaniard and Aztec
fighting......................**45.00**

One Hundred Thousand Pesos

1988-91 Calles/Stag **85.00**

Reform, 1000 Pesos ' 1 New Peso

Ten Nuevos Pesos

1992 Cardenas/Coyolxauhqui **7.50**
1992 Zapata/statue of Zapata.......**4.00**
1994-96, same without Nuevos......**3.00**

Twenty Nuevos Pesos

1992 A. Quintana Roo/Pre-Columbian art
.............................**12.50**
1992 Juarez/statue **6.50**
1994-96, same without Nuevos......**5.50**
2000, same with commemorative bank
inscription **9.50**
2001, as 1994-96 but plastic polymer **4.50**

Fifty Nuevos Pesos

1992 Cuauhtemoc/Spaniard and Aztec
fighting.......................**27.50**
1992 Morelos/fisherman **15.00**
1994-98, same without Nuevos **10.00**
2000, same with commemorative bank
inscription **17.50**
2000, as 1994-98 but vertical security strip
added.......................**10.00**

One Hundred Nuevos Pesos

1992 Calles/stag **40.00**
1992 Nezahualcoyotl/Xochipilli statue
.............................**25.00**
1994-96, same without Nuevos.....**22.50**
2000, same with commemorative bank
inscription **35.00**
2000, as 1994-96 but vertical security strip
added.......................**18.00**

Two Hundred Nuevos Pesos

1992, de Asbaje/temple of San Jeronimo
.............................**45.00**
1995-98, same without Nuevos **37.50**
2000, same with commemorative bank
inscription **70.00**
2000, as 1994-98 but vertical security strip
added.......................**32.50**

Five Hundred Nuevos Pesos

1992, Zaragoza/Puebla Cathedral.**110.00**
1995-96, same without Nuevos **95.00**
2000, same with commemorative bank
inscription **150.00**
2000, as 1995-96 but vertical security strip
added.......................**80.00**

MOROCCO

	VF
1942 1 Franc, star/City of Fez........	**2.50**
1943 10 Francs, star................	**5.00**
1951-58 1,000 Francs, mosque and city view.........................	**35.00**

	Unc.
1965-69 5 Dirhams, King Muhammad V/ man with sheaf	**27.50**
1970-85 10 Dirhams, King Hassan II/ woman sorting oranges	**5.50**
1987 10 Dirhams, similar/mandolin and pillar...........................	**8.00**
1987 200 Dirhams, similar/sailboat .	**35.00**
1996 20 Dirhams, King Hassan II and mosque/fountain	**4.50**

Netherlands 1994 1,000 Gulden

New Zealand 1996 20 Dollars

NETHERLANDS

F

1846 10 Gulden, inscriptions . . . . *rare*
1904-21 25 Gulden, arms and ornate
border. **450.00**
1939-41 20 Gulden, Queen Emma and
sailing ship/church **12.00**
1943 2-1/2 Gulden, Queen Wilhelmina
. . . . *VF* **7.00**

Unc.

1966 5 Gulden, Vondell/mondernistic
depiction of building. **10.00**
1972 1,000 Gulden, Baruch d'Espinoza
. . . .**750.00**
1982 50 Gulden, sunflower and bee **35.00**
1985 250 Gulden, lighthouse **150.00**
1992 100 Gulden, abstract pattern . **75.00**
1994 1,000 Gulden, abstract pattern. **6.00**
1997 10 Gulden, different abstract pattern
. . . . **7.50**

NEW ZEALAND

VF

1934 1 Pound, kiwi, arms and Maori chief
. . . .**60.00**

Unc.

(1967-81) 1 Dollar, Elizabeth II/bird. . . **8.00**
(1981-92) 1 Dollar, similar but older
portrait **3.00**
(1992-) 5 Dollars, Sir Edmond Hillary/
penguin **5.00**
1996 20 Dollars, Elizabeth II 70th Birthday/
bird **200.00**

NICARAGUA

F

1894 10 Centavos, arms **55.00**
1938 50 Centavos, Liberty/arms. . . .**45.00**

Unc.

1962 1 Cordoba, building/Cordoba . **7.50**
1972 20 Cordobas, woman lighting
cannon/treaty signing ceremony **10.00**
1979 1,000 Cordobas, Sandino. **45.00**
1985 1,000 Cordobas, Sandino. **7.00**
(1991) 50 Cordobas, Chamorro/polling
place **12.50**

NIGERIA

Unc.

(1967) 1 Pound, bank building/man
beating plant. **8.00**
(1973-78) 1 Naira, bank building/workers
stacking bags of
grain **12.50**
(1984-) 10 Naira, A. Ikoku/women carrying
bowls on heads. **3.00**

NORWAY

F

1695 25 Rixdaler Croner, inscription with
wax seals **2,000.00**
1877-99 5 Kroner, Oscar II **400.00**
1940-50 1 Krone. **8.00**

Unc.

1972-84 10 Kroner, F. Nansen/fisherman
. . . . **6.00**
1984-95 50 Kroner, A.O. Vinje/medieval
stone carving. **15.00**
1996-2000 50 Kroner, P.C. Asbjornsen/
water lilies **10.00**
1999-2002 500 Kroner, S. Undste at right/
wreath. **85.00**

OMAN

Unc.

(1970) 100 Baisa, dagger and swords **3.00**
(1973) 5 Rials, arms, Nizwa fort **70.00**
1977) 1/2 Rial, same/castle. **4.00**
1985-92 50 Rials, sultan/castle **210.00**
1995 200 Baisa, sultan/port. **1.25**
2000 5 Rials, sultan/Nizwa city view **18.00**

PAKISTAN

Unc.

(1953) 5 Rupees, small boat/mountain
scene. **12.50**
(1964) 50 Rupees, Mohammad Ali
Jennah/2 boats. **10.00**
(1973) 1 Rupee, archway. **3.00**
(1982-) 1 Rupee, Tomb of Allama Iqbal
. . . . **1.00**
(1986) 50 Rupees, Mohammad Ali Jinnah/
Gate of Lahore Fort **6.00**

Nicaragua 1979 1,000 Cordobas

Nigeria 1984 10 Naira

Norway 1999-2002 500 Kroner

Oman 1973 5 Rials

Pakistan 1964 50 Rupees

Palestine 1927-1939 50 Pounds

Paraguay 1952 500 Guaranies

PALESTINE

	F
1927-39 50 Pounds, Crusader Tower/ Tower of David	*rare*
1927-45 500 Mils, Rachel's Tomb l./Tower of David	**150.00**
1927-44 1 Pound, Dome of the Rock l./ Tower of David	**150.00**

PANAMA

	VF
1941 1 Balboa, Balboa	**650.00**
1941 5 Balboas, Uracca	**1,500.00**

PARAGUAY

	F
1856 1/2 Real, flowers and seal	**80.00**
1903 1 Peso, woman in straw hat	**7.50**
	Unc.
1943 5 Guaranies, Gen. Diaz	**15.00**
1952 1 Guarani, soldier/building	**4.00**
1952 500 Guaranies, Gen. B. Caballero/ freighter	**1.85**

	Unc.
1995 5,000 Guaranies, D.C.A. Lopez/ Lopez Palace	**5.00**

PERU

	F
1879 5 Soles, women with children	**10.00**
1922 10 Libras, tapping tree for rubber	**90.00**
	Unc.
1958 5 Soles, Liberty (or Peru)	**6.00**
1962-68 5 Soles de Oro, Liberty (or Peru) std./arms	**4.00**
1977 50 Soles de Oro, Tupac Amaru/town of Tinta	**1.25**
	Unc.
1995 10 Nuevos Soles, J. Abelardo Quiñones/biplane flying upside-down	**7.00**
1996 20 Nuevos Soles, R. Porres Barrenechea/Torre Tagle Palace	**22.50**

Peru 1996 20 Nuevos Soles

Philippines 1985-1994 10 Piso

PHILIPPINES

	F
1852-65 25 Pesos, Isabel II . . . . *rare*	
1908 50 Pesos, woman with flower, "Banco Español Filipino" **500.00**	
1928 50 Pesos, similar, "Bank of the Philippine Islands" **40.00**	

	Unc.
(1942) 10 Centavos, "Japanese Government" . . . . **.50**	
(1943) 5 Pesos, Monument, "Japanese Government" **2.00**	
(1949) 2 Pesos, Rizal. **1.50**	
(1969) 1 Piso, Rizal/1898 independence declaration. **1.00**	
(1970s) 10 Piso, Mabini/Barasoain church **4.00**	
(1985-94) 10 Piso, Mabini/Barasoain church. **2.50**	
(1987-94) 500 Piso, B. Aquino/scenes of Aquino's life. **30.00**	

POLAND

	F
1794 5 Groszy, Eagle and mounted knight *F. Manlinowski* on back **15.00**	
1917 20 Marek, white eagle **20.00**	

	VF
1931 20 Zlotych, E. Plater/woman with children. **2.00**	
1948 50 Zlotych, bust of fisherman . . **1.25**	

	Unc.
1962-65 1,000 Zlotych, Copernicus/ diagram of Copernican view of solar system. **20.00**	
1977-82 2,000 Zlotych, Mieszko I/Chrobry **1.00**	
1994 20 Zlotych, Boleslaw I/Medieval coin **10.00**	

PORTUGAL

	F
1798-99 2400 Reis, walled cities and cherubs . . . . *rare*	
1891 500 Reis, arms/arms **80.00**	
1918-20 50 Centavos, woman holding ship/Justice **6.00**	
1920-25 5 Escudos, J. das Regras/church and convent. **65.00**	
1944-52 500 Escudos, Joao IV/king with crowd. . . . . *VF* **45.00**	

	Unc.
1960 50 Escudos, Pereira/"The Thinker" statue **85.00**	
1971 20 Escudos, G. de Orta/market in Goa **2.50**	
1987-93 5,000 Escudos, Antero de Quental/six hands with rope **50.00**	
1989-91 10,000 Escudos, Moniz/Nobel medal **125.00**	
1996-2000 1,000 Escudos, Cabral/1500s sailing ship **10.00**	
1997-2000 500 Escudos, Joao de Barros **6.00**	

PUERTO RICO

	F
1813 8 Reales, Paschal lamb . . *G* **1,500.00**	
1889 10 Pesos, Paschal lamb and coast watchers/arms . . . . *rare*	
1895 1 Peso, bearded bust l./crowned arms of Spain. **60.00**	
1909 10 Dollars, Ponce de Leon/Liberty **2,500.00**	

QATAR

	Unc.
(1973) 1 Riyal, arms/Port of Doha . . . **15.00**	
1980s-1996 10 Riyals, arms/National Museum **50.00**	
1980s-1996 500 Riyals, arms/oil platform **250.00**	
(2003) 1 Riyal, arms/three different birds **1.25**	

Portugal 1989-1991 10,000 Escudos

Qatar 1980s-1996 500 Riyals

Romania 1947 100 Lei

Russia 1997 100 Rubles

Rwanda 1978 5,000 Francs

ROMANIA

	F
1877 5 Lei, two women std	**250.00**
1877 50 Lei, Ancient Romans	**800.00**
1914-28 5 Lei, woman with distaff/woman picking apples, child at side	VF **3.00**

	Unc.
1947 100 Lei, 3 men with torch, ears of corn	**15.00**
1966 1 Leu, arms	**2.00**
1991 500 Lei, bust of Brancusi/Brancusi std	**3.00**
1993 5000 Lei, A. Iancu/elaborate gateway	**2.50**

RUSSIA

	F
1787-1818 5 Rubles, inscriptions	**500.00**
1866-80 5 Rubles, monogram/D. Ivanovich Donskoi	**350.00**

	Unc.
1909 5 Rubles, arms	**2.00**

	Unc.
1918 100 Rubles, two-headed eagle	**3.50**
same but 5 Rubles	**1.00**

The above two are from the Russian civil war.

	Unc.
1938 5 Rubles, pilot	**5.00**
1961 3 Rubles, Kremlin tower	**1.00**
1991 50 Rubles, Lenin/dome at Kremlin	**6.00**
1997 50 Rubles, monument	**3.00**
1997 100 Rubles, chariot monument/Bolshoi Theater	**7.50**

RWANDA

	Unc.
1964-76 50 Francs, map/miners	**2.50**
1978 100 Francs, zebras/woman and child	**7.00**
1978 5,000 Francs, woman with basket/lake and mountains	**150.00**
1988-89 1,000 Francs, two Watusi warriors/two gorillas	**20.00**

SAUDI ARABIA

	Unc.

1373AH (1954) 10 Riyals, two dhows in Jedda Harbor **225.00**

1379AH (1961) 1 Riyal, Hill of Light/arms **40.00**

1379AH (1968) 5 Riyals, airport/ships at oil dock **45.00**

1379AH (1976) 50 Riyals, King Faisal/arches in mosque **40.00**

1379AH (1977) 10 Riyals, King Faisal/oil platform **15.00**

1379AH (1984) 1 Riyal, King Fahd/landscape. **1.25**

1419AH (1999) 200 Riyals, King Abd al Aziz with glasses/Gate of Al Mussmack Palace **85.00**

1379AH (1983-2003) 500 Riyals, King Abd al-Aziz and Kaaba in Mecca/courtyard of Great Mosque **185.00**

SOUTH AFRICA

	VF

1867-68 1 Pond, arms, "Zuid-Afrikaansche Republiek". . . . . *rare*

1920 1 Pound, arms. . . . . *F* **150.00**

1928-47 10 Shillings. **22.00**

1928-47 1 Pound, sailing ship **20.00**

	Unc.

(1961-65) 1 Rand, Jan van Riebeeck/lion crest. **18.00**

(1966-72) 1 Rand, Jan van Riebeeck/sheep and plow. **10.00**

(1978-93) 10 Rand, Jan van Riebeeck/bull and ram **9.00**

1994-99 100 Rand, water buffalo/zebra herd. **25.00**

SPAIN

	VF

1874 50 Pesetas, D. Martinez . *F* **2,000.00**

1925 (1925-36) Philip II/Philip II in scene **2.50**

1935 500 Pesetas, H. Cortez/Cortez burning his ships. **80.00**

1949 1,000 Pesetas, de Santillan/Goya painting **57.00**

1951 5 Pesetas, Balmes/building **3.50**

	Unc.

1965 100 Pesetas, Gustavo Becquer/woman with parasol. **7.00**

1965 1,000 Pesetas, St. Isidoro/medieval sculpture. **50.00**

1970 100 Pesetas, Manuel de Falla/residence of kings of Grenada **5.00**

1971 500 Pesetas, J. Verdaquer at right/Mt. Canigo. **35.00**

1976 5,000 Pesetas, Charles III/Prado Museum **120.00**

1985 10,000 Pesetas, Juan Carlos I/Prince of Asturias **120.00**

1992 1,000 Pesetas, Cortes/Pizarro . **12.50**

1992 5,000 Pesetas, Columbus/armillary sphere. **50.00**

SUDAN

	VF

1961-68 1 Pound, dam **15.00**

1964-68 10 Pounds, bank building/camel rider. **60.00**

	Unc.

1970-80 25 Piastres, bank building/textile machine **6.00**

(1970-80) 10 Pounds, bank building/ship, plane, train, trucks **65.00**

1981 10 Pounds, Pres. Nimeiri/sugar factory. **75.00**

1987 50 Piastres, instruments, map and peanut plant/bank building. . . . .**.75**

1993 10 Dinars, People's Palace/dome and tower. **3.50**

SWEDEN

	F

1666 10 Daler Silvermynt, inscription **7,000.00**

1802-34 8 Schillingar Specie, inscription **65.00**

1907-17 5 Kronor, Svea std./Gustav Vasa **45.00**

South Africa 1966-1972 1 Rand

Spain 1971 500 Pesetas

Sudan 1970-1980 10 Pounds

Sweden 1996-2002 50 Kronor

	F
1918-52 5 Kronor, similar	**1.00**
	Unc.

1954-61 5 Kronor, Gustav VI Adolf/Svea
  stg. **3.50**
1965-81 5 Kronor, Gustav Vasa/Stylized
  rooster **2.00**
1985-2002 500 Kronor, Carl XI/C. Polhem
  . . . . **75.00**
1991-2002 20 Kronor, Selma Lagerlöf/boy
  flying on goose. **3.50**
1996-2002 50 Kronor, Jenny Lind/violin
  . . . . **8.50**

SWITZERLAND

	F

1907 50 Franken, Helvetia and child
  . . . . **1,000.00**
1924-49 100 Franken, female portrait/man
  chopping tree. . . . . *VF* **55.00**

	Unc.

1979-2002 10 Francs, L. Euler/water
  turbine **8.00**
1961-74 50 Francs, little girl r./apple
  harvesting **50.00**
1994-95 50 Francs, S. Taeuber-Arp/Her
  abstract art **35.00**
1975-93 100 Francs, Francesco Borromini
  . . . . **80.00**

SYRIA

	VF

1919 5 Piastres, Baalbek/lion head . **50.00**
1935 5 Livres, Azam Palace **100.00**
1944 5 Piastres, Citadel of Aleppo. . . **5.00**
1958 1 Pound, industrial worker/water
  wheel. **3.00**
1963-73 5 Pounds, same/Citadel of
  Aleppo **2.50**

	Unc.

1977-91 10 Pounds, palace and woman/
  water treatment plant **1.00**
1997 200 Pounds, Saladdin/cotton
  weaving and energy plant **6.00**
1997 1,000 Pounds, Pres. Assad/oil,
  harvesting and fishing industries **35.00**

TANZANIA

	Unc.

(1966) 5 Shillings, Young Julius Nyerere/
  mountain **12.50**
(1978) 20 Shilingi, Julius Nyerere/cotton
  knitting machine. **4.50**
(1985) 20 Shilingi, Old Julius Nyerere/tire
  factory workers **2.50**
(1992) 200 Shilingi, Pres. Mwinyi/two
  fishermen **6.00**

THAILAND

	Unc.

1955 1 Baht, Rama IX and temple/building
  . . . . **3.00**
1968 100 Baht, Rama IX/royal barge **20.00**
(1978) 100 Baht, Rama IX/Statue of
  Narasuan on Elephant **8.00**
1987 60 Baht, Rama IX enthroned/royal
  family with subjects **6.00**
1997 50 Baht, Rama IX/Rama VI seated,
  plastic polymer **4.00**

TURKEY

	XF

1259AH (1843) 250 Kurush, inscription
  . . . . *rare*
1334AH (1918) 10 Livres, inscription in
  ornamental border. **300.00**
same, WWI British military counterfeit
  . . . . **5.00**
*Note: The counterfeits far outnumber
authentic notes.*
1930 50 Kurush, Ismet Inonu/building **8.00**

	Unc.

1930 (1961) 5 Lira, Ataturk/three women
  with baskets. **60.00**
1970 (1971-82) 10 Lira, Ataturk/lighthouse
  view **4.00**
1970 (1984-97) 10 Lira, Ataturk/children
  giving flowers to Ataturk. . . . . **.50**
1970 (1997) 100,000 Lira, Ataturk/similar
  . . . . **2.00**
1970 (1995) 1,000,000 Lira, Ataturk/dam
  . . . . **12.50**

Thailand 1997 50 Baht

Turkey 1970 (1997) 100,000 Lira

United Arab Emirates 1993-2001 10 Dirhams

Venezuela 1991 1,000 Bolivares

Yugoslavia 1991 1,000 Dinara

	Unc.
1970 (2000) 20,000,000 Lira, Ataturk/ ancient city	6.00

UNITED ARAB EMIRATES

	Unc.
1973 5 Dirhams, arms/Fujairah Fortress	35.00
1982-2001 5 Dirhams, Sharjah market/ tower	2.50
1993-2001 10 Dirhams, dagger/farm.	4.00
1993-2003 100 Dirhams, fortress/Dubai Trade Center	42.50

UKRAINE

	Unc.
1918 500 Hryven, Head between tridents	22.00
1991 1 Karbovanets, Libyd/cathedral	.25
1992 100 Karbovantsiv, Libyd and her brother Vikings on ship/cathedral	1.75

	Unc.
1994-95 1 Hryvnia, St. Volodymyr/city of Khersonnes	1.00
(1996) 50 Hryven, Hrushevsky/parliament	20.00

VENEZUELA

	F
1811 1 Peso, seal	800.00
1861 8 Reales, inscription	rare

	Unc.
1945-60 10 Bolivares, Bolivar and Sucre/ arms	45.00
1961 10 Bolivares, Bolivar and Sucre/ Carabobo Monument	35.00
1974-79 20 Bolivares, J. Antonio Paez/ similar	8.00
1985-98 50 Bolivares, A. Bello/bank building	1.50
1991 1,000 Bolivares, Bolivar/Signing of Declaration of Independence	2.50

Zambia 1973 5 Kwacha

VIETNAM

	F
(1946) 100 Dong, farmers with buffalo	**22.00**

	Unc.
1976 5 Hao, arms/river scene	**3.00**
1980 100 Dong, Ho Chi Minh/junks sailing amid rocks	**8.00**
1994 50,000 Dong, Ho Chi Minh/view of docks.	**8.00**

YUGOSLAVIA

	VF
1920 10 Dinara, progress moving wheel/ mountain scene	**40.00**
1931 50 Dinara, King Alexander/ equestrian statue	**3.00**
1939 10 Dinara, King Peter II/woman in local costume	**8.00**

	Unc.
1944 1 Dinara, Soldier.	**1.00**
1963 100 Dinara, Woman in folk dress/ view of Dubrovnik.	**2.00**

	Unc.
1974 20 Dinara, Freighter ship	**1.50**
1985 5,000 Dinara, Tito/view of Jajce	**3.50**
1991 1,000 Dinara, Nikola Tesla/high frequency transformer	**7.00**
1993 10,000,000,000 Dinara, Nikola Tesla/ high frequency transformer	**10.00**
2000 20 Dinara, Petar II of Montenegro/ statue	**2.00**

ZAMBIA

	Unc.
1963 1 Pound, Elizabeth II & Fisher with net/bird	*rare*
(1968-69) 2 Kwacha, Pres. Kenneth Kaunda/mining facility	**120.00**
(1973) 5 Kwacha, Pres. Kenneth Kaunda/ children by school	**450.00**
(1980-88) 10 Kwacha, Older Pres. Kenneth Kaunda/bank building.	**10.00**
1992 500 Kwacha, Bird/elephant head and cotton pickers	**3.00**

Index

Get the Coin and Currency Collecting Advantage!

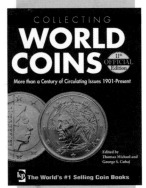

Warman's® Coin & Paper Money
Identification and Price Guide
3rd Edition
by Allen G. Berman

The coins and paper money market is very active, and growing more so with each day. Whether you are collecting for investment or as a hobby, *Warman's® Coins and Paper Money*, covering U.S. and world coins and paper money, is the best reference for getting started or getting ahead in your collecting!

• Provides current information on Middle East coins and paper money

• Contains more than 3,000 detailed photos to assist with identification

Softcover • 8-1/2 x 11 • 320 pages
3,000 b&w photos • 8-pg. color section
Item# WCC5 • $21.99

Collecting World Coins
More Than a Century of Circulating Issues 1901-Present
11th Edition
Edited by Thomas Michael and George S. Cuhaj

This comprehensive guide includes coins from Afghanistan to Zimbabwe, and every country in between. Within the pages of this new edition you'll discover historical and identifying details, values and photos to help you easily and accurately assess your world coin collection.

Key features of this popular guide include:

• An Instant Identifier grid that makes it easier to identify even the most challenging coins

• 25,000 up-to-date values for U.S. state quarters, coins of the Russian Federation states, and new issues from Afghanistan, Iraq, and Africa

Softcover • 8-1/2 x 11 • 888 pages
17,000 b&w photos
Item# CC11• $34.99